NO END
IN SIGHT

Also by Rick Steber

NO END
IN SIGHT

My Life as a Blind Iditarod Racer

Revised and Fully Updated

Rachael Scdoris
and Rick Steber

St. Martin's Press   New York

www.stmartins.com

Design by Phil Mazzone

Captions and credits for the artwork and photographs appear on pages
269–270.

Library of Congress Cataloging-in-Publication Data

Scdoris, Rachael.
 No end in sight : my life as a blind Iditarod racer / Rachael Scdoris and
Rick Steber.—1st ed.
    p. cm.
  ISBN 0-312-35273-5
  EAN 978-0-312-35273-8
  1. Scdoris, Rachael. 2. Iditarod (Race). 3. Women mushers—Oregon—
Biography. 4. Mushers—Oregon—Biography. 5. Sled dog racing—Alaska.
I. Steber, Rick, 1946– II. Title.

SF440.15.S33 2006
798.8'3'092—dc22

                                                                    2005020897

First published by Two Star, a division of Bonanza Publishing, Prineville,
Oregon.

First Revised Edition: February 2006

10 9 8 7 6 5 4 3 2 1

CONTENTS

INTRODUCTION

I am a sled dog racer. I also happen to be legally blind, not that my blindness defines who I am; it is simply a part of me. And yet my blindness is what draws the public's attention.

Strangers often approach me to say I serve as an inspiration to them. Children want to touch me because they think I am famous. I have appeared on *The Early Show* on CBS and the *Today* show on NBC, been chosen as one of the one hundred most outstanding female athletes in the nation and honored with a host of awards. My face has been splashed on everything from magazine covers, to billboards, to sacks of dog food. There have been discussions about turning my story into a Hollywood movie. It can all be rather flattering, but it is also a distraction from my main objective: to become one of the best professional sled dog racers in the world.

With so much attention focused on me I knew it was only a matter of time before someone wrote a book about my life. I did not want to take the chance of someone getting it wrong and decided to take the initiative and tell my own story. I persuaded Rick Steber, a successful writer and a close family friend, to collaborate with me on a book. I told my story to Rick, all my trials and tribulations of growing up, my successes and failures, even my most awkwardly embarrassing moments—and he wrote my book.

If my story serves to inspire others, or if it propels those with disabilities into a positive course of action, or if it makes a significant impact on a young person, then our efforts will have been rewarded. I believe that through hope, courage, and determination each of us can overcome any obstacle we may face in life. Happy reading.

Rachael Scdoris

NO END
IN SIGHT

1

MY PERFECT MOMENT

*M*y *perfect moment: dead of winter, dogs running flat out, air so cold I can taste its brittleness on the tip of my tongue. I know this trail, know it by heart. Ahead is a sharp switchback right, followed by a steep downhill, breaking into a series of tight S-curves. Any of these can cause a musher to wreck.*

I have the overwhelming sensation of speed. A blanket of snow-laden clouds hides the harshness of the sunlight. I squint to see the vague shapes of dogs out in front of me. They are indistinct and one-dimensional. I see a bit of harness over there, a leader's head bobbing, feet flying, a chest lunging, a tongue lolling up and down, the swish of a tail, the rump of a wheel dog. I know from past experience that the dark blobs flashing past on my right are pine trees. To the left is nothingness, a sheer drop-off of several hundred feet.

I have absolute trust in my dogs. Their breathing comes hard and fast. They scream downhill. Full tilt. I tell myself, "Get ready for it." Bending both knees, I drop my center of gravity, getting as low as I can on the runners. The dogs kick up snow crystals that sting my cheeks like shards of glass; cold wind gnaws at my ears. "Stay off the brake! No matter how wild it gets, just stay off the brake!"

Blasting into the switchback, I shift both feet to the right runner, my right leg instinctively extends out as if it were an outrigger, and I throw my weight to counterbalance the centrifugal force that wants to fling us to the outside of the curve. The runners chatter, sharp edges bite into the snow, and we whip around the corner with the sled sliding just a tiny little bit.

Jamming out of the switchback, we plunge downhill. My overwhelming impulse is to mash the brake, dump some of this seductive speed. But this is a race. No time for caution. No time to get conservative. Girl, it's time to get athletic!

Into the first S-curve. Into it and out just as quickly. Staying low. Shifting weight from one runner to the other like a dancer moving across the ballroom floor. Charging through the second S-curve, breaking out and blasting down the long straightaway. I did it. I grin, wildly pump one fist in the air, throw back my head, and shout, "Wahoo!"

I may be young. I may be a girl. I may be visually impaired. But none of that has diddly-squat to do with the fact that I am a sled dog racer. My plan is to become world champion and to someday challenge the leaders of the Super Bowl of sled dog racing: the Iditarod. To me all the other stuff is irrelevant. But it seems that everyone I come in contact with wants to focus on one thing: what I can see or, to be more precise, what I cannot see.

Yes, I am legally blind, but blindness has not stopped me. In fact, it has barely slowed me down. According to the legal definition, a person is blind if she has uncorrectable vision of 20-200. In a clinical setting with controlled lighting, my vision is about 20-200. But when light conditions change, my vision rapidly deteriorates. Doctors estimate my walk-around vision varies between 20-300 and 20-600.

I was born with congenital achromatopsia, a rare genetic disorder caused by a recessive gene from both parents. In technical terms, I have a shortage of rods and cones in my retina. Rods and cones control light, color, and depth perception.

Exactly what do I see? I have been asked that question a million times. All I can say is that I see what I see. It might not be what you see, but I do not think that makes my gift of sight any less distinctive or beautiful to me than what a normal person might see. It is just different, that is all.

In fact, the question of my vision would rarely come up if I gave in to my blindness, but I refuse to. Especially when there are so many activities I enjoy: rock climbing, horseback riding, swimming, running competitively, and racing on a tandem bicycle. But my passion, the reason I believe I exist, is to raise, train, and race sled dogs. I am a musher, a sled dog racer, and I live for those moments when everything in the universe seems to align into a delicate balance of perfection. In those moments my vision is never an issue.

2

LIVING WITH BLINDNESS

People wonder how a blind athlete is able to compete in the demanding world of sled dog racing, where sight is such a fundamental part of the sport. I suppose it is not unreasonable for people to question me, especially if they saw me trip over an exposed root or drag my nose across a printed page trying to read a book. My answer to people who question my ability is: "Watch me." I love my dogs and I am competent in every facet of the sport, except that every now and then I need a little help seeing things out on the trail.

I have a full field of vision, but I lack detail and the ability to gauge distances. I see some colors but cannot always tell what those colors are, especially blue and green. Those two colors seem absolutely the same to me. I see black and white. That is easy to recognize. And I can sometimes differentiate between red, yellow, and orange.

It is difficult for me to describe my vision because I do not know what a person with normal vision sees. You may be able to clearly see a photograph of a loved one. I see a basic image that I recognize as a person. You see distinct features, eyes and hair color. I see an imprecise shape of a face, dark holes where the eyes are supposed to be, and a blurry, nondescript suggestion of hair. The person I see in the photograph is blended together. It is not really fuzzy or distorted, just blended.

The best way for a sighted person to get a feel for what I see is to take Vaseline and apply a liberal coating on a pair of eyeglasses. Spread the Vaseline on thick enough so that you cannot read the print in a book unless you hold it about three inches from your face. When you look at an eye chart you should be able to make out the top letter; it is an E pointing to the right. That is about what I see on a sunny day. At night my vision actually improves, but car lights are difficult for me. I see the two circles of light that are headlights, but there are skinny fingers of light that stretch and radiate out from the fringes of the light source. Oftentimes headlights irritate my eyes and within thirty minutes my eyes will begin to burn. If I close my eyes the pain usually goes away.

Most people refer to my blindness as a disability. To me the word "disabled" means that you are "unable." I am by no means unable. But if you go to several sites on the Internet you can find all sorts of knee-jerk responses to my blindness. Some of the contributors to these sites say that since I have a visual impairment, surely I could never survive the cold or ride a sled or even care for my dogs. They want to focus on what they perceive as my disability rather than on my abilities.

I am convinced that there is more to vision than merely sight. My body finds ways to counteract my blindness, including a reliance on my senses of hearing, touching, tasting, and smelling, as well as my intuition—what my gut tells me. For instance, once a dog has run a trail he remembers all the twists and turns and will diligently follow the same path again the next time. I have run races where a trail has been changed from the route my lead dogs ran two years before and they will want to follow the old route. I respond the same way. When I run a trail I pick up the subtle nuances of the trail, the way the sled moves under me, the long uphill pull where I have to get off and run to lighten the load for the dogs, followed by the downhill, and the sharp switchback at the end of the grade. I store those things in my memory, just like the dogs do. And I read the lay of the land around me, the way sounds echo and bounce around that landscape, the changing aromas as we progress through woods of pine, fir, lodgepole, and cedar. I hear the subtle difference the runners make passing over the trail, chattering on ice in the shadows and whispering softly in the sunny spots.

There are many alternative ways to see. I have worked to hone those skills, and as a result of my successes I am never hesitant about trying something new. You want to rock climb? *I'll beat you to the top.* Want to swim? *Let's get wet.* Ride a horse? *Can we run barrels?* How about trying a tandem bike? *I'm all for it, just as long as I'm not the one steering.* Run a footrace? *Make it a long one, with a lot of hills thrown in. I'm not a very good sprinter, but I've got great endurance and can beat a lot of sighted people from three miles up to a twenty-six-mile marathon. I'm like the Energizer bunny. I just keep going, and going, and going. I love to run.*

What I see seems perfectly normal to me. I do not know what I am supposed to see, because my eyesight has always been like this. I do not know what I am missing. There were times at high school track meets when everything was a blur to me, but a friend would describe how the race was progressing and how the runners were coming around the far corner. I would think to myself, *Wow, you can see what's happening way over there; now that's pretty cool.*

When I run on a four-hundred-meter track I see the white lines that mark the lanes and can see if anyone is close to me by the general form of her body. Sometimes I see the color of a competitor's uniform. I can tell when I am approaching a corner and know the finish line is always at the end of the straightaway. I do not think that my lack of vision, in any way, impairs my ability to run on a track. A track is like a clinical setting: Every track is laid out exactly the same, the surface is flat and smooth, and during the race the pace dictates a certain cadence where sight is no longer a necessity. I run just to be running, not for the ribbons or medals, although I am competitive and do like to win.

In track there is a freedom from obstacles, unforeseen circumstances, and the confusion and distractions of everyday life. In an odd way my visual impairment might even be considered beneficial because it allows me to fully concentrate on simply running.

Cross-country running is another matter. There were times in high school when I missed a poorly marked turn at a cross-country meet and ended up out in the pucker brush. Other times, when the light conditions were particularly bad, I felt compelled to slow my pace rather than risk stepping on an unseen rock and rolling an ankle, running into a tree, or tripping and falling. I have done all those things and skinned my knees and elbows. I've worn the bruises and scars like badges of honor. But I have also embarrassed myself in front of competitors and spectators, and that can be humiliating, especially for a young girl who is merely trying to fit in with the crowd.

If I had to choose between running cross-country and track I would probably choose track. The scenery does not change all that much, but at least I know I have less chance of running into something or injuring myself. Besides, it is difficult to go the wrong way on a track; there is only one right direction: counterclockwise.

A few sports elude me. I will never play tennis on center court at Wimbledon. Never be the goalie on the USA soccer team. Never play point guard in the WNBA. If the sport involves a ball, I am toast. When a ball is thrown to me I generally see it leave the person's hand, then it disappears as if it were in a magic show, only to reappear again a few inches from my face. That is why I always flinch when a ball is thrown at me. When I was young some of the boys used to toss a ball at me just to see my reaction. Usually the ball hit me in the face and I made a slapstick grab for it. The boys, and even some of the girls, thought that was funny. Kids can be so sadistic and mean.

Stationary objects, like parking meters or trees, have a tendency to jump out at me. According to my eye doctors, I have better peripheral vision than straight-ahead vision. When I am racing dogs, looking straight ahead, I will not see a trail marker until it flashes past next to my sled. And then there are ropes, cables, and guy wires. I never see them and will usually trip and fall as ungracefully as a goose on ice. Guy wires are the absolute worst; they get me every single time.

There are times when I am able to avoid making a fool of myself and people are unaware that I have a visual impairment. When that happens it makes me feel as if I have accomplished something of significance. If I am standing close enough when people find out, I can actually see the look of surprise and shock sweep over their faces. Sweet. Otherwise I have to settle for the tone of voice as someone says, "Really?" or, "You are?" or, "Is that true?" or, best of all, "You're blind? I never would have guessed."

If I were sighted, the world I live in would be neater and more orderly. I did not invent the disorganization that surrounds me. Visually impaired people, in general, have a tendency to be messier than sighted people, who instinctively know, or can quickly see, where they placed a particular item. A visually impaired person puts one thing down, another article on top, and the first thing is lost until an inordinate amount of time is spent going through stuff until the lost item is found. I accept the fact I do not possess any of those skills it takes to be organized, and yet it frustrates me when I look at my room, or my locker at school, or the binder where I keep my homework. I ask myself, *How did I let this happen?* and vow to work harder at my organizational skills. But I fear that I am doomed to a life surrounded by a jumble of clutter.

During my high school years I acquired the label of being "aloof" and sometimes even "stuck up" because I did not greet or acknowledge people by name as we passed in the hall. I guess they figured that since I was capable of completing a five-hundred-mile sled dog race I should certainly be able to recognize someone standing five feet in front of me. The fact is, I forget that people see me a whole lot better than I see them. At one point I was going to have a

T-shirt printed with the words: "I'm not a snob—I'm just blind."
But I never did.

Often I can recognize a friend by the way she stands or maybe a
distinctive gait or hairstyle, or maybe he always wears a letterman's
jacket or a backpack or smells of a certain cologne. These little things
allow me to recognize particular people without actually seeing
them. Of course the easiest way is to hear a voice. A voice is as distinctive as a fingerprint, and so is a laugh. No two laughs are exactly the same.

When it comes to interacting with my peers I cannot make any
assumption on looks and appearance because I have to get uncom-
fortably close to become aware of that kind of detail. I never judge
people by superficial things: how they look or what they wear. Instead of physical features, I see characteristics in people: personality, strength of character, ability to talk, listen, and formulate
opinions, sense of humor, level of self-confidence, and their sense of
spirituality. As a result I have a cross section of friends that blows
most people's minds. My friends range from a girl with purple hair
to the prom queen and boys from the most popular athlete in school
to one who has never had a date in his life. I would not trade my diverse group of friends for anything in the world.

I wish I knew how many times I have left the house wearing the
most mismatched clothes known to mankind. I did not have to look
at my outfits, so it never much mattered to me. Not until the girls at
school began teasing me. It took awhile, but I finally figured out that
black or white tops and jeans go with everything. I could never go
wrong with that.

In my opinion makeup is highly overrated and something I have
never really fooled with all that much. Every once in a while, if I'm
out with a girlfriend and she has some makeup in her purse, I might
throw on a little dab of mascara. Or if I am attending an important
event I will have Mom help me look pretty. Really, at this stage of
my life, I do not need makeup. When I no longer have color in my
lips and wrinkles begin to show around my eyes you can bet I will
sing a different tune. Until then the world gets me natural.

I consider myself as normal as anyone. I only feel blind on an especially bright day when surrounded by a crowd. When I find myself in such social situations I generally stick close to the person I came with. There is no worse feeling than being alone in a crowd, when all the faces look the same and I cannot differentiate between them unless I get within a few inches of the person. If I do that and it proves to be a stranger it can be rather awkward. Put me in a crowd and I am lost, but out in the woods I can find my way because my other senses kick in and I can identify tangible landmarks: trees, rock outcroppings, mountaintops, the skyline, the general lay of the land. Away from people I am perfectly fine and content.

Generally I am comfortable with my level of vision. I was once asked a hypothetical question: "If an operation would give you a fifty percent chance for perfect vision, and a fifty percent chance for total blindness, would you take the risk?" My answer was a definite, "No." I am satisfied with what I have. And no, hypothetically, I would not be willing to trade sight for any of my other senses. Taste—I never would be willing to give up the cold, creamy sweetness of soft ice cream on a hot summer day. Hearing—I could not live without music and the sound of puppies yipping and carrying on at feeding time. Smell—I want to be able to breathe in the tang of evergreens and sweet fragrance of a meadow of flowers in springtime. Feel—I want to be able to stroke a dog and feel the warmth beneath my fingertips and the way the muscles squirm with happiness. I am content with my level of vision.

If I could change one thing it would be the general assumption of most people: that legally blind means that a person cannot see anything. There are subtle degrees of vision, whole ranges of sight, and countless terms to describe them: "low vision," "partially sighted," "visually impaired." To be politically correct, I am a visually impaired person. In my opinion being politically correct is highly overrated. You can call me whatever you like, visually impaired or blind—just as long as you never call me handicapped or disabled.

I know that one of the main reasons people are curious about me is because I am a legally blind girl doing something unusual. It would be nice if the media focused their attention on my beautiful dogs and my skills as a sled dog racer. But that will never be the story. My blindness is what captures the interest, the part that sells newspapers, books, and the products I endorse. I will always be Rachael Scdoris the blind sled dog racer.

Some people try to put limitations on me because they want me to fit into the legally blind box. There are the naysayers out there who say I have no business being out on the trail, or running dogs, or doing any of the other activities I am involved in. A perfect example of this occurred during my freshman year of high school. I was running a cross-country race and got clotheslined by a guy wire. One minute I was running and the next I was on the ground, flat on my back. Once I got over the shock I jumped up and continued to run. A woman standing near Dad admonished him with, "Your daughter is blind. How could you let her do something so dangerous?"

Dad came back with the greatest answer: "What would you like for her to do? Sit on a couch with a white cane over her lap and be blind?"

I refuse to sit back and let life quietly slip past me. I want to be involved. I want to try things. I want to live and experience everything I possibly can. I know there are dangers out there. I accept them. No, I embrace them. Dangers present us with fear. And fear is my fuel. It makes me go. If I did not meet the dangers of this world head-on and come to grips with my fear, I would be cheating myself.

Those people who are content to sit on the couch and say, "I'm blind," or, "I'm deaf," or, "I'm sick," are missing something—a life.

My blindness gives me a sharp contrast between easy and difficult. It forces me to push past the limitations other people try to place on me. Over and over again I am obligated to prove my competence and, as a result, I push harder to achieve than anyone else I know.

I hope this book will provide a window of understanding of the fact that just because a person has a physical impairment or certain limitations that person is not helpless. Those of us who are impaired or limited must cling to the possibility of hope. Hope that today's challenges will be overcome, hope that we can find the personal strength to face yet another battle, hope that our individual lives will become more rewarding.

Kids have told me that I am an inspiration to them. They consider me a role model. I never sought to become a role model, have never thought of myself in those terms, but if people say I am, then I am comfortable with their assessment. Although such a label does put a certain amount of pressure on me, because I know I have a responsibility to make sure I behave myself and act in a proper way. I need to be constantly aware of my words and actions. But that is a mission all of us share. We all serve as role models to those younger than us.

I plan to live my life to the fullest, challenge myself at every opportunity, never give in, never give up, and always fight for what is right and just. If I do those things I will be successful. That's how I see it.

3

A BEAUTIFUL BABY

I was born February 1, 1985, the same year Libby Riddles became the first woman to win the Iditarod. According to my parents, I was an incredibly beautiful baby, but, of course, all parents say that. I was nearly a month late and had to be taken by cesarean section. I weighed ten pounds, eight ounces, measured twenty-four inches, and was the largest girl baby born up to that time at St. Charles Hospital in Bend, Oregon. I came into this world with a full head of blond hair.

Since I was too young to know what was going on during that time, I have relied on what my father, Jerry, and mother, Lisa, have told me about this period of my life. According to Dad, within a few days of bringing me home he began to notice something abnormal about my eyes. When he held me close and cooed to me, he said I was not able to focus on his face. It was as if I was searching for the source of the sound but unable to locate it.

Dad actually returned to the hospital and asked one of the

nurses in Pediatrics about his concern. She told him, "It's not uncommon. It takes some babies a few weeks, or even a month, to be able to focus. Don't worry." She showed him other newborns, and when a few did not look directly at him when he spoke this seemed to put his mind at ease, at least for a while.

My parents claim I was an easy baby to care for, that I slept when I was supposed to sleep and rarely cried unless I was hungry or needed my diaper changed. But Dad was plagued by what he perceived to be a problem with my eyes. The day I turned one month old he called the doctor and said, "Something is definitely wrong with her vision."

"Each baby develops differently, at his or her own pace. There is nothing to be concerned about," the doctor reassured him.

"No, you don't understand. Her eyesight isn't normal," Dad insisted.

"Mr. Scdoris, your baby is developing. It just takes time. Give it a few months," the doctor said.

My condition never changed. And while Dad was adamant that I had a problem, Mom was more patient and accepting. She thought I was flawless in every way.

"Come over here," Dad told Mom one evening. He was holding me in his arms. "Say something to Rachael and watch her eyes."

"Hey, pretty girl. How's my pretty baby?" Mom babbled. I turned my head searching, even grinned at her, but my eyes never found her.

"See that. She hears perfectly but her eyes can't find you," Dad said.

Having heard this same discourse for the past four months, Mom lost her patience and said, "Okay, tomorrow I'll schedule an appointment with Dr. Berube. We'll get to the bottom of this. He can run tests or whatever he has to do. Promise me one thing: If he says Rachael is fine, I don't want to hear another word out of you. Agree?"

"Fine," Dad told her.

That appointment proved to be the first of an endless string of appointments at doctors' offices. When we met with Dr. Stacy Berube at Central Oregon Pediatric Associates, Dad told him, "Please don't placate me and tell me she is just slow developing her eyesight. Something is definitely wrong."

"Describe the problem she is having," Dr. Berube said.

"I'll show you," said Dad. He went through what he later described as his little dog and pony show, speaking to me and me not looking directly at him. He had Mom do the same thing.

The doctor used a pencil-thin instrument with a light on one end to peer into my eyes. Then, without saying anything to my parents, he walked out of the room and returned with another doctor. This doctor went through the same procedure. The two of them stepped into the hallway and conversed in muffled voices. When Dr. Berube returned to the room he said, "I can tell you this right now, so you no longer have to worry needlessly. . . ."

Dad claimed a wave of relief swept over him because, for an instant, he believed I was fine. That he had been wrong. That everyone else was right. My eyesight was fine, just slow developing. And then Dr. Berube dropped the bombshell.

"I don't believe she is totally blind. She may be partially sighted."

After that announcement, life would never again be the same for any of us in the Scdoris family. Dad, in a state of shock, responded with anger. "What are you talking about? My baby's not blind."

Dad told me that at that moment he felt as though he were back playing football at David Douglas High School and some 250-pound lineman had blindsided him. It was difficult for him to breathe. He could not say anything else.

"What does that mean?" Mom asked.

"At this point I'm not totally sure," Dr. Berube said. "I want Rachael to see Dr. East. He's an ophthalmologist. His office is just up the street. If it's all right with you, I'll call and see if we can come up."

"I don't think we ought to be in a rush. We've already waited four months. Maybe we can come in next week. I really don't want to do this right now." Dad was in denial. He did not want an ophthalmologist to confirm that his daughter was nearly blind.

Dr. Berube was gentle but firm. "This needs to be done immediately. I would like for an ophthalmologist to substantiate what I found. Perhaps there is some treatment available for your daughter." He made the call, hung up the phone, swept me up, and carried me in his arms the short half block to Dr. East's office. My dazed parents trailed behind like sad afterthoughts.

Dr. Sam East had Dad sit in a chair and hold me while he conducted a comprehensive examination of my eyes. When he finished he turned his attention to my parents and told them, "I detected limited vision and estimate your baby has eyesight no better than 20-200."

"What does that mean?" Dad wanted to know.

"She is most probably in the category of legally blind."

"Whoa, just a minute. Legally blind? What are you talking about?" Dad cried.

Dr. East gave an audible sigh. "When she is older she may be able to function normally, but she will always require special accommodations."

Dad claimed a thousand thoughts were racing through his mind. He wanted to know what the doctor meant by the words "special accommodations." He wanted out of the room. He wanted to go back in time, to when he only suspected something was wrong, before it had become a medical certainty. He wanted me to be healthy and normal, his perfect baby girl. He mumbled, "I don't want this thing."

"I know you don't. None of us do," Dr. East said.

"Is it correctable? Can't she just wear glasses?" Mom asked.

"At this point we don't know, not without further testing."

"It won't get any worse, will it?" Mom asked.

"It's impossible to tell," the doctor said, and then, searching to soften his diagnosis, he added, "We hope it doesn't."

My parents were totally devastated by the news their baby was legally blind. I've always had a nagging suspicion that at the moment the doctors gave my parents the news a tiny fissure began to form between them. In time it split them apart. I don't know if that is true or not, but I don't think the news helped bond them together. Little by little they grew apart, and when I was three years old they divorced and went their separate ways.

I lived with Dad. We had a cabin in the woods, ten miles from the town of Sisters and five miles from the nearest paved road. I still remember the house perched on top of a hill facing west, overlooking the beautiful panorama of the Cascade mountain range. Even I could see the mountains. The sharp, snowcapped peaks of the Three Sisters seemed close enough to reach out and touch.

Dad was a sled dog musher. As a boy he had fallen in love with the *Sergeant Preston of the Yukon* television show. He would pretend he was Sergeant Preston and run around calling out, "On, King, on you huskies. Mush!"

Sled dogs were nothing more than a child's fantasy until Dad went into the Army during the Vietnam War. Several Indians from Alaska were in his unit and he talked to them about sled dogs. Before snow machines became popular, everyone in the North drove dogs. It was a way of life in those days.

When Dad was discharged from the Army in 1970 it was his dream to settle in Alaska, file on a homestead, and put together a team of dogs. But first off he enrolled in college and graduated with a degree in education. His first job was teaching at Gold Beach on the Oregon coast. Here he met a fellow from North Bend who was training sled dogs with a cart on the beach. Shortly after that encounter Dad got his first sled dog, Jenny. Within a couple years he had seven dogs.

In 1978 he ran the Sisters Sled Dog Race, and according to the story that he loves to tell it was one of those magical nights, ten below zero, the moon was out, and it was snowing. It was so perfect that right then and there, he made up his mind what he wanted to do with his life. He returned to Gold Beach and quit his job—although he honored his contract and finished out the year—and moved to Central Oregon to train and raise dogs.

Some of my earliest memories are of our little cabin on the top of the hill, surrounded by thirty-two dogs chained to stakes driven into the ground. Each dog had his own individual doghouse. I played with the puppies and helped Dad feed and water the dogs and do cleanup chores.

The year I was born Dad had acquired a sled dog sponsor, Elliott Dog Food. They were in the process of developing a complete nutritional formula for working dogs and used our kennel to conduct research. Dad trained dogs, competed in sled dog races throughout the Northwest, and made public appearances to promote Elliott Dog Food. I went everywhere with him. On training runs Dad tied my car seat onto the basket on the sled and slipped dog booties on my hands as mittens. I was happy as could be. But I cannot remember much about the rides, because as soon as we started on the big loop that wound around through the forest I fell asleep. I'm not sure why; maybe what made me drowsy was the motion of the sled or the feeling of speed, or perhaps I just felt sheltered and secure.

Sometimes I spent weekends with Mom, but usually I was with Dad at the cabin. And there were the trips we took back and forth to Portland. We made a lot of trips to Portland, meeting with doctors at Oregon Health & Science University and Devers Memorial Eye Clinic. One of the leading retinal specialists in the world, Dr. Richard Weleber, a professor of ophthalmology and medical genetics with a specialty in congenital and hereditary eye diseases at the OHSU Casey Eye Institute, took a special interest in me. He tested, retested, and tested me some more.

For a time we worked with two researchers who were conducting post-doctoral work in the field of genetics. They wanted to know about our family history, if there had ever been any member of our family who had been blind or had vision problems. Dad and Mom tried to trace their genealogy, but it seems as if our ancestors were mostly farmers or common laborers, and if they had had problems with their vision it was never noted.

Dad had accepted the clinical diagnosis, that I was legally blind, but what he kept trying to find out from Dr. Weleber was what, as a father, should he do? How could he help me? Would I have trouble interacting and socializing with other children? Would I ever be able to take care of myself, hold a job, and lead a normal life? What could he do to help me prepare for adulthood? How could he make my life easier and more fulfilling?

Dr. Weleber would shrug his shoulders. "I don't know."

Dad would press him for information. "Will she be able to learn? Will she have to read Braille? Will her classmates accept her?"

"I'm a doctor. I'm a scientist. I specialize on what is inside the eye. Beyond that, I do not know about such things."

It seemed that every specialist who looked at my eyes gave me another prescription for eyeglasses. I was only nine months old when I was fitted with my first pair of glasses. We have pictures of me, this little baby wearing glasses with lenses as thick as a Coke bottle.

The first glasses I remember were pink. That was my favorite color at the time and they had the image of Minnie Mouse on each corner of the frames. I was constantly taking off my glasses, laying them down, and losing them. Anyway, they were not very effective in helping me see, and I stopped the charade of wearing them when kids my age began teasing me.

Even though we continued to make regular visits to Portland, the doctors were unable to determine a diagnosis. Finally we received a partial answer, or at least a postponed possible answer. Dr. Weleber said that when I turned six years old I would be able to respond to cognitive questions. He promised that at that point he could make a definitive diagnosis. And so we went home and waited.

During this interval Dad was forced to make one of the most difficult and heart-wrenching decisions of his life. He came to the conclusion that living out rural like we did was not in my best interests, that I needed to have a more traditional home environment near kids my own age, and that we should live close enough to town to take advantage of the various state and federal programs available to blind children.

Dad made two telephone calls. One was to Jeffrey Mann in Alaska and the other to John Patten in Minnesota. Both were close friends and fellow mushers. Dad put it to them straight: "I need a favor. I want you to come get my dogs."

They dropped everything and came as quickly as they could. Neither stayed very long. They just loaded up the dogs and departed.

I recently asked Dad about that day, because I do not remember anything about what happened. I just came home and found the dogs were gone. Dad confessed he had sent me away to stay with friends. He was trying to protect me.

I picture Dad loving the dogs, saying his good-byes to Lester, Jagger, Nellie, Mickey, and all the rest, standing there alone, watching his dogs and his way of life going off down the road. He said when the trucks, with his dogs inside the dog box, pulled away from the cabin he stood there watching their progress toward the highway by the dust trail that rose and floated above the tops of the trees. And he cried.

He gave up everything for me. I genuinely admire and have the deepest respect for Dad, that he was willing to make such an enormous sacrifice for me. Those dogs were almost like children to him. They were some of the finest sled dogs in the world. In fact, John Patten took a team of dogs that included many of Dad's dogs to Alaska and raced the Iditarod in 1988. He finished eighteenth, which at that time was the second-highest finish for a team made up of dogs from the Lower 48.

By giving away his dogs Dad had put my welfare above the way of life he had chosen and enjoyed so much. He set aside his personal dreams, his wants and desires, for me. I think that is the genuine measure of love, real true love.

. . .

We moved to the growing town of Bend and Dad snapped up the first job that was offered: furniture salesman. He had been in the Army and he had been a schoolteacher. He did not have any experience in sales, and especially not in retail furniture. His notion of furniture was a chair that was comfortable to sit in and a couch he had picked up for ten bucks at a yard sale. But Dad had an innate belief in his abilities and a quiet confidence that he could do anything he set his mind to doing. He was committed to working regular hours, making enough money to live comfortably, and taking good care of me and my special needs.

One of the first significant events that occurred after we moved to town was when Dad signed me up for the Central Oregon Regional Program for the Blind. Dusty and Jeanine Johnson administered the program. They visited our house and explained the services that were available to the visually impaired. Jeanine talked about school and the importance of Braille, saying I should begin learning the skills as soon as possible. That would have been hard enough for Dad, but then Dusty really threw him for a loop.

"The most important component for any blind child to become successful in life is mobility. Rachael needs to learn to get around on her own. When you go places how does she get around now?" Dusty asked.

"I carry her, or she walks and holds my hand. When I'm not with her she is either at her mother's place or in pre-kindergarten, and they have a fenced yard and everything in order."

"I'm sure that works well. It's wonderful that the two of you have such a tight bond. And I have to commend you on arranging your work schedule so that you can spend as much time as possible with your daughter," Dusty said. "That's really good. But I have one question for you, Mr. Scdoris: When are you going to let go of her hand?"

Dad sensed he was being set up. "Well, she plays with friends and she's active and does things without me."

"Exactly how long do you plan on holding her hand?" Dusty was relentless.

"What's the point here? What are you driving at?"

Dusty shrugged. "Nothing. One of the hardest things any parent has to do, and this is especially true if the child has a physical impairment, is to allow that child independence. Whether you acknowledge this fact or not, and this is an absolute certainty, Rachael will have to learn to get around on her own. I think we need to introduce her to a cane. She needs to become a cane traveler as soon as possible."

"I beg your pardon. A cane traveler?" Dad was insulted.

"Yes. A cane will give her mobility and independence."

"Rachael will not use a cane."

Dusty stared at Dad, waiting for him to blow off more steam and eventually come around to his way of thinking.

"You've got to be out of your mind."

"Maybe I am," Dusty countered. "But one question for you to consider: Do you plan on holding her hand in high school? Will you walk Rachael across the stage to the podium when she is presented with her diploma at graduation?"

"Of course not." Dad knew that Dusty had backed him into a corner and it frustrated him. "Why don't we skip the cane and just make up a sign: 'Please Excuse Me—I'm Blind'! Rachael can wear it around her neck. No! My daughter will not use a cane."

"Your reaction is not abnormal, Mr. Scdoris. It is difficult to admit that someone we love might have certain limitations. But you have the opportunity to give Rachael the most precious gifts possible: mobility and independence. With the aid of a cane she can walk down a sidewalk and feel comfortable in her footing and cross safely at intersections, because motorists have respect for a white cane."

For several weeks Dad resisted the introduction of the cane. Dusty and Jeanine were so incredibly dedicated to their program and to the benefits of cane traveling that they finally convinced Dad. I take that back. I do not think he was ever convinced; they just finally wore him down and he gave in.

4

MOO-MOO COW

Amy McCormack arrived at our house with a little tele-scoping device. It looked like a small, unobtrusive white stick, but with a simple flick of the wrist it became a white cane. To me, it seemed like a magic wand. I thought it was pretty cool.

Mrs. McCormack taught me the basics of how to use my cane and not just play with it like a toy. When it was extended, the top of the cane came up about chest high. I was to grip the slender shaft, index finger pointed down and the thumb wrapped over the top of the other three closed fingers. As I walked I was to shift the point of the cane in a side-to-side motion, keeping the tip in contact with the ground as much as possible. She explained this technique would al-low me to "feel the ground," all the little imperfections that might otherwise cause me to trip and fall.

We practiced stair steps. Ascending I was to hold the cane close to my body, more upright than normal, and once I had located the step and how high it was I simply stepped up, repeating this maneuver until I reached the landing. To descend I was to tap my way down. For me the experience of becoming a cane traveler was not demeaning in any way; actually, it was kind of fun.

When I became proficient with the use of the cane throughout our house and around our block, Mrs. McCormack said it was time for me to test my skills crossing streets and making my way in unfamiliar territory. When Dad was informed of this development he insisted on accompanying us, but he was under strict orders from Mrs. McCormack that he not interfere in any way. He even had to agree to the stipulation that he walk several steps behind us.

As a teacher Mrs. McCormack was very composed and diligent. On a downtown street she directed me to tap my way along the sidewalk to the end of the block and identify the curb, but I was not to step down. I was to remain standing with my cane extended in front of me and listen to the traffic. When the cars stopped I was to proceed, very slowly, by tapping my way into the street, pausing again as I neared the midway point and listening for traffic coming the other way. Only when I was sure it was safe to cross was I to advance.

Mrs. McCormack escorted me on my first attempt. The second time, I was to solo. Even though I could hear Mrs. McCormack shuffling along a few steps behind me and Dad a few steps behind her, it seemed as if I were finally on my own. *Tap. Tap. Tap.* I made my way down Wall Street to the corner. Locating the curb, I paused, just as I had been taught, with my white cane extended in front of me to warn anyone driving by that a four-year-old blind girl was attempting to cross the street.

Drivers whizzed past, completely ignoring me. I waited. The flow of traffic continued. Finally a car turned right and passed so closely to me that it nearly ran over my cane. This was the final straw for Dad. He lost his patience and sprang into action, bellowing at the top of his lungs, "You stupid fool. Open your eyes. Can't you see this little blind girl with her white cane?" He raced forward and banged his fist on the side of the car. And the driver responded by tromping on the gas to get away from this madman.

A City of Bend policeman had witnessed the altercation and he pulled over and tried to reason with Dad. But Dad was infuriated. He exploded at the officer, "Go arrest him. Arrest all of them. They're supposed to stop. It's the law. What's wrong? Are they blind?"

"Sir, you're overreacting. Calm down."

"No, I'm not overreacting and I'm not gonna calm down. I'm gonna jerk the next inconsiderate slob who refuses to stop out of his rig and beat him to death with—with that white cane."

Our lesson was cut short that day and, miraculously, Dad was able to avoid an arrest and the humiliation of being carted off in handcuffs and tossed in jail. Word of our escapade reached the Johnsons. Dusty had a heart-to-heart talk with Dad and suggested that since inconsiderate drivers made him so mad, perhaps he should leave the training sessions to Mrs. McCormack.

"When I stood there and watched those cars whiz past her I realized that if I weren't her strongest advocate, if I didn't stand up for her, then nobody was going to," Dad lamented.

"All her life Rachael is going to encounter other people's ignorance. She has to learn to deal with it," Dusty counseled.

"She's so young, and so vulnerable. She's just a little girl," Dad said.

"I know, but she won't be a little girl forever."

I thought up a name for my cane. It looked, at least to me, like a skinny black and white dairy cow. I mistook the red as black. I called it Moo-Moo Cow. Every time we left the house Dad would ask, "Where's Moo-Moo Cow?"

Sometimes the other kids played with Moo-Moo Cow. They closed their eyes and walked around tapping the ground, playing blind.

Eventually I did learn the power of my white cane. It commanded a certain amount of respect, and equally as important was that it had the potential to pack a real wallop. Both those realizations were brought to my attention one morning as Dad walked me to the school bus stop. He was holding my hand and in the other hand I was carrying Moo-Moo Cow. We reached the crosswalk and waited. Several other kids gathered behind us. I could hear a car speeding up the street, and the driver had no intention of stopping, let alone slowing down. I raised Moo-Moo Cow and defiantly whacked it on the ground, whacked it really hard. That got the driver's attention and he slammed on his brakes. There was the screech of tires on pavement. He shuddered to a stop a few inches into the crosswalk. I could smell the stench of burned rubber.

I triumphantly led the way forward, the others following behind like meek lambs. The driver lowered his window and called an apology: "Sorry, I didn't see you until the last minute. Sorry."

When we reached the other side the kids erupted in cheers. They pounded me on the back. I felt ten feet tall, as though I had accomplished something really noteworthy. I had power. I had prevailed over the forces of ignorant drivers and mechanical monsters. I was the hero.

From that day forward, anytime I came to a crosswalk I violently whacked the pavement with my cane, demanding that I be seen and the law of the land be observed. Without fail, drivers slammed on their brakes. For a time Dad thought this was cute, but before long he informed me that whacking the pavement was not considered proper etiquette for a cane traveler. After that, crossing the street was not nearly as much fun.

I discovered another improper use of the cane the day Dad and I were walking on the sidewalk in a residential section of Bend. A woman, attempting to back out of her driveway, apparently did not look behind her, because she very nearly backed over the top of us. Instinctively I smacked the fender of her car with Moo-Moo Cow. And not just one smack, either, but smack-smack-smack. The lady stormed out of her car, but when she saw my white cane she became so apologetic it was very nearly embarrassing.

With that confrontation it became readily apparent to Dad that I had the capacity of becoming dangerous with my cane. He told me, "I don't want you to strike anything with your cane ever again, not a car, not the pavement, and certainly not a person." He made it abundantly clear that, from that moment forward, Moo-Moo Cow was to have limited power. It was to be used for aiding my sight and nothing more. But secretly I think he kind of enjoyed my standing up for myself, although he never would have admitted it, not in a million years.

Unable to unleash the magic power anymore, my Moo-Moo Cow became a liability. I grew tired of lugging it around and it was a real pain to have to keep track of where I happened to lay it down. And when I was frustrated with having to use it or could not find it, I called it Stupid Moo-Moo Cow. One time I even tried to break the darn thing. My friends and I kicked it, stepped on it, and tossed it on the ground. But the cane was resilient and refused to break.

It seemed that Dad and I were constantly at odds over that infernal cane. Dad wanted me to carry it at all times. I wanted to throw it away, throw it as far as I could, especially when the kids at school wanted to know, "Why do you have that thing?" or, "Is that a walking stick?" or, "Why do you have to use that? Can't you see?" It was bad enough that I was wearing clunky glasses, but the white cane made me stand out even more. My life became almost unbearable. I felt like a freak. I felt blind.

The last time I remember using my cane was on a trip we took to Los Angeles. Dad and I flew down, and as we walked through the airport I could hear the reaction of people as we passed. I was tapping my way with Moo-Moo Cow. "Oh, look at the blind girl," and, "Isn't that so sad; she can't even see," and, "She is so adorably cute with her miniature white cane and all." Dad heard them, too. One thing that neither of us has ever been able to stand is pity.

After we returned home we never fought about the cane again. Whether Dad finally gave up on spending his entire adult life fighting with me over a piece of fiberglass or he had suddenly been forced to confront the treatment I faced every day I will never know. But for some reason we called a truce between us. I never used a cane again and he never asked what happened to it.

5

THE DIAGNOSIS

Shortly after my sixth birthday we visited Dr. Weleber in Portland. I was taken to an examination room and helped into an enormous chair. The armrests were so tall that when I placed my elbows on them my shoulders shrugged up around my ears. There was not so much as a pinprick of light entering this room. I felt claustrophobic and had an unreasonable fear that if I should try to breathe too deeply I might suck the blackness into my lungs and suffocate.

Dad was in the room with me. Knowing he was there reassured me, but still I felt alone and vulnerable. A bad thing could happen and Daddy would not be able to find me in the dark. Any old monster could be lurking in the evil darkness. I squirmed in the leather chair and could feel the bottom of the headrest touching the top of my head. I had a suspicion the chair might try to swallow me.

"Daddy." My voice seemed puny in all the blackness.

"I'm right here, sweetie," he called. His voice was strong and re-assuring. It helped to bolster me.

"Daddy, do you want to sing with me?"

"Sure. What do you want to sing?"

At that time I was obsessed with *The Sound of Music*. I was con-stantly playing the sound track. We sang "Do-Re-Mi" and "My Fa-vorite Things," and we sang "Climb Every Mountain." As our voices blended together the blackness was not nearly so oppressive.

I don't know how he found his way into and across the room, but Dr. Weleber was suddenly there, standing next to me.

"How are we doing today, young lady?"

"Fine," my voice squeaked.

Someone else was in the room, and from the lightness of the foot-steps I assumed this other person was a woman. Dr. Weleber spoke, saying they were going to administer a series of tests. "Relax," he di-rected. He said it would take only a few minutes. I felt hands on my head and fingers probing here and there. I think they applied some type of goop and then fastened tiny suction cups to my scalp with wires running from them. I knew about the cups and wires because I reached up and felt one of them. An apparatus was fitted over my head. Dr. Weleber called it a spaceman's helmet. That made it fun. I fantasized I was a spaceman floating in the black void of the universe.

After handing me a handheld device and instructing me how to push a button in the center, the doctor and his assistant exited the room. I was left with Dad, out there somewhere, and the raspy sound of my own breathing.

I was thinking that I wanted to scratch my scalp and was won-dering how I could go about it when a small light exploded in front of my eyes. It was like a tiny star exploding. This was followed by more bursts of light.

"When you see the color red, push the button," Dr. Weleber's voice commanded.

I saw a red light, pushed the button, and Dr. Weleber asked me to describe where, in my field of vision, I had seen it. And then I was sup-posed to respond to other colors when I saw them. It was wonderful, incredible, mind-boggling, this show of pulsating lights that sparkled, twinkled brightly, and winked out. For the first time in my life I witnessed the entire spectrum of color as though it were a sparkling rainbow painted across a galaxy of shooting stars. The vivid images of light and color burned into my retina and into my mind.

All too quickly the test was concluded and the overhead fluorescent lights were flipped on. The harshness of these lights gave me an instant headache, a headache so acute I thought I was going to be sick to my stomach. The spaceman's helmet was removed and they pulled off the electrodes and tried to wipe away the goop that had affixed them to my scalp.

When Dad and I left the office that day we still did not have any answers about a diagnosis of my visual problems. Dr. Weleber sent us home with a single request: "Can you come back next week? We will have the results of the tests by then."

After years of waiting, Dr. Weleber had a definitive answer. We met him in his office the following week and he did not waste time on idle chitchat or preparing us for the results. The minute he entered the room he started talking.

"Without a doubt Rachael has a rare disease called congenital achromatopsia. It causes nearsightedness, farsightedness, and color blindness.

Dad wanted to know, "What can we do about it? Is there a cure?"

"As I said, this condition is extremely rare," explained Dr. Weleber. "It was only discovered in the past couple decades. Fewer than one hundred people have been diagnosed. We estimate about one out of every one hundred and eighty thousand people in the world will be stricken with congenital achromatopsia.

Mom was with us that day and she asked, "How did she get it?"

Dr. Weleber was blunt. "Congenital achromatopsia is a genetic condition and both parents must have recessive genes to pass it on to their offspring."

"Will she get better?" Dad asked.

"To be frank, we know very little about congenital achromatopsia. But I can tell you we believe the eyesight she has is stable. But anyone stricken with this condition is susceptible to any, and every, change in light conditions. Tracing past history of patients diagnosed with congenital achromatopsia, we find nearly all have complained that teachers, employers, and even spouses have accused them of faking their lack of vision. Most individuals report they have suffered socially, academically, and financially. We have only scratched the surface of researching and learning about this particular condition."

"What can we do?" Mom asked.

Dr. Weleber shrugged his shoulders. "Sunglasses might help, but only so much."

Dad came upright in his chair. "Sunglasses? That's all you have to offer? Sunglasses?"

"I'm afraid so," Dr. Weleber stated.

We had waited six years for a diagnosis, and now that we had an answer Dad wanted to know, "Can you tell me how this is going to impact Rachael?"

"No. That is beyond the scope of my knowledge. I know about the science of retinal diseases. I do not know about the social implications. But there are other people who can help to answer your questions."

Dad was trying to wrap his mind around everything that had transpired and gauge what the future might hold. "So you're basically saying Rachael will just have to adjust to being blind?"

"Precisely. And now that we have made the diagnosis there is nothing more that we can do here at OHSU. But rest assured, if there are any scientific developments you will be notified. And of course, it goes without saying, if your daughter has any significant change with her vision, which we do not anticipate, please advise us immediately."

With that said, Dr. Weleber stood, shook hands with Dad and then Mom, patted me on the top of the head, and, as he walked from the room, tossed over his shoulder, "Well, good luck and good-bye."

And then he was gone. My parents sat for a few moments, their faces drawn and colorless. Dad was the first to rise. When we left the room that day I was between my parents, holding hands with both of them.

6

SPINNING IN CIRCLES

On my first day of kindergarten we arrived at Bear Creek Elementary a half hour early. Dad walked me to the playground and pushed me on the swing. We spun on the merry-go-round, swung on the monkey bars, played, and laughed like we had no cares in the world. And then the bell rang.

The parents and their children gathered in Marie Madden's classroom. Ms. Madden asked the students to say their names and introduce who was with them. Since I could not tell when I was supposed to talk, Dad gently laid his hand on my shoulder and whispered, "It's your turn." I dutifully recited my name and introduced my father. After every child had an opportunity to speak, the parents were instructed to say their good-byes and leave.

I'm sure Dad had every intention of following the directive, but I found out later he walked to his pickup and instead of driving away he just sat and worried about me. Would I be able to follow Ms. Madden's instructions? Would I be able to do the work, find my way around, and what would happen at recess? Would the dynamics of group interaction be a nightmare for me? Dad could not overcome his anxieties. He returned to the school and peered through the window. I was sitting cross-legged on the floor playing with toys like all the other children.

When Dad told me what he had done that first day of school, he said the comical part was that he fitted in perfectly with the doting mothers who were hanging around in the hall, unable to turn loose of their sons and daughters. In fact, they forged themselves into an informal group that became the nucleus of volunteers who helped out when they were needed at the school.

Dad arranged his work schedule so he could take me to school every morning and pick me up every afternoon. All through the primary grades he made that commitment, and I loved it. No matter what had transpired during the day, I always knew he would be there to pick me up. I counted on him. Weekends I spent with Mom.

In kindergarten, for the first time, I began to realize there were real differences between myself and the other kids. Ms. Madden read stories to us, and even though I sat close to her, I could never see the pictures in the book when she held them up to show the class. But she helped me in every way she could. When we learned letters of the alphabet she always enlarged the papers for me. She did the same with drawings when we colored. And when I sometimes stumbled into a desk or tripped over a backpack that had been left lying on the floor, Ms. Madden addressed the class and in a very loud voice said, "Maybe Rachael has difficulty seeing, but class, what can she do very, very well?" And the class answered in unison, "Hear."

Kindergarten through second grade was a fun time, but not without a few bumps and bruises along the way. During that time Dad fell in love and got married. But they soon divorced and Dad and I were on our own again.

The most significant and exciting news, from my perspective, was that Dad got back into the sport of sled dog racing. He bought twenty dogs and had another twenty given to him. He started a business, Oregon Trail of Dreams, taking paying customers on sled dog rides around Mount Bachelor. I spent all the time I could with him. I was happiest when I was riding on the sled or playing with the dogs. I loved the mountain and the snow, but most of all I loved the dogs.

When there were chores to be done I pitched in and helped any way I could; packing small buckets of water to fill the dogs' water pans, taking turns stirring the dog food, and even using my little plastic scoop shovel to clean up messes. And when we had puppies it became my job to care for them. I was their first human contact. As soon as I stepped inside their pen a throng of yapping, yelping, hyper puppies descended on me and in their excitement they jumped on me, scratched me, and pulled at my pant legs until they knocked me down. And once I was on the ground they were like a pack of playful wolves, licking me, nuzzling me, tickling me, nipping at me.

Dad taught me how to handle the puppies. Whenever I went into the puppy pen I took a little switch with me. Any puppy that jumped on me I swatted on the top of the head. Dad always said if you swat a dog on the behind he will look at his behind. But if you swat him on the head he will look at you. I never swatted a puppy to hurt him. I would never, could never, do that. I just tapped a misbehaving puppy to get his attention. It worked.

We kept the dogs at a friend's farm until Dad bought a place way out in the country, away from everything and everyone. We moved to forty acres in the middle of the Badlands of Central Oregon, a National Wilderness Study Area. It was twenty-three miles to Bend, twenty-eight miles to Prineville, and twenty-five miles to Redmond. We lived in a trailer with no running water and no electricity. The water was trucked in and pumped into a cistern. We ran a generator for power. But the most difficult adjustment for me was that I had to change schools.

I had been perfectly content at Bear Creek Elementary. But now, enrolled at Buckingham Elementary on the outskirts of Bend, I began the most difficult period of my life. Many of the students at Buckingham Elementary came from privileged families, and cliques developed by the third grade. I did not fit into any of their exclusive cliques.

The popular kids dressed in trendy designer clothes. I threw on whatever was clean, and it never mattered if it matched; green and purple, blue and red, pink and green. Besides, I wore clunky glasses with incredibly thick lenses. I was always squinting at people and things, trying to bring them into focus so that I could see. As a result I was ostracized and ridiculed. Sometimes it went beyond normal childish teasing and I was the center of a cruel and deviant form of entertainment. In the hallway between classes, boys ran up from behind, grabbed my arms, and spun me in circles. In an effort to try to keep from falling I lurched this way and that, like a gangly moose on an icy pond. They tossed their caustic laughter and insults in my direction. "What's the matter, stupid blind girl, can't you see?" or, "Four Eyes, look where you're going!"

After an attack I stumbled around, trying to gain my bearings, trying to figure out where I was and in exactly which direction I was facing. If I made a mistake and started back the way I had come from or, heaven forbid, staggered into something, the kids whooped and hollered like this was the most hilarious thing they had ever witnessed. And as their laughter and jeering washed over me I felt like crawling into a hole and dying.

There was another visually impaired girl at Buckingham Elementary. Her name was Stacy. She had an additional strike against her because she was also an albino. Stacy suffered the same type of treatment I did; but when the boys spun her, she fought back like an enraged badger, screaming, shouting, and cursing until a teacher came on the run to see what the crisis was about. I was timid and passive, suffering in silence and allowing myself to be dominated by these hooligans who took such a perverse glee in exploiting my weaknesses.

Dad never knew what was happening at school, because I did not want to be a snitch and tell him. And so the struggle to survive continued until one day Dad happened to see a neighbor boy, Jimmy, walking along the road. Dad pulled over. "Hey, Jimmy, need a ride home?"

"Sure."

Jimmy climbed into the pickup and Dad, making small talk, inquired, "How's school going?"

"Fine."

"Been staying out of trouble?"

"I didn't do anything."

Jimmy's reply was so quick and defensive Dad knew something was eating at his conscience. Dad turned his head and saw that a tide of emotions was welling up behind Jimmy's eyes. "I was just joking. What's wrong?"

Jimmy blurted out, "I just feel real bad about what's happening at school with Rachael."

Dad's demeanor was very calm, but inside he was seething. "What's happening to Rachael?"

And that was when Jimmy broke down and started crying and all the ugly things that were happening poured out into the open. "There's this group of fifth-grade boys and every time they catch Rachael alone in the hall they pick on her."

Dad pulled off to the shoulder of the road and stopped. "Really? So what are they doing? How do they pick on her?"

Tears were spilling down Jimmy's cheeks. "They run up behind her in the hall, grab her by the arms, and spin her in circles. If she falls down, or stumbles into something, it's a big joke. And they call her names, too. They tease her all the time."

"Really?"

Jimmy wiped at the tears with the heels of his hands. "Mr. Scdoris, I'm not one of them. I swear. I just feel bad for Rachael, that's all."

"I believe you, Jimmy."

Jimmy whimpered. "I've wanted to tell someone for the longest time. I'm really sorry, Mr. Scdoris."

I was unaware that Dad knew about my personal problems until he asked me, "What's going on at school?"

"Nothing. Everything's fine."

"What's happening in the hallway? Tell me about the fifth-grade boys."

At that point I knew that he knew, but I tried to make light of it. "They're just playing. They're having fun. It just happens to be at my expense."

"I'm taking you to school tomorrow and we're going to sit down and talk to the principal. We're getting to the bottom of this and I guarantee you this crap won't be happening again. Not to you, not to anyone else."

"No, Dad. Don't say anything. You'll only make it worse." I argued with him, but secretly I was glad that the boys' outlandish behavior had been exposed. I hoped, I had secretly prayed, that something might be done about it. But I was also scared, scared of what the boys might do to me in retaliation. I could not sleep that night. I was that fearful.

The following morning Dad was on a mission. He marched me into the principal's office, informed the principal what was going on, and very forcefully stated, "Either you monitor the halls and make them safe for my daughter or I promise you that I will be here to monitor the halls myself. It's up to you."

"I had no idea such a thing was going on. You can be assured we will take care of the situation," the principal said.

I was excused to attend my first-period class, but midway through it I was called to the principal's office. The special education teacher was there, and so was Stacy. Stacy had already described the injustices we had been subjected to and I confirmed that what she said was true, as well as adding that the trouble was not confined to the hallway. "Some boys give me a hard time at recess. They run around and scream in my face and pull my hair. They're just boys being stupid. That's the way boys are."

The special education teacher wanted to know, "Can you tell me who's doing this? Can you give me names?"

Stacy and I never saw faces. Perhaps we could have identified exactly who was terrorizing us in the hallways and on the playground, but even if we knew for a certainty I do not know that we would have named names. At that point both of us felt pretty much scared to death.

The principal made a solemn promise to have the staff monitor the situation. But as far as I could tell, nothing really changed. Each evening when Dad asked if there had been any problems, I would lie and tell him no, that everything was hunky-dory.

While the boys were sadistic barbarians, the girls were even meaner and more hurtful. They fought a war against anyone who was not a part of their particular clique, and their weapons of choice were intimidation and manipulation. What they could say with a few sharp words was often more insulting and offensive than being spun in circles. "Rachael, why don't your clothes ever match?" or, "Rachael, why don't you wear pretty things?" or, "Rachael, why do you smell like dog poop?"

Usually I tied my hair in a ponytail. That was the way Dad liked me to wear it. Every morning he brushed my hair and tied it in a ponytail. The girls at school said things like, "Why do you always wear your hair in a ponytail?" or, "Do you know what's under a pony's tail? A horse's butt," or, "Why don't you ever fix yourself up cute?"

Again, no one in a position of authority knew about the abuse and the taunting. I felt powerless to affect the behavior of my peers and so I kept my mouth shut, endured the situation the best I could, and tried to be submissive and as inconspicuous as possible.

The only time I felt comfortable was when I sang. I loved to sing and I was good at it. And when it came time for the Christmas show I was chosen, along with four other girls, to present the musical portion of the show. I was so proud to be there singing Christmas songs to the audience.

Dad attended and he saw what happened. I walked onstage, me in the middle with two girls on either side of me. The music started. I was animated and sang from my heart, sang loud and with perfect pitch. Midway through "Joy to the World" the other girls began to imitate me; raising their hands, tilting their heads upward, rolling their eyes like I have a tendency to do, and squinting when I squinted.

After the last song concluded, the crowd clapped politely. Dad, who was standing next to one of the teachers, turned to her and whispered, "I can't believe what I just saw."

"Wasn't that wonderful," the teacher said.

Dad replied, "Either you're blind or I'm imagining things."

"What do you mean, Mr. Scdoris?"

"Didn't you see them mimicking Rachael? They were making fun of her. It was obvious. You can't tell me you didn't see it."

"You're way too sensitive," said the teacher. "You read too much into things. It was just a case of 'kids will be kids.'"

Dad responded, "I am appalled at what the kids did, but what concerns me the most is your level of toleration. You allow, no, you accept discrimination. They were making fun of Rachael's blindness and you rationalize it by saying kids will be kids."

Dad walked away. Later that evening a mother of one of the students in my class came up and told Dad how shocked she had been at what had transpired onstage. She said, "If those four girls were mine, I'd take them out and whip their behinds until they couldn't sit down for a month of Sundays."

Dad hugged her.

One day, out of the clear blue, one of the most popular girls at school (I will call her Sally) approached me in the hallway and struck up a conversation. She caught me completely off-guard. To be perfectly honest, I was flattered at her attention and, after a few minutes of chitchat, I naively began to imagine she would ask me to join her and her group of Buckingham princesses at their lunch table.

It was such a treat to be talking to Sally but so out of character that she would waste her time on me. I thought maybe she was up to something but did not know what it could be. Setting aside my suspicions, I began to consider that perhaps Sally had come to her senses and was finally recognizing that I possessed all those worthy and enduring qualities required for inclusion in her elite circle of friends. The next words out of her mouth proved how desperate my thinking really was.

"Rachael, why don't you ever talk to Henry?"

Her question was comparable to waving a red flag in the air. Henry (not his real name) was a nice kid, but he was a little on the slow side. Actually, he was labeled "retarded" and was every bit the social outcast that I was. "Why do you want me to talk to Henry?"

"It's just that he needs a friend."

"Why don't you be his friend, Sally?"

"He likes you. He wants you to be his friend."

I found myself saying, "Yeah, well, who couldn't use a friend? We all could use a friend." I knew I was being manipulated. Sally was playing cupid—matching up the blind girl with the retarded boy. How pathetic was that?

"He's right over there. Go talk to him," coached Sally.

"I can't."

"Sure you can." Sally placed an arm around my waist and exerted enough pressure that she gently pushed me across the hall to where Henry was standing in front of his locker. She whispered to me, "Tell him hi." Her hand was now at the small of my back, coaxing me within a few inches of Henry.

"Hi, Henry," I said.

Henry did not move. His head was down as he self-consciously stared at his shoe tips. The door to his locker was open. It was messy inside.

"Give him a hug," Sally whispered along with a giggle that she was unable to stifle.

"No, I don't want to."

Sally was persistent. "He wants to be your friend. Come on, Rachael. Just touch him." She took my hand and guided it toward Henry. As my fingertips came in contact with his skin he recoiled as if bitten by a rattlesnake and scuttled away. I quickly lost sight of him. Sally was gone, too. I hesitated, not knowing if I should walk away and not knowing in which direction to go.

Before I did move, Sally appeared in front of me. She was holding on to Henry, pinning his arms to his side. She thrust him forward at me. He tried to pull away, but Sally held on to him firmly. She triumphantly exclaimed, "Here he is!"

"Please, Sally, let him go. He's afraid."

I sensed people around me, heard the shuffle of their feet, a silly laugh, a snicker, hands reaching, hands pushing me. I lost my balance. To my mortification, I found myself bumping into Henry. He burst into tears, yanked free of Sally, and fled down the hall.

Sally made a mocking gesture by holding her hands together in front of her, and in a voice laced with fake sincerity she said, "There for a few seconds I was thinking to myself—the two of you made such a cute couple. Quite a pair of darling lovebirds."

The popular girls jostled me and laughed at me, laughed in my face. Tears stung my eyes. But I refused to cry. I was too embarrassed, and too mad. Anyway, I was not going to give them the satisfaction of witnessing me break down.

"You are an awful person," I snapped at Sally. "You are mean-spirited and stupid." I spun away and pushed through the ring of girls.

Although this sad episode should have ended right there, it did not. It continued through the week as Sally and her lunatic friends took every opportunity to prolong this miserable drama with their asinine antics. Each time the group passed near me they rushed over and said things like: "Did you and Henry break up?" and, "Is Henry still your boyfriend?" and, "The two of you are so absolutely perfect. You should get back together."

Each time the girls confronted me I simply tried to pretend they did not exist. Our exchanges served to underscore my own lack of confidence and self-worth. Why was I so desperate to have Sally as my friend? What had I been thinking? And yet what made me the angriest was that Henry had been manipulated and used as an unwitting pawn. He was a meek, sensitive boy and the ridicule he had suffered because of me had been humiliating and must have hurt him deeply. I was profoundly sorry for the pain I had forced on him in my misguided endeavor to become one of the popular girls.

7

NEW BEGINNINGS

During summer vacation Dad and Mom talked it over and decided that because of my difficulties at Buckingham Elementary I should transfer to a new school. Starting in the fall I would spend weekends and vacations with Dad and live with Mom during the week so I could attend fifth grade in Redmond.

The first day of school at Lynch Elementary, during physical education, we were required to run relay races. Between runs I stepped into the shade to sit down and take a short break. Coming from the sunlight into the shade is always difficult for me because my vision literally disappears. As I went to sit, someone was already sitting there and I fell directly on this person. It turned out to be Lauren Sprenger. We laughed about it at the time, and in the coming weeks, as our friendship developed, I think we each began to truly believe the accident was caused by divine intervention. Lauren helped me in class, reading to me, helping me organize my work, making sure my assignments were turned in on time. She was my ally. She was my best friend.

Don Duncan was our fifth-grade teacher. He had been a carpenter for twenty years but had a calling to go back to college, get his degree and teaching credentials, and become a classroom teacher. He had a passion for helping children. He made fifth grade a turning point in my life and helped me rediscover that learning could be fun.

Fall turned to winter and I spent every minute of the weekends with Dad and the sled dogs. When he was training dogs Dad allowed me to ride the tandem sled. He drove the dogs, while I brought up the rear on the trailing sled.

Dad served as my eyes, calling to me, "Look out, low branch." And I ducked. "Hard left corner coming up." I bent my knees, got low, and shifted my weight to counterbalance the centrifugal force that pulled at us.

These training runs proved to be a terrific learning experience. I had my feet on the runners and was learning the nuances of balance, how to take corners without tipping over and push on the uphill slopes, and how and when to use the brake. I watched Dad and did whatever he did. And the best part was that, at times, I visualized being alone with the dogs. Dad ceased to exist; it was just the sled, the racing dogs, a wide-open trail, and me.

Dad's former racing partner, John Patten, came out from Minnesota for a visit. I was fascinated with John. We sat up late into the night and I listened intently to him, totally mesmerized by his stories, especially of the time he ran the Iditarod. He talked about driving his dogs through howling blizzards, enduring temperatures of fifty and sixty degrees below zero, encountering moose, and having to load up a dog that gave out and carry him on the sled to the next checkpoint. John described the camaraderie that developed between mushers as they fought their way across the Alaskan wilderness. And he told stories of points of interest along the trail, what made them special or memorable or difficult: the confusion and chaos at the start of the race in downtown Anchorage, the lack of snow in The Burn, crossing the Alaska Range at Rainy Pass, leaving McGrath and facing the push across the interior, the celebration at Unalakleet, running the pressure ridges of Norton Sound, and finally the last 150 grueling miles between Koyuk and Nome. John had gone without sleep for days on end. He had driven himself to the point of utter exhaustion, had endured hallucinations and pushed himself far beyond what he ever imagined he could endure. But more than anything John talked about his dogs, how special they were to him; and whenever he talked about his dogs his eyes brightened and he became passionate, intense, and his gestures more animated. Sometimes, as memories of special dogs that had passed on came floating back to him, he became misty-eyed.

Because of John's passion, the skill of his delivery, and the power of his stories, I began having dreams. These were dreams that were dynamic and full of energy and life. I was the superhero, and when a deranged moose attacked my team I fought him with my bare hands. When I became disoriented in a blizzard I stumbled into a checkpoint, caked with ice on my hair and eyebrows. We fell into open water and I climbed out onto the ice and saved my dogs. One of my favorite dreams was reaching Safety, the last checkpoint of the race. Other mushers were there, gathered around the wood stove, while the wind howled outside. Nobody wanted to leave Safety and face the horrible wind and the deadly cold. Taking the lead from Libby Riddles—she had gone out in a storm when no one else had dared—I stood and announced, "I'm going out." The other mushers pleaded with me to wait until the storm broke, but just as Libby had done, I went anyway. After I got a few miles under my belt the wind miraculously died, the sun came up, and the end of the race loomed ahead. I would awaken just as I neared the finish line, but close enough to know I was the winner of the Iditarod.

To me, the thought of being able to ride a sled and drive a team of dogs became an obsession. I began to believe that God had put me on this earth and granted me this passion, but it was up to me to accomplish this goal. I made myself a promise—someday I would run the Iditarod, not just to compete in the race, but to try to win it. And when I accomplished that impossible mission I would be fulfilling my dream.

During the week I went through the motions of going to school and turning in my assignments. I lived for the weekends. Then I could spend time with my dogs. They were the most important things in my life. They were always happy to see me. They were my boys and girls. They loved me and I loved them back.

Any chance of my ever being able to compete in the Iditarod was a million miles away, especially considering that Dad refused to allow me to run the dogs. I pleaded with him to give me the opportunity to take them out on my own.

"Dad, do you think I do a lot of work around here?"

"Sure. And I appreciate it," he would say.

"Then when can I drive a team alone?"

I tried being rational: "Dad, I can't learn to drive a team any younger than I am right now, so why not let me do it today?"

"Someday, maybe."

Finally I resorted to indiscreet begging: "Dad, just let me drive the dogs. Please, please, pretty please."

I tried affection: "I love you, Dad. Will you please let me take out a team?"

"No!"

And yet, little by little, I thought I detected tiny chinks beginning to form in his resolve, in his tough exterior. Sometimes he actually talked to me. We progressed from a flat "No!" to a three-word response: "I said no!" From there we evolved to full-fledged, back-to-back sentences: "Honey, stop asking all the time. Someday I'll let you drive the dogs, but not today."

Spotting a moment of weakness, I would close in for the kill: "Can I drive them tomorrow. Can I, Daddy?" But it looked like tomorrow, or someday, would never arrive.

Dave Sims worked for Dad. Dave was more than just an employee; he was also a close personal friend. Lots of times I went on rides with him, either on a tandem sled or as a passenger. Since I was unsuccessful in swaying Dad, I set my sights on Dave and began pestering him. If I convinced him I was capable of driving a dog team, maybe he would put in a good word for me.

But with the passing of time I came to believe that I would never be allowed the opportunity to drive a team of dogs, that I would never be given the chance to be on my own, that I would never run the Iditarod.

All my life, my entire life, someone had always been with me. Either I was in the company of an adult or I was operating under the buddy system with a responsible friend at my side. In school I was surrounded by other kids, and on the playground I was under constant supervision. I had never gone for a walk by myself, had never run on a trail through the woods without a companion. Not once had I been given the freedom of being alone, really alone.

One Saturday in mid-December it snowed a good six inches on the mountain. The trails were slow and the dogs, after working all day, had lost their nervous energy and were settled down. A member of the ski patrol stopped to visit for a moment and Dad asked him to make a pass on his snow machine and pack the Kid's Trail, a little one-mile loop that circled through the woods. I figured Dad was thinking that we might get a family who had grown tired of skiing and wanted a short sled dog ride before heading down the mountain. What I did not know was Dad had whispered to Dave, "This might be a good time to let Rachael make a run."

"Not a bad idea," Dave responded.

"She's eleven years old; think she's ready?" Dad asked.

"Ready as she'll ever be."

Dad and Dave hooked two of our best dogs, Coyote and Shane, to a sled. Both were leaders. Both had run the Iditarod. Coyote was an Alaskan husky, strong, dependable, and levelheaded. Shane had led a team that won the Yukon Quest. He was one of Dad's favorites and possibly the best dog Dad ever owned.

"Hey, Rachael," Dad called to me. "Do you want to make a run?"

"Sure," I said. I was always up for a run. I walked over to where Dave was holding the team, paused to pet Coyote and Shane before proceeding to the sled where Dad waited. "Who's going with me?"

"Just you," Dad said.

It took a second for that to sink in. And when it did, I assumed I had not heard him correctly. When I asked, "Just me?" my voice was more timid than I wanted it to be.

"Just you."

I moved quickly, before Dad could change his mind. My feet found the runners and my fingers gripped the handlebars. Dave stepped away. I spoke to the dogs: "Coyote. Shane. Hike!"

Instinct took over. From having run the tandem sled so many times I knew exactly what to do. But this was an entirely new sensation, to be alone, with only the dogs out in front. It was the coolest feeling. Fantastic. Exhilarating. I could use a thousand other adjectives and never begin to do justice to the incredible joy I felt at that moment. It was the thrill of a lifetime.

The start of the one-mile Kid's Trail is a fairly steep incline. I had been over it hundreds of times, but always in the basket or riding a tandem sled. It was an entirely new phenomenon to be doing it on my own. The shift of the runners beneath my feet was unlike any time before. The dogs ran faster. In fact, it was a little scary.

"The brake!" I could hear Dad's voice drifting to me from a long distance away. I knew he wanted me to slow down, but, quite the contrary, I wanted to go faster. I wanted the wind in my hair and the ice crystals kicked up by the dogs stinging my face. I wanted to race these dogs into the woods and never come back. I was intoxicated with this strange power of freedom, of being in command of so much raw energy, of being on my own. What did it matter that only two old dogs comprised my team, that we were on the Kid's Trail, that six inches of new snow was slowing the sled? The true significance of the moment was that finally I was taking my first step toward realizing my ultimate dream: to someday run the Iditarod. From inside me a noise began to emanate, bursting forth in an invigorating shout that caused me to throw back my head: "Wahoo!" It was a spontaneous thing, uttered in a moment of total exhilaration. Even I was surprised by it.

The trail dropped off the hill and we raced across an open flat. I rode the runners like a veteran musher as we careened into the first corner, and when we started the uphill climb I crossed over to one runner and used my free leg to pump, pushing to save my dogs and increase the sled's speed.

And just that quickly the mile run was over. We were back at the staging area and Dave was taking hold of Shane by the collar. We had barely come to a stop when I piled off the runners and sprinted to my dogs. I loved my two boys to death, threw my arms around their necks, hugged them, and showered them with kisses. I had never been so happy. I lavished every ounce of my affection on Shane and Coyote. They had taken me out and brought me back safely. One mile. The significance of that single mile was that if I could run one mile, it opened the possibility that I could run twelve hundred miles. The Iditarod had never been as close to a reality as it was at that moment.

Dad reached me. He was breathing hard and beads of sweat lined his forehead, but in my moment of ecstasy I never questioned why. Not until later did I learn that he had watched me heading out into the world alone and it frightened him. He yelled at me to ride the brake. But I had other ideas. I think that terrified him even more, that I had my own ideas. My whoop had sent him over the edge. He turned to Dave and said, "What have we done?" Then Dad took off on foot, sprinting, trying to chase me down. He ran the entire one-mile loop and only caught a couple quick glimpses of me. I'm glad I never knew—it might have spoiled my run knowing he was following me.

"I want to do it again."

"Not today," Dad huffed. "We're going home."

When the dogs were put away, Dad and Dave exchanged a few words about my accomplishment. They let me know how extremely proud they were of me.

Several years later Dad confided to me that he and Dave had a private conversation after I was in the truck. Dad said, "Every time she comes to the mountain she's going to want us to hook up a team for her. I'm afraid we've unleashed a monster."

"You know, Jerry, when she took off she reminded me of a bird that has suddenly gained its wings and learned to fly. I think she tasted freedom in that mile. And if I were you I'd be a whole lot more concerned about that than being afraid you'll have to hook up a team for her." Dave was joking, but Dad never laughed.

The next time I was allowed to drive a sled, Dave took Dad aside and gave him a little more advice. Once again Dad had run behind me. Dave told him, "Jerry, you're going to kill yourself trying to keep up with her. Leave her be. She's a natural dog musher. She'll be fine."

From then on, whenever I went on a run, Dad and Dave grilled me. They went over everything that could possibly go wrong and had me recite how I would handle any difficulties that might arise: If the dogs became tangled I would stand on the brake and holler for help; if the sled tipped, I would hang on and tell the dogs to whoa; if I lost the sled, I would stay on the packed trail; if I ever felt lost, I would stand in one spot and they would find me; if I heard a snow machine driving fast, I would assume the driver was crazy and I would immediately slow and move to the far edge of the trail.

I must have run that one-mile loop a thousand times. It became routine, almost boring, and I pleaded to be allowed to try one of the longer runs, the three-mile or seven-mile loops. Longer trails meant more independence. I also wanted to add more dogs to the team. Dogs equaled speed. I was like the kid who drives an old beater car but hungers to slide behind the wheel of a Ferrari. My Ferrari was longer runs and more dogs. Dad flatly refused to consider anything but the Kid's Trail, but little by little I was able to inch him forward in his thinking and eventually he allowed me to run three dogs and finally four.

For Christmas that year John Patten gave me a special gift—an Iditarod sled. It was called the Hornet. It weighed only twenty pounds and was superfast. One time I ran four dogs hooked to the Hornet and did the entire one-mile loop without ever once stepping on the brake or the drag. To do that was like gaining a red badge of courage. We flew around the loop in less than four minutes. After that I felt as though I were ready to handle anything that could be thrown in my direction. But it would be another year before Dad allowed me to run the three-mile loop.

8

RUNNING BLIND

In fifth grade we took an overnight field trip to Portland. We did all the things country bumpkins do when they go to the big city: visiting the water fountains, the parks, the Rose Garden, the Oregon Historical Society, and the Portland Art Museum. We even spent a night at a downtown hotel.

Normally I was paired with Lauren, who acted as my eyes and described in detail everything she saw, but on the second day we were placed in separate groups. I walked with our teacher, Mr. Duncan, holding his hand as our group strolled the sidewalks of downtown Portland.

We were talking and having fun. I really do not know what happened except that, I guess, Mr. Duncan forgot I was beside him and relying on him to be my eyes. He accidentally walked me into a parking meter. It hit me forehead high. *Thunk.* It didn't take my feet out from under me, but it definitely knocked me back a step.

Tears of shock and pain welled up in my eyes, and a goose egg swelled on my forehead.

Mr. Duncan was so apologetic. He ducked into a nearby restaurant and returned with a small bag of ice, directing me to hold it to my forehead to reduce the swelling. After about his hundredth apology I told him, "Mr. Duncan, don't worry about it. That sort of thing happens to me all the time." And really it did. I was always running into something; it comes with the territory when you are visually impaired.

Once the swelling went down, the incident would have been nothing more than an amusing footnote to a fun trip. But two boys, I will call them Timmy and Kevin, witnessed the accident and they refused to let it go. They kept up a steady banter, saying things like, "Rachael, look out for that parking meter," and, "Rachael, there's a power pole coming up," and, "Rachael, look out for that forty-story building; it's going to fall on you."

If their comments had been said once and dropped, it would have been one thing. But they repeated the comments with irritating regularity, reaching the point of torture and torment. I asked Mr. Duncan to please make them stop. And they did, for the remainder of the trip.

Once we returned to school those two imbeciles went out of their way to harass me and make my life a living hell. Compared to Timmy and Kevin, the kids at Buckingham were totally incompetent, nothing but a pack of rank amateurs.

One day in physical education class the teacher was introducing us to the various events in track and field. We were taking turns long jumping, and when my name was called I stepped forward and started running down the approach. I was concentrating on trying to pick up sight of the takeoff board as soon as I could, so I could adjust my steps if necessary.

"Look out for that parking meter!" Timmy screamed at me from only a few feet away.

I reacted like any visually impaired person would, ducking and throwing up my hands to protect myself. I tripped and fell. Everyone laughed, including the PE teacher, who had heard the story of my running into the parking meter in Portland. I approached her to complain. She saw me coming and said, "What can I do for you, girl with the squinty eyes?"

The following year I attended sixth grade at Obsidian Middle School in Redmond. The school was nice, but the kids were out of control. Timmy and Kevin continued to pester me and they added a new recruit to the cause; I'll call him Bill. Bill was a crude, loud-mouthed bully. Every time he passed me in the hall he shouted at me, calling me Blind Bitch and other even more vulgar names. If the three of them were together, Timmy, Kevin, and Bill, they egged one another on to see which one could be the most gross. It did not matter to them if other students or even teachers were around, because there was very little discipline at the school and absolutely no accountability.

As early as September I was praying for snow, because once winter set in I would be back on the mountain every weekend doing something I enjoyed, away from the school and my tormentors. I thought this would be the year Dad would allow me to run the three-mile and maybe even the seven-mile loop. I brought up the possibility to Dad, but he said I had to go out for the cross-country team at school. Then and only then would he consider the possibility of allowing me to progress past the Kid's Trail.

When it came to running dogs, Dad had a hard and fast rule: If a musher runs a fifty-mile race, he has to be able to run twenty-five miles, just in case he loses his team at the midway point. Furthermore, Dad held to the theory that the musher in the best shape has the advantage in any race. It was hard to argue with him, because he kept in good shape and had established himself as the most dominate musher in the Northwest.

Dad told me on more than one occasion that if he and another musher had equal dogs he prayed for a steep hill. Dad always got off his sled and sprinted to the top of the hill. That was how he won so many races. It was not that he always had the best dogs; it was just that Dad "out-toughed" the other mushers.

His point was that if I was serious about running dogs, then I had to be physically fit. In Dad's estimation, the best way to become physically fit was by running. He laid down an ultimatum—if I wanted to run the dogs on the three-mile loop, I had to be able to run a mile and a half.

I did not sign up for the school cross-country team right away. Instead I expended all my energy trying to persuade Dad to change his mind. He refused to budge: "You can do the three-mile loop when you can prove to me you can run a mile and a half. I won't even consider it until then."

I knew I had some athletic talent as a runner. My very first race was the Little Foot Run held in Drake Park in Bend. I was only six years old. I ran with my cane in one hand and holding on to Dad's hand with my other. It was a two-mile event, a long way for a child, but I did it and finished ahead of many of the sighted kids.

After the race Bob Latham, the track and cross-county coach at Bend High School, came up to me. He got down on one knee so he was close to my height and said, "You're about the most amazing runner I have ever seen in my entire life. I'm the running coach at Bend High and I can hardly wait for you to come and run for me."

After Mr. Latham said that, Dad picked me up and held me and it looked like he had tears in his eyes. When I asked him why he was crying he told me some dust must have blown in his eyes.

But I was in the sixth grade and in my estimation too old to be told what to do. I did not want to run cross-country. I was against it for all the obvious reasons: I was afraid of running into something and hurting or embarrassing myself, did not like being short of breath, hated when my leg muscles burned, and disliked all the other pain and discomfort associated with the crazy sport of distance running.

One day I complained to several friends that Dad was trying to force me to go out for cross-country. My best friend, Lauren, said, "Cool, I'm going out. We can run together." And another friend,

Gretchen, said she was thinking about trying out for the team. Suddenly running did not seem quite so bad.

Running cross-country proved to be a unique experience. I actually enjoyed the training and the socializing with friends as we leisurely ran the trails around Redmond. But the races were entirely different. I refused to run with a guide runner because I did not want to impose on a teammate and have her alter her pace for me. It seemed my best alternative was to run with a guide dog. I chose Sitka. She was not a sled dog but was my pet. She was the first puppy I ever raised and she was a wonderful dog. But I soon discovered she was not well suited for cross-country racing.

At our first cross-country race the contestants lined up and the starter fired a blank round into the air, signaling the start of the race. This scared Sitka. She darted between my legs, tripping me. She was so frightened I had to pick her up and carry her for a ways before I could set her down. By then the field of runners had left me in their dust.

Within the first half mile I had overtaken and passed several of the slower runners. This fueled my competitive juices and it became a challenge to see how many more I could overtake. I was running as fast as I could as we approached the finish line, which was in the vicinity of the start of the race. Sitka, remembering the sound of the shot, shied once again, and to avoid tripping over her I scooped her up in my arms and hugged her across the finish and into the chute. All things considered, I felt it was a relatively good showing for my first cross-country race. The bonus was that I had run the entire way, thereby proving to Dad that I was ready to drive the dog team on the three-mile loop.

The following week I carried Sitka the first fifty yards of the race before setting her on the ground. During the race there were a few times Sitka pulled me, but more often she was not the least bit interested in following the designated course. Other times she was reluctant to run as fast as I wanted and I dragged her along. Once again, as we neared the finish line I carried her. This time the crowd cheered me.

The last race Sitka and I ran together was after a rainstorm. Puddles dotted the course and in some places, where there was no way around the water, runners were forced to plod through it. We reached the first puddle and Sitka stopped suddenly, causing me to trip and fall face-first into the muddy bog. I popped up, drenched to the bone and spitting putrid, brown water. After the race I told Dad, "This is stupid. I'm not going to run with Sitka ever again."

That winter Dad allowed me to run the three-mile loop. At first I could use only two dogs, but as I gained experience and proved myself I was able to add an additional dog, and then two. As my skills improved I became more confident, and I think that carried over and helped me deal with the problems I was facing at school.

Kevin had grown up and for the most part left behind his rude antics, but Bill had reached an all-time low, even for Bill. He began running up behind me in the hallways and attempted to grope me in inappropriate places. The first time or two he got away with his repulsive assaults, but I devised a plan to deal with him. I confided in my friend Anna and told her what I planned to do and enlisted her help.

The next time Bill came running at me in the hall Anna had time to whisper, "Here he comes." I prepared myself.

"Ugly blind bitch," he screamed in my face as his hands went out to grope my pitifully flat breasts.

I was old enough to know that a boy has a certain location on his body that is particularly tender. If not protected, he can be quite susceptible to a retaliatory attack. Armed with this knowledge, I employed my newfound strength as a runner and musher to bring up my knee, aiming it at Bill's groin. There was a sickening sound as my knee made contact. Bill grunted, groaned, and collapsed in a pool of pain. I stepped over him as if he were nothing more than an annoying obstacle and continued on my way.

But even this did not stop the taunting, rude behavior and physical attacks. Nor was it limited to Bill. Timmy and some of the other boys joined in. It became a favorite game for some students to wave several fingers in front of my face and ask, "How many fingers do you see?" For the most part I ignored their insensitive remarks. But one day, when nothing seemed to be going right, one of the boys went through the irritating and all too familiar routine: "How many fingers am I holding up?"

I told the boy, "You're not my ophthalmologist. You don't need to give me vision tests. I don't know, or even really care, how many fingers you're holding up. But maybe you can tell me something: How many fingers do you suppose I'm holding up?"

With that said, I extended my middle finger. I flew that finger proudly in the face of my offender, with as much fierce pride as any war veteran ever felt running up the Stars and Stripes on Flag Day. It was a bold statement, an exclamation point to mark the end of years of passively shouldering the teasing and ridicule of my peers. In the span of a few days I had kneed Bill in the groin and I had flipped somebody off. I felt liberated and giddy.

Shortly after that incident Dad got a call from the principal's office. The principal explained what had happened and concluded by saying, "I understand there might have been some provocation, but, Mr. Scdoris, your daughter cannot go around flipping people off simply because they tease her."

Dad replied, "For your information, kids have been intimidating and browbeating her for years. Through it all she has never retaliated. Let me tell you this: I'm proud as hell she finally stood up for herself. If you want to punish her, fine, but if you do, then you're going to have to deal with me."

"Mr. Scdoris, I'm not finding fault or threatening anyone." The principal had suddenly become amicable. "I was just hoping you could talk to your daughter and tell her that flipping people off is not appropriate behavior for a young lady."

9

FROG LAKE TO WYOMING

The snow hook is a double-crampon device. When jammed into the snow it will, in theory, hold back a team of sled dogs. It will hold them if the snow is not too powdery or too icy and if the snow is deep enough. A snow hook can be dangerous to use if not set properly, and the musher has to be fairly strong in order to pull it.

For these reasons Dad refused to allow me to use a snow hook until I was twelve years old. That meant if I was out on the trail and had any trouble with the dogs getting tangled or an equipment problem, all I could do was stand on the brake and call for help.

I signed up to race in my first sled dog competition, the Frog Lake Race, in the three-dog novice division. My twelfth birthday was only a month away, but Dad would not fudge and allow me to use a snow hook.

Before the race several things made me nervous. Not having a snow hook was one, but also I had never run the trail, a four-mile loop through the Cascade Mountains near Mount Hood.

Helping to allay my concerns was my team—King, Big Guy, and Gus. They were reliable and fast. King and Big Guy were seasoned veterans. Gus was young, but, as Shane's son, he came from good bloodlines. He was part of the team Dad was taking to race in Wyoming in less than a month. Dad called these three dogs a "push-button" team, which meant any novice musher could take them out and, even without a snow hook, would have no problem.

Most of the mushers and spectators thought it was cute to have a blind girl entered in the novice class, but one fellow questioned whether it was safe for me to be on the trail. Dad told him, "Rachael has miles of experience behind her. She has done everything I asked her to do. She is a runner. She is strong. She is determined. I can't see holding her back just because she happens to be legally blind."

Frog Lake was a two-day race. The first day, my dogs started off like a dragster burning rubber off the line. I held on and we went flying down a long hill and into a looping corner. I rolled the sled on that first corner, but that was not a problem. I held on to the handlebars, dug my elbows and toes into the snow, and yelled, "Big Guy. Whoa. Whoa." He never stopped, but thankfully he slowed enough that I was able to get my knees under me and jerk the sled upright. Only a minimum of time had been lost.

There was a keyhole turnaround at the end of a two-mile run. We went into it a little iffy, but Big Guy figured it out and pulled us through. Out of twelve mushers in the race we crossed the finish line in third place. The following day I swore I would stay off the brake and keep the sled upright. I had a burning desire to win.

The second day, my "push-button" team failed me. We made it down the hill without overturning, but when we hit the turnaround things got sketchy. Usually when a dog goes on a trail the route is imbedded in his memory. Big Guy forgot. He tried to go straight. I stomped on the brake and managed to stop before we had gone too far off the trail. I called to one of the race officials and asked him to stand on the brake while I turned the team around. I assumed the man knew to stay on the brake until I returned to the sled. I went up, turned the dogs, took one step toward the sled, and the official stepped off the brake. The dogs shot forward and the sled went past me before I could grab the handlebars. I called to the dogs to whoa and started sprinting after them. With a little help from a competitor I was able to get back on my sled and finish the race. The delay cost me valuable time. Instead of challenging for first place, I slipped a spot in the rankings and took home the fourth-place trophy. But still, I was thrilled. I had completed my first race and it seemed as though nearly all the mushers had accepted me. As long as I was the little blind girl, running the three-dog novice class, everything would be fine.

I was given an excused absence from school to become a member of Dad's support team for the Wyoming International Pedigree Stage Stop Sled Dog Race. The dogs were well trained and Dad was primed for the challenge. He had not lost a race in the Northwest in fifteen years and believed he had a legitimate shot to win the Stage Race.

We arrived in Wyoming and the race director, Frank Teasley, took a genuine liking to me. Once the race started, Dad spent long hours on the trail while I idled away the time with Frank and flitted around like a social butterfly. Only when Dad came in from a run did I work to help make sure his team was well cared for and ready for the next day. And then I was off being entertained at the banquets or sitting around the campfire visiting with the officials, mushers, and visitors.

Dad was running a strategic race, staying in the middle of the pack. I assumed he was positioning himself and saving his dogs for a hard push on the last couple legs. I thought everything was going well. I failed to read the dogs and see that the race was becoming an ordeal for some of them. I did not comprehend the quit in their eyes.

On the seventy-seven-mile run over the mountains from Pinedale to Lander, Dad's lead dogs gave out. They quit and refused to go. Dad hitched himself to the lead position. For thirty grueling miles he dragged the sled, and his team, toward the finish line. But two miles shy of Lander his strength was gone and he collapsed onto the snow. He could not endure another step, let alone two long miles. When an official came along on a snow machine to check on him, Dad said, "It's over. I'm scratching."

That afternoon, while Dad had been struggling over the Rocky Mountains, I was oblivious to any potential problems he might be facing on the trail. I flitted here and there, having a grand time, enjoying myself to the utmost. I had not a single care or concern as I waited. Other mushers finished and I fully expected to see Dad at any moment. But afternoon grew toward evening and still Dad was nowhere to be seen.

Out on the trail Dad had watered and fed his team and allowed them to rest. After several hours he determined they had regained enough strength to make a final push for the finish. Two snow machines escorted him and the riders helped when they were needed.

Finally, just before dark, I heard the whine of a pair of snow machines and then someone shouted, "Here he comes."

The snow machines came in and a few minutes later I spotted Dad's team coming down the hill at a painfully slow pace. Dasher, one of our lead dogs, was riding in the basket. I knew something had happened, but I was naive and never picked up on all the telltale signs that spoke to the heartbreak and misfortune of the day.

I took Dasher to the truck, gave her food, water, and lots of attention. Our handler snipped at me, "Leave her alone. Stop fussing over her."

Jessica's remarks were insulting to me. Dasher was one of our lead dogs. I could touch her and give her love if I wanted. I vowed to have a talk with Dad about Jessica's attitude, just as soon as I got him alone. But people were crowding around him, mushers shaking his hand, telling him they were sorry, wishing him well. This scene seemed so melodramatic, so blown out of proportion, to me. Dad had come in with a dog in the basket. So what? There were still miles to go. The race was not over.

When the hullabaloo calmed a little Dad took me aside and told me, "It's over."

"What do you mean, it's over? It can't be over."

"I scratched," he said.

"Dad, you can't pull out. You have to keep going. Maybe you didn't do very well today, but you can come back tomorrow. You can win this race. Dad, you've never quit anything in your life."

"Today I did. That was my only choice. I accepted outside help and if I don't scratch I'll be disqualified. It's over."

Finally it hit me. This was not about me or the terrific time I was having. This was about the dogs, Dad, and the bitter taste of his defeat. The dogs had quit. Given up. I could sense Dad's disappointment, frustration, and absolute exhaustion.

Later, when I found out that he had taken up the harness and led the team for thirty miles, that he had done everything he could to make up for his team's deficiencies, I was so proud of him that I bawled. I made a promise that day—to return to Wyoming and complete the race. And when I crossed the finish line, I would dedicate all my miles, my pain, misery, and happiness, to Dad.

Back at school it was the same old thing. Bill and Timmy would push me and jump away. They called me every vile name in the book and some that were totally original. They took advantage of every opportunity to torment me. Finally, I had had enough of their bizarre form of entertainment. I went to the principal and told her what was happening.

The principal called Timmy's mother to school. She listened intently to the evidence and asked her son, "Is this true?"

"Most of it," he admitted.

His mother was very apologetic and promised that, in addition to any discipline imposed by the school, Timmy would also be disciplined at home. He was forced to write me a letter of apology, admitting to his stupidity and immaturity and promising it would never happen again. I wadded up the letter and threw it away.

When Bill's father was notified he reacted quite differently. He threw a tantrum and was antagonistic toward the principal, telling her, "This is bogus. You think you can call a man away from his work for some ridiculous little thing like this? You're accusing my son of name-calling, a little teasing? This girl was probably egging him on. Hell, she was probably asking for it. I don't have time for this kind of crap. If you want to talk, talk to my attorney."

And then he addressed Bill: "Come on, son. Let's go home."

As Bill passed me on the way to the door he was grinning as if he had won the decisive battle of the war. He never came back to school and I never saw him again. Thank goodness.

That spring I turned out for track and participated in two running events—the 800 meters and the 1500 meters. I never beat anyone and finished every single race in last place.

"Don't sweat it, honey," Dad told me. "The important thing is to keep running. If you do, I promise, you'll improve and your times will get better. You'll start beating some people."

He was right, but it took a lot longer than either of us expected.

10

FITTING IN

I began to show some potential my last year of middle school. I had difficulty running cross-country, but in racing sled dogs my star began to shine. I entered the four-dog novice class and I won every race: Frog Lake, Chemult, and Diamond Lake. Most of the other mushers still thought it was cute to have the blind girl racing, but there was also a bit of undercurrent in the world of Northwest sled dog racers. I was aware that my winning had changed a few things.

One musher said to me, "Well, sugar, you've certainly proved you're the best novice. Too bad you can't run that class anymore. Oh well, nothing wrong with being a spectator."

At school the ranks of my antagonists had thinned considerably. Bill was gone. Kevin had stopped being a jerk. It was down to Timmy. He was still trying to build himself up by tearing me down. But a series of events occurred one day during fifth period that put an end to Timmy's reign of terror. Fear will do that.

It began with a friend, Scott, getting kicked out of class. Scott was a big kid with a great sense of humor, but sometimes he could be a goofball. Scott was being disruptive in class and the teacher sent him to stand in the hall. But rather than stand there looking like a dork, Scott squeezed himself inside his locker.

I happened to be walking down the hall alone. Timmy spotted me, sneaked up, and bonked me on the head. "Watch out for that parking meter." He danced away.

"Stop it, Timmy."

"You don't know who I am. I could be anybody. You can't see me. You're blind."

Timmy was right. I knew his voice, but he stayed far enough away from me that I could not say I had actually seen his face. I advanced toward him. Timmy backed up, keeping his distance.

He mocked me: "You can't see me. You can't see me. The pathetic blind girl can't see me."

I noticed something behind the hazy outline of Timmy and squinted, trying to focus on what it could be.

"You're squinting again, blind girl."

A locker door banged open and something, or someone, appeared to engulf the form of Timmy.

"I've got him," Scott's voice boomed. "He's not going anywhere. Maybe you'd like to make a positive ID, Rachael?"

Scott had Timmy's arms pinned to his side and it was obvious that at long last I had the upper hand. I used a rigid pointing finger to thump Timmy's exposed chest. "Timmy, you are a total coward. I am sick and tired of being the target of your stupidity. My blindness is not something I can control. But you don't have to be a coward, or so utterly stupid.

"I turned you in once, got you kicked out of school, and your mommy had to take you home. If you give me one more ounce of trouble, if you do anything to me ever again, I guarantee I'll turn you in. You'll be out of this school and never come back. Do I make myself completely clear?"

"Yeah. I won't bother you. I'll leave you alone."

"Okay, turn him loose," I told Scott.

And then I said to Timmy, "Get out of here." I felt like Clint Eastwood in a Dirty Harry movie and was tempted to add the word "punk," but I held back.

My entire world changed the summer before I started high school. I grew six inches and put on thirty pounds of muscle. I started lifting weights, ran every day, and because of my physical changes, I gained a tremendous amount of self-assurance. It seemed as though I had endured years in a dormant stage as a reluctant, bashful little girl and now I was emerging from my cocoon as a powerful woman. Dad took notice and his favorite saying became, "Pity the fool who messes with you."

My goal was to make the varsity cross-country team. Before the start of the season we were to meet at running camp at a lakeside campground in the Cascade Mountains. The first day we mostly messed around and got to know one another. Two of the older girls, Ginny and Jessica, decided to rent a paddleboat and go out on the lake. They asked me to go with them and I said I would, of course. I was thrilled that older classmates would include me in their fun.

We paddled around for a while, sunbathed, and visited. We did not realize it, but the wind had come up and pushed us far out into the lake. When we tried to get back, no matter how hard we paddled we could not make any headway into the wind, and, in fact, we were being blown backward. I tied a rope around my waist, dove in, and swam, pulling the paddleboat to shore. That evening around the campfire Ginny and Jessica told the story of how I had saved them. Of course they embellished it and made me, the lowly freshman, nothing short of Wonder Woman.

But the luster on my star lost a little of its shine when we went on our first run. We were on a trail in the woods and I failed to see a small log that all the others were able to jump over. I stumbled and fell. And while I was trying to get to my feet all the others passed me. A couple of the slower girls stopped and asked if I needed help.

"I can't see much in this light. This is going to take a while. You'll go crazy waiting for me. Don't worry. I'll find my way. Go on," I told them.

After they departed, the woods became eerily quiet. I had no idea where I was or how I was going to find my way back to camp. I never considered sitting down, staying put, and waiting for one of my teammates to find me. That is not in my nature. It was never even an option. Do that and what? Run a headline in the newspaper: "Poor Pathetic Blind Girl Lost in the Big Bad Woods." I kept running.

For thirty minutes or so I was separated from the others, and then a junior, Nichole, doubled back and asked how I was doing. I told her, "Fine, but I can't see much of anything." She stayed with me and we ran the rest of the way to camp.

Camp was a fun place. We had a fire in the evenings and Coach Davidson talked to us about the various aspects of competitive running, from training to nutrition, and from race strategies to proper care of typical runners' injuries. We roasted marshmallows, told jokes, and swapped stories. I had never been a part of a group bonding experience before. It was terrific. And there was a boy there who paid a lot of attention to me. He tried to sit with me at every opportunity and offered to cook marshmallows for me. It was pretty obvious he was attracted to me, and that, too, was a new experience. Up until then I had had a few boys who were friends, but boys mostly just wanted to tease me and try to make my life miserable.

The day we had arrived at camp the campground host paid us a visit. He said, "I don't mean to alarm you, but we have a troublesome black bear in the area and sometimes she can make quite a pest of herself. I advise you to keep a clean camp. Don't leave anything that smells like food lying around. Always store your food in your vehicles and make sure the windows are rolled up."

With a little encouragement from Coach Davidson we had followed the host's warning. At the end of the first night, camp was clean as a whistle. The second evening, Dad came up for a visit and brought us candy. That night a few wrappers were left scattered

around on the ground. The third and final night we were convinced
that the bear was a myth, a bunch of hooey.

Since it was the last night of running camp, we stayed up later
than usual; singing songs, playing traditional camp card games, and
performing skits. Finally we called it a night and went to our tents.
I got in my sleeping bag but kept my flashlight on in order to make
a few notations in my daily journal. I was tired and after fifteen
minutes or so I gave up on writing, telling myself I would finish the
entry in the morning. I turned off the flashlight and lay back on my
pillow. A few minutes passed and then I heard a strange noise right
outside my tent. It went *crunch, crunch, crunch.*

The fire was still burning, throwing off a glow around our
camp, and when I looked in the direction of the noise I could see
someone hunched over, moving slowly. My first inclination was that
one of the boys was up, attempting to play a trick on one of us girls,
and I thought, *Don't get caught.* Coach had made it abundantly
clear there was to be no tepee creeping. Once we went to our tents,
we were to stay there.

Crunch. Crunch. Crunch. The vague shadow lumbered past my
tent and out of sight. It had an odd appearance and moved with a
shuffling gait. Judging from the size of the shadow, this thing was
huge, bigger than our biggest runner. Then it made a snorting
sound, almost like a *woof,* and it hit me. Bear!

The bear knocked over something, rattled some papers, and
chewed the contents. I thought about running over to the next tent
so I did not have to die alone. I could hear the girls over there laughing and giggling, totally unaware a bear was in our camp. I decided
to stay where I was.

Oh my gosh, do I have any food in my tent? I made a mental inventory of everything and did not think there was any candy or
snacks, but I was not absolutely sure. I thought maybe I should
scream and warn my teammates, but what if that scream frightened
the bear and she ran into someone's tent in the dark and got tangled
up? Someone could get seriously hurt. What if I were to throw
something at the bear? All I had was my pillow, some clothes, and

my running shoes. A shoe might work. But I was afraid to unzip the flap, and besides, I did not know exactly where to aim. If a miracle occurred and I did hit the bear, that would probably only make her mad. The noises continued for a long time and then I could not hear anything anymore. The voices, the laughter and giggling, had ceased. Everyone, except me, was asleep. The fire slowly began to die. Light flickered and shadows fluttered. Fatigue tugged at my eyelids and finally sleep washed over me.

The next morning I thought I was the first one up, but then I saw Coach Davidson. I wished him a good morning.

"Good morning back at you," he said. "Did you hear the bear during the night?"

"Oh yeah, I heard her. And I saw her, too. Anyway, I saw her shadow. She was right outside my tent."

I trailed along with Coach and we surveyed the damage. The bear had torn apart some of our food. While we picked up the litter, Travis crawled from his tent and said, "I saw the bear. She came around not too long after we went to bed. I got scared and threw her a bag of Fritos."

We found the bag. It had been torn open and the contents devoured, except for a few Fritos that lay scattered on the ground.

After training camp we got down to the serious business of preparing ourselves for the cross-country season. On the first day of mandatory practice Coach Davidson divided us into groups according to our running ability. We went for a run and I was staying up with my group until my shoe came untied. I stopped to tie it, and when I stood up, everyone was gone. I tried running in the direction I thought they had taken, but all I got was lost. Finally I had to ask someone how to get back to the high school.

By the time I returned, practice had long since ended and Dad was waiting to take me home. He demanded to know, "Where have you been?"

"I got lost," I told him.

Coach Davidson approached and Dad let him have the brunt of his anger. "I entrusted my daughter to your care and this is what happens? Do whatever you have to do, but don't let Rachael wander around lost ever again. Have I made myself clear?"

"I understand your concern perfectly," said Coach Davidson. "And I'm in complete agreement. It will not happen again. I promise."

At the next practice Coach Davidson told me point-blank, "I know you can stick with me, or whoever I assign you to, when we run. You did it at camp; you can do it now."

"Okay. I'll try."

"Trying isn't good enough. You will keep up."

For the next ten days I ran either with Coach or with a group of girls. But then one afternoon I forgot my sunglasses. We were running directly into the sun and I had a hard time seeing anything at all. I did not want to run into a tree or get hit by a car, and I slowed my pace. Again I found myself alone. But this time I knew where I was and returned to the school. Coach Davidson's wife was waiting there. By the time I reached her it was pretty obvious that I was upset.

"What's the matter?" she asked.

"Your husband warned me to stay up. But I couldn't see where I was going. He's going to kick me off the team. I know he is."

She tried to console me, but it did not help much, because I knew I was gone. What hurt most was that for the first time in my life, I had felt like I was part of something. I had a whole group of new friends. They were almost like family and now I was going to have to leave and it was just so dreadfully unfair. I wanted to stay on the team. I did not want to lose my friends and the camaraderie that bound us together.

The different groups of runners began returning and I tagged along with them to the weight room and began lifting weights. I was hoping Coach was unaware I had come back early, but to be on the safe side I enlisted one of my friends to warn me when he arrived. She dutifully whispered, "He's coming."

Coach marched straight to me. "Rachael, come with me right now."

I tagged along as he went to each person who had been in my group and motioned for her to follow. Once we were outside I knew he would launch into a tirade, and trying to deflect some of his anger away from my teammates I mumbled, "It was my fault. I forgot my sunglasses. I couldn't see anything."

He put a hand on my shoulder and left it there. He took a big breath, held it, and expelled it as a *whoosh*. "I understand, Rachael. But here's the deal. I'm responsible for you. It's a liability issue."

He squeezed my shoulder then.

"I know you can do this; I know you can keep up. And you are going to stay with the group to which you're assigned or you're off this team."

Then Coach removed his hand from my shoulder and turned his attention to the girls who were in my running group. When he spoke, his words were distinct and the message emphatically clear: "If there is any reason that Rachael cannot run, you will all wait for her. If she will not run, you are to come back and tell me she will not run. I'll kick her off the team. Now get back to work, all of you."

I felt as though I had dodged a bullet. I was still on the team, but just barely. If I did not give my best, it was over. I decided that even though I detested the pain of running, I would rather suffer than let down my wonderful teammates.

From that day forward I picked up my pace. I really tried. Sometimes we came in from a run and I was in a complete stagger. But there was no way I was not going to stay with my group.

The first meet of the cross-country season was halfway across the state in Hermiston. We arrived several hours early and jogged the course to warm up. I found the layout of the course to be confusing. In one place there was a figure eight and the runners were to double back around on one leg, but the other leg was run only once.

During our race the spotters at the apex of the figure eight allowed me to take the wrong turn. I ran both loops twice, and when I came around the last time they were about to send me around again, but one of our assistant coaches intervened and pointed me in the direction of the finish line. I had already run three miles. I was tired. I wanted to quit.

"You're not in last place. There's at least five girls behind you," the assistant coach called to me. "And there's a runner less than fifty yards in front of you. Catch her."

I took off for the finish. Just before I got to the chute I passed the girl and it felt so good, but at the same time I felt so absolutely awful. My legs were the consistency of wet spaghetti, my lungs had been set on fire, I could not breathe, and I had a pounding headache. But all the same, when it was over I was as happy as I had ever been. My time was thirty-eight minutes, which was not bad considering this was my first high school race and I had run an extra mile. Maybe I did have potential.

Every race I ran I was able to lower my time, and, little by little, finishing did not hurt quite so much. There was even an outside chance I would make the varsity and win a letter. It came down to the last week of the season before the district meet.

Coach Davidson said he was going to take only ten runners to District. The final spot would be determined at the Broken Top Golf Course race in Bend. If I beat my friend Haley, I went. If she beat me, she took the last varsity spot and ran at the district meet. I had never beaten Haley. The stage was set.

Haley started out like she always did, sprinting at the start and getting into her racing pace early. I was more like the tortoise, slow but steady, and I knew if I pushed myself I could eventually catch her. The question in my mind was: *Will I have enough gas left in my tank to pass her?*

We were into the last mile when I finally spotted Haley's familiar ponytail bobbing up and down in front of me. I slowly reeled her in. As I drew alongside I could hear her praying, asking the Lord to help her. She was hurting real bad.

"Haley, you can do this," I encouraged her.

She shook her head. "No, I can't. You go on."

During the season Haley and I had become best friends. She had been my visual interpreter and every day we had trained together.

Once, at a race in The Dalles, I was having a bad day and Haley had actually taken hold of my arm and tried to pull me along, but it did not help me run any faster. Afterward she apologized and told me how sorry she was she had beaten me so decisively. I told her, "No way, kid. This is a race; if you can run faster, do it. Don't be waiting around for a slowpoke like me."

And now I felt compelled to assist Haley. I took hold of her wrist and tried to pull her along. She twisted away. "Go. Just go."

As I accelerated, I took one quick look over my shoulder at her, saw the tears glistening on her cheeks, but I did not have the energy to feel bad for her. I did not feel anything but the pain of the race. I charged ahead, sprinting all the way to the finish line. I made varsity and ran at District, did not do worth a dang, but I was awarded my letter. My success proved to me that if I stayed with it and worked real hard, I might improve enough to win a few races by the time I was a junior or senior.

11

STANDING OUT

Going into winter I was in terrific shape physically, but that did not help with my first sled dog race of the year, a cart race held in Sheldon, Washington. This is a cart race because Sheldon is located on Puget Sound and rarely gets so much as a dusting of snow.

I made a practice run over the trail with the cart and the dogs. Dad rode in front of me on a 4 wheeler and served as my visual interpreter. With his help it seemed like a piece of cake, and that was probably why, as the race drew near, I told Dad I did not need his help.

"I know what I'm doing. I'll get along just fine. Besides, the dogs have been over the trail and they'll remember which way to go," I said. More than anything I did not want Daddy always hovering around and fixing all my problems. I wanted to stand on my own two feet. What a mistake. I definitely was not ready for that kind of independence. Not quite yet.

I ran the race without a visual interpreter. Maybe it would be more correct to say that the race ran me, because within the first mile I was in serious trouble. Most of the blame I put on inadequate trail markers. They were small paper plates tacked on trees, nearly impossible for me to see, and complicating matters further was that a red plate meant turn at the next intersection while a green plate meant stay on the main trail. I do not see colors, especially green and red. They tend to blend and become the same indistinct color.

I failed to see one of the red pie plates. We went straight through an intersection when we should have turned. The trail quickly petered out and the dogs went into a patch of windfalls. The cart became high centered. I had to pull the dogs over the downed trees and muscle the cart back on the trail. All this cost me time and I expended a great deal of effort and energy.

This was not my only wrong turn. Not by a long shot. It happened over and over and over again. Most of the time it was my fault, because I could not see the turns and kept confusing the dogs. I messed with their heads until they did not know what direction they were supposed to be going. I finished the race next to last. I was lucky not to be the bottom rung on the ladder.

After the race, people said nasty things. The musher who finished just in front of me complained, "The only reason I didn't win was because I spent the entire race worried about that blind girl."

Others said they had wasted time trying to fix my problems. They said I had no business being in the race. Well, to set the record straight, I was appreciative of their help and concern, but really, I never asked for it and was perfectly capable of finishing my run on my own, without help. Sure, I found myself facing a little adversity, but never was I, nor my dogs, in any danger.

The toughest part of the race was for me to swallow my pride and admit to Dad that he had been right; I had desperately needed a visual interpreter. All I could do was chalk this race up as a good learning experience.

·   ·   ·

My first sled dog race of the year on snow was a four-miler at Frog Lake. I entered the four-dog class and got out of the starting gate fine, but soon noticed one of my wheel dogs, Powder, was not pulling. I kept trying to see what the problem was and finally figured out that his tugline was not snapped. I should have just let it go; three dogs pulling a four-mile sprint race was plenty of dog power. But it was driving me crazy to have a hard worker like Powder not able to do his job.

I slowed them with the brake, set the snow hook, got off the sled, and fastened his tug. This stole valuable time and I ended up four minutes from first place. That was about how long it took me to fix the snap. Live and learn. More experience to tuck under my belt. You cannot buy the type of experience I was learning.

The next race was Chemult. I entered the six-dog main class to be run over a seven-mile course. It was two days of competition and without a doubt I was taking a step up in competitive terms, but it was definitely not an unreasonable step to take.

I had grown to five feet, seven inches tall and was packing 130 pounds of muscle. I was physically capable, had been battle scarred and tested, and was ready and willing to race. I could handle almost any situation as well as a man. But the officials called a meeting and made it more of a showdown by throwing a barrage of confrontational questions at Dad and me.

"How old are you?" one official asked me.

"Fourteen, but what does that have to do with anything?"

"Do you realize this is a seven-mile race, run over two days?"

"Sure we do. That's the race we entered," Dad responded. "The course is well marked and there's a spotter on every corner. Rachael has a great team, excellent leaders, and she knows exactly what to do."

I jumped in then, just to let them know I could handle any situation that might arise. "If I fall, I hold on. If there is a tangle, I set my snow hook, go up, and fix it. If I lose the trail, I get back on it. What could go wrong?"

"What if your dogs fight?"

"Our dogs don't fight," Dad stated.

"What if you get in someone's way?"

"Hopefully their dogs will be as well trained as mine," I said, "and they will be able to go around me, just as they would any other musher on the trail."

And then the questioning became more personal. One official said, "Just what can you see?"

I felt like saying, "I can see that you're prejudiced against visually impaired people," but I bit my tongue and said nothing.

When I refused to answer, they turned their attention to Dad, asking him, "Why are you letting her do this? You're setting her up to fail."

"I don't think so, not at all. The bottom line is, she wants to be a sled dog racer. This is what she does. She has trained more than a thousand miles. Not to be disrespectful, but I'm absolutely sure she can handle your little seven-mile race."

They took a vote. I was allowed to race.

I wanted to make the most of my opportunity at the Chemult race and went flying out of the starting gate. But it was an especially bright day and I could hardly see a thing. I had trouble on a number of corners, never knew they were there until we were in the middle of them. I dumped the sled twice and burned time trying to get the sled upright. That day I finished near the back of the pack.

The second day I made a glorious comeback. Everything went smoothly, the dogs ran fast, and I stayed off the brake. We challenged the leaders, and when we finished I was pumped. Really pumped. I felt as though I had the ability to run with anyone in the open class, I told myself, "Iditarod, here I come!"

My success on the second day was especially sweet after all the negative things the officials had thrown at us. A reporter from the Bend *Bulletin* newspaper caught up with me and asked for my reaction to the race. I shot off my mouth when I should have taken a moment to compose myself and really think about what it was I wanted to say.

The following day, Sunday, my photograph graced the front page of the Klamath Falls *Herald and News*, the Eugene *Register-*

Guard, and the Bend *Bulletin.* The caption in the *Bulletin,* which was an accurate quote from me, read: "I may be a kid. I may be a girl. I may be blind. But I can still kick butt."

I cringed when it was shown to me because I knew Dad would be furious. He did not surprise me. "Who do you think you are, coming across so cocky? This is not the way a Scdoris acts. We are modest. We act like winners. We don't need to go around bragging that we kick butt."

Not only was he angry with me, he was also upset at the newspaper reporter for taking advantage of a fourteen-year-old. Dad questioned how they could quote a minor making such a brazen statement. He snapped at me, "Does this mean I have to be with you every second, so you don't shoot off your mouth and say things like , . . like this." He rapped a knuckle on my photograph in the newspaper.

I was properly contrite, promised it would never happen again and that in the future I would avoid purposely drawing attention to myself. I apologized for my arrogance. But to be honest, I was thrilled with my impressive splash of publicity. I tried to imagine the scene at school in the morning. I assumed every kid, at that very moment, was reading about me and gazing at my photograph. I was going to be the most popular kid at school, everyone's shining star. There would be a special announcement over the intercom. Surely every teacher would hold up the articles and talk about my success. Maybe there would be a school assembly. All the wild possibilities, and the headiness of fame, delighted me.

Come Monday morning, much to my chagrin, absolutely nothing was said. All my grand publicity was totally ignored by the teachers and my peers. Not a single friend came up and said, "Way to go!" or, "Atta girl!" or, "Read about you in the paper." I did not have a single request to sign an autograph. Nobody waved my picture in front of my face. Nothing had changed, nothing at all. My star had fizzled before it ever started to rise. By afternoon I had dealt with my disappointment and deflated ego. So, I was not going to be a celebrity. I told myself, *Okay, deal with it.* And I did.

The same thing happened when *Teen* magazine did a major feature on me. Only one girl mentioned that she had seen the article. Not that it was a good article or a good series of photographs, not even, "It really sucked." It was just, "Saw your article in *Teen* magazine," and that was it.

It was kind of funny, the day before the photographer from *Teen* came to take photographs I was with Dad getting a load of straw to put around the kennels for the dogs to sleep on. The farmer, Bill Robinson, loaded the truck with a forklift and afterward, while Dad and Bill were visiting, I came around the side of the truck and walked right into one of the forklift tines. I had to wear my hair down over the side of my face to hide the ugly red welt across my forehead. I looked like Cousin It from the *Addams Family* television show.

Then on the day of the shoot I had more problems. We were on the mountain and the photographer had me running the dogs back and forth so that he could get shots with the sun at the right angle and the mountains behind us. At one point I set the snow hook, thinking it was good snow, but it was ice and I slipped and smashed my face against the handlebars. If you look closely at the photograph in the magazine you can see a tiny trickle of blood running down my cheek. But you have to look real hard to see it.

It seemed that every time I turned around someone wanted to take my picture or write an article about me. The media loved me and I really did not understand why I was being singled out for all this publicity, except that every caption or article mentioned my blindness. They viewed me as someone who was overcoming obstacles and the limitations society attempts to place on people with disabilities. If I had not been blind I would never have made the media's radar. Other factors that played in my favor were that I was a girl, I was young, and I did not fit the picture of a stereotypical dog musher. I was not the Grizzly Adams type with icicles hanging from my beard. But mainly the media was interested in my blindness.

"Can you tell me what you see?"

"Describe what you see right now."

"Can you read that billboard over there?"

"Have you ever missed a turn?"

"What do you do when you get lost?"

I wanted to shout at them, "Ask about what it feels like to be out on a trail racing dogs. For cripesakes, ask about my dogs." But instead I patiently answered their questions, no matter how ridiculous they might be. "Can't you wear contacts or glasses to correct your vision?" "When you're racing is being blind an advantage?"

Over and over again I explained about my blindness: that I had been born with a rare genetic disorder, slowly spelling the words "congenital achromatopsia." To simplify the disease I said it was merely a shortage of rods and cones in my retina and that rods and cones control light, color, and depth perception.

"So you're totally blind?"

And I went through the whole song and dance about how my vision changed with light conditions and how it rapidly deteriorated in sunlight.

"Can't you just wear sunglasses?"

"Yes," I said, "sunglasses can be beneficial under certain conditions, but there is a limit to the amount of light which can be filtered out with sunglasses."

Educating the media was an ongoing process. I had to be clear, concise, and factual. I had to spoon-feed them the information without appearing to be self-serving or coming across as impertinent or egotistical. I made some mistakes, but I learned in a hurry and tried not to repeat those mistakes.

The local television station, NBC Channel 21, did several stories on me. I was the only blind girl running sled dog races in Central Oregon and the reporters and anchors seemed to be captivated by my story. So were the viewers. They voted me the Sports Story of the Year. Some of my friends took notice of that, which goes to show, kids pay a whole lot more attention to television than they do to newspapers.

Whenever my newfound popularity gave me a case of the "big-head," something came along to burst my bubble. One of those guaranteed downers was to mention the word "driving." I knew I would never be able to have a driver's license, and that fact weighed heavily on my mind, as it would with any teenager. All my friends were getting their learner's permits, taking driver's education classes, and talking about what cars were their favorites and what they might be driving in the near future.

Having a car and being able to drive was everything. If you had your own set of wheels, you had freedom, mobility, and independence all rolled into one sweet package. I was more envious of my classmates than I had ever been of anyone in my entire life.

Dad understood this and sometimes permitted me to drive home once we turned off the oil road. It was a thrill to be behind the wheel. I crept along and he instructed me when, and in which direction, to turn. "Not so much." "Easy." "Straighten it out." "Good going, girl."

Without these small opportunities to be an ordinary teenager it would have been harder to accept that I would never have a car of my own, never be able to slide behind the wheel and cruise Main Street. Deep down I knew the limited amount of driving that I was allowed to do was nothing more than an illusion. It was not as if I could jump in a rig and go for a spin, or drive to the Alfalfa Store for an ice-cream bar, or dash into town to catch a movie, or to a fast-food joint for a burger and fries. I would always have to rely on someone to run me here or there.

I did find out about a powerful bioptic telescope that visually impaired drivers were using. It was a three-inch eyepiece that could be fitted into an eyeglass frame and worn over one eye. Some states allow the visually impaired to use a bioptic device to qualify for special driver's licenses. But that never seemed like an option for me. I had used a monocular, which was like a pair of binoculars but with only one lens, to try to see the blackboard in school. It was a hassle and I never really could get the hang of it. I got frustrated and quit using it. I figured a bioptic was little more than an accident waiting to happen, and besides, Oregon was not one of the states that allowed the use of a bioptic device.

Nearly all teenagers, after driving a few times, develop a distorted view of their newly acquired abilities and skills. Just because they have learned the complexities of operating the gas pedal, clutch, and steering wheel does not automatically make them good drivers. Most young drivers become overconfident, drive too fast, and take too many chances. They reason fast reflexes will make up for any lack of experience or judgment. My perception of teenage drivers comes from hearing my friends talk about their experiences. But I, too, was struck with this common teenage affliction for speed, carelessness, and overconfidence.

Mom has always had a difficult time accepting my blindness. She wanted me to see what she saw and continually pointed out things, saying, "See that? It's right there. You can see that, can't you?" She desperately wanted me to be normal and do all the things normal kids did. She was a soft touch when it came to allowing me to drive.

One time we left Dad's place with me behind the wheel. I knew that road by heart because I regularly trained cart dogs over it. I was cruising along, feeling cool and in control. I pushed down on the gas pedal. We went faster and faster.

Mom barked out a warning, "Corner."

When I run the dogcart I take this particular corner fairly wide. I never cut to the inside or else the cart ends up running over rocks and clumps of sagebrush. With that thought in mind, I swung wide and started to sweep through the corner. I took my foot completely off the accelerator. We were just coasting.

"Brake!" Mom shouted.

I tried to stomp the brake but missed and instead jammed the accelerator pedal to the floor. The car shot forward. I was aware of a juniper tree looming in front of us, dangerously close. Mom grabbed the steering wheel, cranked it hard to the right, and we did manage to slide past the tree, but the front tire on the passenger's side struck a huge root, throwing the car airborne. When we came down, the root tore into the underside of the car. There was a horrific sound of grinding metal being mangled and shoved backward.

The engine stopped running. A cloud of dust seethed around us.

I looked at Mom and for the first time in my life I said a cussword in front of her.

She ignored it. "You okay?"

"Yeah, just a little mad at myself. I was going too fast, wasn't I?"

"A little. Well, we better hike back and get your dad."

"No way," I said. "We can take care of this."

We had to dig our way out. And when we finally had the car free and back on the road, Mom told me I was driving. This time I went a lot slower. Five miles down the road the car quit running, and after all our hard work digging the car out from the tree root we still ended up walking all the way back and having to face Dad.

12

IN THE SPOTLIGHT

Because of the press I had received and my achievements in cross-country, track, and sled dog racing, the United States Association of Blind Athletes (USABA) invited me to be one of the featured athletes to participate in an exhibition 400-meter race during the Olympic Trials in Sacramento. The 400 meters is a sprint. I have never been a sprinter, only a long-distance runner, but I was thrilled to have the opportunity to participate and to rub shoulders with the elite athletes who would represent the United States in Sydney, Australia, at the 2000 Olympics.

After making arrangements for the care of our dogs, Dad and I headed our pickup truck south. It was a long, hot drive. We stopped at Lake Shasta, and after a swim to cool off a bit we continued on. As soon as we reached Sacramento we checked into the hotel, because we knew the room was air-conditioned.

It was a swanky hotel and everything was fine, except that during the night Dad snored. When I woke him it was as though I had interrupted his sleep to tell him we were in the middle of a major earthquake. He was defensive and claimed he never snored. But I did manage to get to sleep before he started snoring again.

The following morning we met with representatives of the US-ABA and I had the chance to meet the other athletes I would be competing against: Pam McGonigle, ranked number five in the nation by the USABA in the 5000 meters; Sonya Bell, ranked number one in the world in both the 100 meters and the 200 meters; and Rana Mikkelson, who competed internationally in the heptathlon, a grueling two-day, seven-event competition for women. It hit me that I was up against some pretty stiff competition. I hoped I would not embarrass myself.

We were presented our Olympic credentials and given our race uniforms. And then we were ushered onto a practice field so we could do a little running and practice coming out of the blocks. Being a distance runner, I had never used blocks, but after I was invited to participate at the Trials I had worked with Dave Hood, the coach at Mountain View High School, and he showed me how to set the blocks, drive out of them, and get into my sprinter's stride as quickly as possible. He also coached me on a solid strategy for running the 400. The technique was foreign to me: running on my toes, with arms pumping like pistons to help drive my legs.

During this practice session I felt a twinge in my right calf and at first I thought it was probably a cramp caused by the heat. I drank several glasses of water and stretched my calf muscle. I tried jogging, but any movement caused so much pain it forced me to stop. When I told Dad, he sent me to the trainers' tent. One of the trainers worked on my leg and it did help some, but I was leery about trying to run. I thought maybe I should stay off my feet and save myself for the race. The discomfort I was feeling really bummed me out, because we had come a long way and this was a once-in-a-lifetime experience. I had to suck it up. I had to be ready to compete.

An hour before I was scheduled to run we were given our race numbers and Dad called me over to the fenced area where he was standing so he could take pictures of me on the track at the Olympic Trials. After that I chose to be alone. I needed to gather myself. While I pondered the upcoming race Dad took a series of photographs of me being nervous; gnawing at my fingernails, toying with my hair, yawning, playing with my sunglasses. The last photo on the film roll was of me changing into my running spikes. At that point my calf muscle was killing me. I had real reservations whether I was going to be able to run at all, let alone finish the race.

But a strange thing happened when I stepped onto the track—the pain in my calf disappeared. Maybe it was the straight shot of adrenaline that coursed through my veins as twenty-seven thousand spectators rose to their feet and cheered. We were led down the straightaway like expensive racehorses at the Kentucky Derby, and when my name was called I raised my right arm and waved to the crowd.

I was assigned to lane three. I reached my blocks, stood in front of them, and waited for instructions from the starter. From this point forward the race became a dream sequence, flashes of sequential moments: settling myself in the blocks, the command "Set," my body coming up, fingers poised behind the line, leaning slightly forward, holding, muscles tensing, waiting, waiting.

The gun popped. I got out fast, pumping my arms and hitting my stride as early as possible. I powered around the corner. On the straightaway I eased up and tried to glide, just as Coach Hood had advised me to do. When I reached the back corner the sun hit me square in the eyes. It was difficult to see anything at all except for two white lines a few feet on either side of my lane. I swept through the corner and two shadow forms became visible in front of me. I told myself I was catching up to the pack and tried to come out of the corner with enough momentum to carry me down the straightaway.

The two shadows became more solid. They were running together and I knew it had to be Sonya Bell, the 100- and 200-meter champion, and her guide runner. My body screamed with fatigue, and though I wanted to slow, I reached inside myself and found a desire I never knew existed, a desire to win. Pain was consuming me. My heart pounded. My breath came in ragged gasps. Out there beyond me somewhere was the din of clapping hands and shouts of encouragement.

I put everything I ever was, everything I will ever be, into that final drive to the finish line. The intensity of the crowd became a roar, like diving under a waterfall and hearing the muffled, thundering reverberation of water pouring into a pool. I prayed. Prayed not to stumble. Prayed that God give me the strength and endurance to finish this race. Prayed for speed.

Sonya and her guide runner were still ahead, but I was gaining. How much farther? I had no concept of distance, or time, or anything else. I was suspended in this surreal moment, floating above the track, feeling only the raw agony of my muscles tightening, knowing that, stride for stride, I would fight Sonya all the way to the finish.

God, keep me going.

God, give me strength.

God, don't let me give up now.

Lactic acid was building, turning my veins as hot as an acetylene flame. Nerve endings screamed. My legs were dying, but I fought against the paralysis and, somehow, I summoned the strength to actually run faster. As I accelerated, my fatigue seemed to fade. I drew even with Sonya's shoulder and for several strides we matched each other, arms and legs pumping in unison, and then slowly, ever so slowly, Sonya and her guide runner began to drop away. I could not see them but could hear their labored gasps and the pounding of their feet, only a step or two behind me.

I sensed the finish line was near. I saw the timers and officials to my left, on the inside of the track. And then a man was grabbing me, wrapping his arms around me, telling me, "It's over! Great race! What a tremendous finish!"

As soon as I stopped running my legs went rubbery. I leaned over, panting for a taste of precious air and some relief from the agony of the searing heat consuming my lungs and legs. My head pounded to the beat of my heart. I mumbled, "Thank you, God. Thank you."

I became aware of the crowd and the continuous clamor as they saluted us for our effort and our hard-fought struggle down the straightaway. I saluted them with a wave. Sonja and I had proven that blind athletes could compete just as hard as sighted athletes. Sonja never backed off. Neither had I, and in the end I had a little more conditioning, speed, determination, or maybe it was heart. Whatever was the deciding factor, I knew I had gutted it out, laid it all on the line, and exposed myself like I had never done before. In that battle at the Olympic Trials I discovered something about myself that I had only suspected—I was a warrior.

Without my really being aware of what was going on, I allowed myself to be led to the awards stand. My name was called and I stepped up and onto the stand. I was presented with a bouquet of fresh-smelling flowers and then a man slipped a red, white, and blue ribbon with a heavy bronze medal attached to it over my head. I had won third place and received an official Olympic medal, the same medal the athletes would compete for in Sydney.

Rana was introduced. She took her spot and received flowers and the silver medal. And then Pam was introduced as the winner. She reached down and took my hand and Rana's hand and raised them into the air. We were all winners and we basked in the glory. Tears of joy spilled shamelessly down my cheeks. I said a silent prayer, that this feeling would last forever.

Pam wanted the three of us to run a victory lap, but the finals of the women's 5000 meters were ready to start and we were quickly ushered off the track and into the media area. Several members of the media had questions for us. We reveled in our moment in the spotlight and answered each question posed to us.

As I was ready to leave, a reporter for the *Oregonian* newspaper approached and said, "If you're serious about getting into running, let me give you a little advice: You're not a sprinter. You need to run distances."

I had just run the most exciting race of my life. I was the one with an Olympic bronze medal around my neck, and this reporter was dispensing advice when she knew absolutely nothing about me. I had to laugh at the absurdity of the situation, because I had never pretended to be a sprinter.

Later I used my credentials to return to the stadium. I had my picture taken with Sandra Farmer Patrick, who won the silver metal in the 400 hurdles. One look at her and you could tell she was an athlete. Her body was a mass of perfectly defined muscles and she had a way about her that exuded confidence. I also walked stride for stride with Marion Jones, the Olympic champion sprinter. As I was leaving I was not watching where I was going and actually bumped into C. J. Hunter, one of the best shot-putters in the world. He was so big and solidly built that running into him was like bouncing off a brick wall.

My experience at the Olympic Trials proved to be a springboard to meet another famous athlete, Marla Runyan. I first saw her on television when she ran at the World Championships in Spain the year before the Trials.

Marla was a world-class runner who was also visually impaired. At the age of nine she suffered a juvenile form of macular degeneration known as Stargardt.

Her vision was comparable to mine. She was living in Oregon and training in Eugene. I decided to write her a letter. She was nice enough to write back. We exchanged e-mail addresses and phone numbers. We communicated several times.

I asked her advice about the trouble I was having from the recreational mushers who thought I had no business competing in the sport of sled dog racing. Marla told me, "Don't sweat it. There will always be people like that. Just make sure you never give in to them."

When Marla qualified for the Olympic team, members of the media besieged her, focusing not on Marla the world-class athlete but on Marla the visually impaired runner. This frustrated her and she balked at why they could not spotlight her accomplishments without always dwelling on her impairment. She told one television producer she would grant him an interview, but she wanted to have a visually impaired girl she knew from Central Oregon to be a part of the story.

Dad drove me to Eugene. The television producer interviewed me on camera. Really, all I wanted to do was meet Marla, but the producer explained they wanted to control the moment we met, saying they had only one shot at it because a spontaneous meeting was always more believable and effective than a staged event.

The meeting was to take place on the track at Lane Community College. I had run there before. It is a blue track, very unique, because most tracks are a darker color, rusty red or a forest green. The producer told me to take my time and warm up slowly. I was just dorking around, stretching my leg muscles by touching my toes and doing side bends. Dad came up to me and whispered, "They want you in lane three. Just jog up the track and try to act natural."

I assumed they were getting some file footage of me. I did not know Marla was anywhere in the vicinity. After going thirty or forty steps I saw a runner coming straight at me, also moving slowly. I squinted and tried to see who it was, but the runner was too far away. We both kept moving in slow motion toward each other. We were about fifteen feet apart when I recognized Marla's tall, lean physique and the way I had seen her carry herself on television, her head tilted and her arms swinging loosely at her sides.

She spoke first. "This Tara?"

"Marla?"

We hurried toward each other and hugged. I forgot all about the cameras and the television crew. She was my hero and I was getting to meet her.

"It's so good to finally meet you," she said, and suggested, "Do you want to go for a little run?"

"Sure," I said. She led and I followed. She went nice and slow for me and we chatted as we jogged. She told me how her training was going and a little about the Trials.

I had watched her fifteen-hundred-meter race on television. Coming down the straightaway of the third lap, a runner in front of her had tripped. Marla stumbled and it looked as if she were going to fall, but she put her hands out, caught her balance, and went on to finish third and make the Olympic team. I told Marla, "It must have been pretty scary when you fell."

She laughed. "I didn't actually fall. Someone went down in front of me. I put my hands down and sort of vaulted over her. But it was funny, after it happened all I could think about was that fall was going to be shown on television, over, and over, and over again and the analysts were going to pick it apart and try to assess blame to one of the runners. Americans were going to be sick of seeing it, hearing about it. I had to laugh, because those things happen so fast. It's part of racing. I was glad to get third, happy to make the team."

After a couple laps we did some accelerations, starting out easy and building to sprinting speed over one hundred fifty meters. It was clearly evident, when Marla took off and left me after about twenty meters, that she was a world-class athlete and I was a high school runner with limited ability. And even though she was so fast it made me look stopped, it was still a thrill to be on the same track with her.

I ran the entire workout with her, although quite a bit slower. I made sure that I gave the same effort she did, and when it was over we sat on the infield grass and talked about things that two people who have shared similar experiences can enjoy and relate to. We had to overcome so many of the same things in life.

Before we parted, Marla told me that I should follow my dream. If I really wanted to run the Iditarod, I should push forward and never give up. I wished her well at the Olympics. She came in eighth. I was as proud of her accomplishment as if I were the one who had run the race.

We stay in touch with each other, despite the fact that we both have really busy schedules. Most often one of us will drop the other an e-mail. The Internet is the easiest way for us to communicate.

13

FACING ADVERSITY

I planned to build on my achievement of the summer by having a great year running cross-country. But that was not to be. I ran and competed, but I was never the star, not by a long shot. I was a solid varsity performer and contributed to the team with consistent running and solid work habits. We thought we might have a chance to make it to the state cross-country meet, but the competition in the Intermountain Conference was too strong and our team did not have the talent to advance to State.

After cross-country season ended, all I could do was wait. We needed snow in the mountains so I could begin training dogs for the upcoming sled dog race season. Without any reason to rise early, I slept late one school morning in November. Dad hollered, "Better get a move on or you'll miss the bus."

I continued to dilly-dally, and when I was finally ready Dad drove me three miles to the bus stop. I got out of the pickup and Dad drove away. That time of the year it is dark when the bus arrives. It was dark that morning, but as I waited, and waited some more, the eastern sky began to turn color. I was not sure if it was pink or green.

Occasionally the bus is late, never early, but I began having doubts. Maybe this was the day it had come early. Or, maybe I had been too late.

When the sun finally broke free of the horizon, I knew for sure. As I saw it, I had two choices, and neither was particularly appealing: either hike up the road and face Dad and his "I told you so," or run twenty-six miles to school. I thought to myself, *That's a long way, but on the bright side, it's only twenty-six miles, and that's a few hundred yards less than a marathon.*

Mom's place was at about the fourteen-mile mark. I knew I could make it fourteen miles. If she was home, she would drive me to school. I wavered between the alternatives. I had on my running shoes. I could handle fourteen miles. I had run nearly that far in running camp. Fourteen miles. Okay.

I started running along the shoulder of the road, listening for any oncoming traffic. There were very few people traveling on the Alfalfa road; once in a while a tractor pulling a trailer of hay passed me, or a farmer heading into town in his rattletrap pickup, but most often curious livestock were the only living creatures around. Cattle bellowed and came to walk the fence line as I passed. Horses nickered softly. Sheep ran away. One time a dog came partway down the lane from an isolated residence, stood stiff legged, and barked at me. Songbirds sang. The cool wind whistled. The sun made a feeble effort to warm the day.

I never was worried about any dangers, like some weirdo stopping and trying to abduct me. Creeps that prey on young girls lurk around Portland or Salem or Eugene. They don't waste their time driving the back roads between Alfalfa and Redmond looking for a victim. That scenario never entered my mind. I just ran. And to be perfectly honest, it was fun. I was not running for time. I was not running because a coach told me to run. I just ran.

Once I got to the main highway there was a little more traffic, but it was not too bad. Nobody stopped to say, "Hey, where you going? Need a lift?" I just ran in peace and quiet, listening to the sparrows, juncos, and crows. The sun had finally warmed the air a few degrees. The only unpleasantness was that whenever a car came past, for a few seconds afterward I breathed the stench of exhaust fumes. I got to the point that whenever I heard an approaching car I waited until it drew close, took a deep breath, and held it until I absolutely had to breathe again.

When I became tired of running I walked, but I tried to keep the walking to a minimum. It was too much fun to run.

I reached Mom's house. She was not there, but I went in and got a drink of water, rested a few minutes, glanced at the clock, and noticed it was not even noon yet. I could still make it to school before the last bell. Twelve miles more—that was doable. I had done twelve miles a lot of times. Never after going fourteen miles first, but I thought, *What the hey—twelve miles, better get going.*

I arrived at school as the bell rang for last period. My friends crowded around and wanted to know, "Where have you been?"

"Missed the bus," I told them.

"How did you get to school?"

"Ran."

"From your mom's place?"

"No, from Dad's."

"How far is that?"

"Twenty-six miles. Something like that."

"Twenty-six miles? That was twenty-six miles? Wow!"

Dad has always been my biggest fan, as well as my toughest critic. But I gained enough of his trust and confidence that he allowed me to enter the twelve-dog, mid-distance race at Frog Lake. My entry fee was mailed. But the organizer of the race telephoned Dad: "I can't accept your daughter's entry."

"Why not?"

"This is the twelve-dog, mid-distance class. Jerry, your daughter is blind. Are you crazy? She can't handle it."

Dad responded, "You know me. If I didn't think she had the experience, the strength, and the ability to deal with any situation she might encounter, I would never have paid her entry fee."

"It's not going to happen. I can't allow it."

"You have to let her run."

"Oh no, we don't. If she's out on the trail she's going to be a distraction, she's going to get in people's way, and she's going to be a liability for the race."

"Is your problem the fact she is a girl, or that she is only fifteen, or because she is visually impaired?" Dad wanted to know.

"I don't have to answer that. All I have to say is we are not accepting her entry. Period."

"Legally, you have to allow her to participate. Have you ever heard of the Americans with Disabilities Act?"

"We thought you might react this way," said the organizer. "We decided if you tried to threaten us and to throw the law in our faces, then we have no choice but to cancel the race."

"Cut off your nose to spite your face? Now that's real intelligent." Dad was angry. "Whoop-de-do. That really hurts. Tell you what, we're coming and we'll be ready to race."

When we got to the Frog Lake race we were told I could not run the twelve-dog race, it was out of the question. Their compromise was an offer to allow me to run the six-dog race. We turned that down and stuck to our guns.

"All right," the organizer told Dad. "The only way we can let her run the twelve-dog race is if she doubles up and you ride the trailer sled."

Their ultimatum was crazy. How was I supposed to be competitive when the two of us, along with the sled, weighed in excess of 350 pounds? It was unfair to me and unfair to the dogs. But it was that or nothing—they would cancel the race and everyone would be mad at us for ruining their party. The organizer had effectively boxed us into a corner and ultimately we were forced to accept his proposal.

I ran twelve dogs and double-sledded with Dad on the trailer. The extra weight and the double friction of two sleds cost me time, but I came out of the first day, after running thirty-two miles, in second place and only two minutes out of first.

The next day I made a flawless run. To lighten the load I ran every uphill and Dad used a ski pole and pumped. But we were not able to overcome our handicaps and finished where we started, in second place. Still, I considered this to be a major victory.

The following week I was scheduled to run a six-dog team over the twenty-mile course in Chemult. In order to avoid a rehash of the problems at Frog Lake, Dad negotiated a compromise ahead of time. He would ride a snow machine and be my visual interpreter, keeping in constant communication with me over a two-way radio. He would alert me to trail conditions, whether there was a downhill or an uphill, and warn me of upcoming corners, low branches, and other circumstances that a normal sighted person automatically recognizes and is able to react to.

We arrived in Chemult the day before the race. The weather was mild. But the morning of the race a cold front had moved in and the air temperature was several degrees below zero. I was dressed for the conditions. Everything would have been fine if I had not dumped the sled within spitting distance of the starting line.

I came out with six screaming dogs and was not aware of a sharp corner less than a hundred yards into the race. The sled went over, I held on, and the dogs dragged me a good two hundred yards before I managed to slow them enough to right the sled. In this process snow went down my coat, my boots, and was even packed inside my gloves. I lost my hat.

I tried to dump the snow as best as I could, but it was a little difficult trying to ride the runners of a racing sled and undress at the same time. We were seriously flying and the wind made me even colder. I waited for an uphill, so I could run and get warm, but the course was flat. Finally I decided to pump a little with one leg, hoping that effort would warm me, but we were moving too fast.

Ten miles into the race I was so cold I began shaking and fatigue set in. Dad kept talking, telling me about trail conditions. I was tempted to get on the radio and let him know I was freezing. But that did not seem quite fair. Besides, what was Dad going to do? Outside help was not allowed. If I accepted dry gloves, boots, hat, or a coat I would be breaking the rules and subject to immediate disqualification. I made up my mind. I was going to tough it out. No matter how bad it got, I would fight through the agony of slowly freezing to death.

"Uphill," called Dad.

I was relieved. This was the opportunity I had been waiting for. But when I tried to run my legs refused to respond. My feet were too cold. I could not feel them any longer as they dragged along behind the sled. Luckily, I had enough upper-body strength to hoist myself onto the runners before we broke over the crest of the hill.

My hands and feet felt like logs. They were no longer a part of my body. My teeth chattered so loudly they sounded like an old truck shaking itself silly on a washboard road. I recognized the telltale signs that I was in trouble. Hypothermia was setting in, but I really did not appreciate the seriousness of the situation until I had the peculiar sensation that warm liquid was oozing from my ears. I had no idea if it was blood or something else. It occurred to me I might be hallucinating. Either way, real or imagined, the discharge from my ears scared me. But I was even more concerned I would fall and not be able to finish the race. I prayed, "Let me finish. Just let me finish."

When my feet finally did slip off the runners, I no longer possessed the strength to pull myself back into position. My stamina was shot. Sheer willpower kept my fingers wrapped around the handlebars. How much longer could I hang on? I was aware of the whine of the snow machine, heard Dad's voice yelling at me, "Get up!" But I could not get up. All I could do was hang on and let the dogs pull me a few more yards, feet, inches.

And that was the way I came across the finish line, on my knees, being dragged behind the sled by my dogs. It was one of the most inglorious finishes in the history of sled dog racing. But shame never entered the picture, not then. All feelings were gone. I was left with an unwavering thankfulness that I had not dropped off somewhere on the trail and immense gratitude that my dogs had not suffered the indignity of pulling an empty sled into the chute at the finish.

Dr. Wes Lewis, a friend and supporter, rushed to me and pulled me to my feet. "Sweetheart, let's get you to the warming hut."

All I could muster was a single word: "Great."

Dr. Lewis wrapped my arm around his neck and mostly carried me to the warming hut. When we got there he peeled off my gloves. A lady handed me a cup of hot chocolate, but I could not hold the cup; all I could do was clamp my frozen hands around it. And as the warmth began to penetrate, my fingers warmed and intense pain shot up my arm. I wanted to scream. But I did not. Instead I bawled.

Dr. Lewis helped me to the pickup, started the engine, and turned the heater on full blast. He pulled off my boots and socks, pulled back my hair. He told me, "You have a little frostbite on your fingers and toes. Your ears are a little more serious."

I looked at my ears in the interior mirror. They were discolored and hideously swollen. I shook my head and my ears flapped. I looked like Dumbo the elephant.

Dr. Lewis used his cell phone to call the emergency room at St. Vincent Hospital in Portland and talked to the trauma doctors. He lanced my ears as they advised, and a clear liquid poured out and ran down my neck. But with my fingers and toes hurting so badly, it did not seem as gross as it probably was. When we arrived back at the motel, Dr. Lewis rubbed medicine on my ears and bandaged them. From my reflection in the mirror I could have passed as an alien child.

The following morning I wanted to continue the race and, I hoped, redeem myself, but Dr. Lewis said there was no way he would allow me to compete. In fact, he forced me to stay at the motel.

Dad returned to the race. Later he shared with me what people were saying about my disgraceful finish. Many were up in arms, some actually gloating, saying they had been right all along, that I had no business in the race. They insinuated the frostbite I suffered was because I was blind. One person went so far as to vow he would make sure I never raced in Oregon again.

Over the course of a few days feeling slowly returned to my toes and fingers. They were only mildly frostbitten. But my ears turned completely black. I had to wear a ski hat at school in order to hide them from public display and a steady stream of ridicule.

That weekend I was honored at the Bend Winterfest, crowned with a glittering tiara and given the title "Snow Princess." I sang the "Star-Spangled Banner" in front of a crowd of five thousand people. I have a photograph of that event. I am wearing a white headband to hide my black ears.

14

REDEMPTION

Dad talked to Frank Teasley, race director of the Wyoming International Pedigree Stage Stop Sled Dog Race, and told him about the problems I was having racing in the Northwest and the negative things that were being said. Frank's response was, "Come to Wyoming. We'd love to have Rachael run our race."

Dad warned him, "Think about it for a minute, Frank. You're opening yourself up to a lot of criticism from the mushing world for letting a fifteen-year-old visually impaired girl compete in your race."

"I don't have to think about it," said Frank. "I'll take the heat. She has every right to compete. We'll take whatever steps are necessary for her to be on equal footing with other racers. If you want to use a visual interpreter on a snow machine, that's fine by us."

We accepted the challenge and I went from failing at a twenty-mile race to attempting a ten-day, five-hundred-mile race that snaked back and forth over the Rocky Mountains at elevations exceeding eleven thousand feet. It was the only race that Dad had never finished. And when he scratched I had vowed to run it someday. And now, four years later, Someday had arrived.

The first step to running in Wyoming was to put together a support team. I called Dan MacEachen in Colorado. I met Dan at the Wyoming race in 1997 and we had become the best of friends. He had run the Wyoming race numerous times, as well as competed in the Iditarod. He also owned Krabloonik, the largest sled dog kennel in the Lower 48 states. I asked Dan to accompany me on a snow machine and act as my visual interpreter. His answer was quick and to the point: "You bet." He even offered me his leaders: Johnny, Copper, and O.J. They were well-seasoned dogs and had run Wyoming as well as the Iditarod.

"I love you," I told Dan. It is one thing for a person to offer to help (in itself that is remarkable and a true test of friendship), but it is quite another to loan another musher your best dogs. That is above and beyond simple friendship. In my book it is a heroic gesture. I will always be indebted to Dan for the gift of his time, expertise, and, of course, wonderful dogs.

I trained through Christmas break, and when vacation was over I worked out a plan with my teachers and the principal at Redmond High School. I was granted an excused absence from school to train for and to run the Wyoming race. But I would have to make up any work that I missed. The next hurdle was to raise the necessary money to make my participation possible. A lot of people stepped forward to help: American Nutrition, the U.S. Association of Blind Athletes, even Dan MacEachen contributed. Many individuals around Central Oregon made donations, as did school kids who took money out of their piggy banks. Every cent that was contributed was greatly appreciated and put to good use.

The Wyoming International Pedigree Stage Stop Sled Dog Race is actually a series of sprint races, with three campouts thrown in to give racers a taste of the Iditarod, where every night is a campout. Each racer is allowed a pool of sixteen dogs, but no more than twelve dogs can be used at any one time.

I used six dogs for the three-mile ceremonial start held on the main street of Jackson, Wyoming. I figured I could control six dogs a lot easier than twelve. It proved to be a wise choice, because a huge crowd lined the route with a ton of distractions. We made a flying run through town, and almost as soon as we had started the short race it was over.

The actual race began at Moran Junction, elevation seventy-seven hundred feet. As the handlers brought my dog team toward the starting gate I felt as though I were being swept away by my emotions and anxieties, remembering back to when I was still a little girl and how everyone had been so nice to me, the trauma of Dad's having to scratch from the race, and my vow to return to Wyoming and run this race for him.

I was more than a little scared. What had I gotten myself into? I had never run any of these trails. I knew nothing about the terrain. Was I ready to tackle a five-hundred-mile race, where every day meant climbing above ten thousand feet? How would my body handle the altitude?

I was only fifteen years old. No fifteen-year-old had ever attempted a five-hundred-mile sled dog race. Was I mature enough to tackle it, mature enough to handle the physical strain? What about the emotional side? Sometimes an athlete has to push her body past what she thinks she can endure. I had done that in running. Could I do it now over a ten-day sled dog race? Did I have what it takes to be a competitor?

The one thing that counteracted my self-doubts was my unflagging faith in my dogs. With the addition of Dan's three leaders my team was seasoned, well trained, and ready to meet any challenge we might face out on the trail. I told myself, "Give it your best shot, girl."

I moved to the starting line, set the snow hook, got off the sled, and petted each of the dogs, encouraging them for the long run that lay ahead. They were anxious to run and their enthusiasm helped to motivate me. While I concentrated on my dogs, the announcer, holding a hand microphone, began the countdown. Noise besieged me: dogs barking, fans wishing me well, the announcer barking out seconds. My nervousness and misgivings about what might lie ahead began to dissipate as I returned to my sled. "Five." Forget the jitters. "Four." Get rid of the doubts. "Three." I'm as ready as I'll ever be. "Two." Let's race. "One." I pulled the snow hook and we were off in a rush of flying snow and wild cheering from the spectators lining the chute.

The trail out of Moran Junction headed into the heart of the Wind River range. Dan was in front of me on the snow machine, calling out instructions as we climbed toward 10,800-foot Union Pass. I was running ten dogs and they were charging hard. The sun was bright and there were lots of light variables as we plunged in and out of shadows. My vision was constantly changing. I could hardly see the shapes of my leaders.

I relied on voice commands from Dan. His voice was hoarse, like gravel shaken in a metal bucket. He was sick with an upper respiratory infection that was hovering dangerously close to pneumonia. The night before the start of the race, Dan had checked into the hospital and checked out after five hours because he refused to miss the start.

That first day we covered forty-seven miles. Coming into the checkpoint at Dubois I was tired. I had run a good share of the twenty miles of uphills in order to save the dogs. That night I stayed with a nice family, had a room to myself, and got a great night's sleep.

In the morning I filled my pockets with bite-sized Snickers bars, and I snacked on them during the day's run. That night was our first campout. I fed and watered the dogs, massaged the ones that needed it, and tended to the feet of every dog. When the work was finally done I grabbed a bite to eat and trundled off to make my bed in a pile of straw. It was bitterly cold, thirty below zero, and I tried to snuggle with the dogs, but they were balled up and ignored me. Through that long night dogs barked, people talked, and there seemed to be constant noise and commotion. I lay there awake, cold, and anxious for morning so I could get back on the trail and start running to get my blood circulating and warm my body.

As soon as I heard others stirring and tending their dogs, I leaped from my sleeping bag, fed and watered my dogs, and tended to their needs. I walked each of them individually to make sure they had no problems with their muscles or feet. I got ready to race. On the way to the starting line I dropped a glove and had to backtrack to retrieve it. That put us behind. When I did get to the chute I had to hurry. If a musher misses the count it costs valuable time, but I made it to my sled at "One!," ripped loose the snow hook, the handlers stepped aside, and we were off and running on what would prove to be one of the most trying days of the race.

Pre-dawn made the mountains blush a soft pink, but soon the sun emerged and splayed great bars of golden light across the snow that forced me to squint. The dogs were full of energy. We came to a long hill and I got off and ran enough so by the time we topped out I was warm and feeling good. I thought that thirty-two miles on a day like this would be a snap.

An hour into the race the sunlight dimmed. I could see a few wispy clouds streaked across the powder blue sky. I was not concerned about them. We were moving fast, the runners gliding over the packed snow with a smooth hissing sound, and our progress seemed almost effortless. We could outrace any storm.

Two hours later the wispy clouds had been joined by a roily mass of thick-bodied clouds that filled every corner of the sky and turned the day dismal gray and gloomy. The north wind huffed and puffed. It was a cold wind. I chose to ignore it.

Dan was ahead of me. "Wind," he hollered over the radio.

Yeah, I know. No big deal, Dan, I thought to myself.

I popped around the shoulder of a long hill and a blast of wind hit me full force. It was like the prop wash of an airplane and it nearly knocked me off the sled. And as the gusts continued to buffet me, long, cold fingers of cold crept down my parka hood and inside my layers of clothing, making me shiver. Blowing snow and ice all but obscured my dog team.

"A bad gust," I told myself. "Give it a minute and it'll slack off."

But if anything the wind intensified, picking up a notch or two and drifting the trail over. The dogs wanted to turn and run with the wind. Dan's voice was attempting to communicate something to me, but the wind tore the words away. Besides, I could not deal with what he was trying to tell me. I had to concentrate on bringing my dogs around.

The trail followed above the route of a state highway, and because the trail had drifted over the dogs made a beeline for the road. My brake was of no use on the icy pavement. I had lost control of the dogs. Other dog teams were there, too. Mushers shouted. Horns honked. Traffic continued; cars and pickup trucks weaved around and through the teams. There was confusion, and hysteria. The wind roared, kicking up snow and making visibility next to nothing. I heard Dan over my radio imploring me, "Get back on the trail!"

Out of nowhere the front bumper and chrome grille of a giant semitruck appeared, ghostlike and frightening. It loomed over me, sliding past on my right at thirty miles an hour like a huge, silent ship bearing down from out of a thick ocean fog. It was a miracle that my dogs and I were spared. We were a whisker away from certain death. Coming that close freaked me out.

Hands reached for my leaders. A group of volunteers appeared. They took hold of my dogs, as they had for other mushers, helping redirect my team off the highway and back onto the windblown trail.

After we fought the wind for another half mile the trail mercifully changed direction, swinging away from the highway, and a quartering wind blew us to the checkpoint and the end of the run. What a day!

After I tended to the dogs, my host family for the evening accompanied me to the local banquet. A herd of kids descended on me, wanting my autograph on shirts, hats, programs, and scraps of paper. I was called to the stage and asked to say a few words. I spoke about the problems we had faced that day on the highway and answered questions from the audience. People wanted to know about my blindness and what it was like for me to race dogs, all the normal things people want to know. After we ate, I signed more autographs until Dad finally rescued me, saying that I had a race to run and needed my rest. On the way out the door the kids had to give me hugs and wish me luck. I fed off their energy.

Having been forced to face some of the nastiest weather Mother Nature could hurl at me and somehow surviving a near-fatal collision perked up my self-confidence. But it was false bravado, and as soon as we reached our host family's house, a wave of exhaustion swept over me. I started to shake and then cry.

Dad wrapped an arm around my shoulders, "What's wrong, honey?"

"I'm tired."

"You haven't slept in two days. I imagine you are," Dad said.

For some strange reason his words set me off. I wailed, "Just leave me alone."

I think Dad figured I would get over my little snit, but when I went to bed I was still blubbering. I was too tired to sleep. All the images from the past couple days played across my mind. The wind, the blowing snow, but most of all that looming silver image of the semitruck robbed me of my sleep. And tomorrow would be another campout in the cold followed by what the other mushers had described as "The Trail from Hell," filled with switchbacks and rugged terrain.

Dad opened the door a crack to check on me. He saw my eyes were open and whispered, "You still awake?"

"I can't sleep."

"You've got to. If you don't sleep you'll burn out."

The tears came. I could not stop them. Dad kissed my cheek and told me he loved me. He promised that when I got to Lander I could call some of my friends. That would be the day of my sixteenth birthday. That helped bolster me. If I could talk to someone my own age, a friend, I could pull through this.

"Remember, I never made it to Lander. But you're going to come barreling into town and you're going to finish this race. I know you can do it. First, you've got to get some sleep. Want me to sing to you?"

I nodded my head. When I was little Dad sang me to sleep every night. The song that was guaranteed to put me under was called "Daddy's Lullaby." Grandpa Scdoris wrote it and he used to sing it to Daddy when he was a young boy. Dad had changed a few words from the original song to fit my love in life: sled dogs.

> *Cares of the day have fled, my little sleepyhead.*
> *The stars are in the sky, time that your prayers were said,*
> *my little sleepyhead, to your daddy's lullaby.*
> *Harness up your puppies, your lead dog's here, to guide*
> *you down the trail of dreams.*
> *Time that you closed your eyes, my little sleepyhead, to*
> *your daddy's lullaby.*

The words and the tone of his voice, a lot like Perry Como, soothed me. The cares of the day were washed away. Tomorrow was of no concern. I closed my eyes and fell asleep even before the last refrains were sung in my ear. I never heard Dad as he tiptoed from the room and pulled the door closed behind him.

The next thing I knew, Dad was gently shaking me awake. I still was not feeling myself, but my team of handlers was up and working and they were such a great bunch of guys that I supposed everything was going to be okay. Dan made sure I had food and water. Dad checked my clothing and rattled off a list of things for me to do that would make my campout more tolerable: pad under and around me with plenty of straw, put my down jacket over my sleeping bag instead of wearing it, thus creating another air pocket, and curl up like the dogs do instead of sleeping as if I were stretched out in a bed.

A television crew followed me that day on a snow machine. The run to Blucher Creek went without any trouble whatsoever. The crew filmed me at the campout: tending the dogs, eating, and even sitting around the bonfire with the other mushers talking and singing songs. The crew followed me when I turned in, and finally Dan had to tell them it was time to call it a night.

I stayed warm through the long, cold night and slept well. When

I got up I discovered one of my dogs, Dot, had chewed through her line and found the sack of snacks I kept to feed the dogs on the trail. Dot did not get any breakfast that morning.

Because I spent a couple minutes repairing the damage Dot had done, I was a tiny bit late feeding the dogs. Dan, who was still sick and fighting pneumonia, grumbled, "Now you're going to start out slow. This'll ruin your whole day."

I just smiled. "Dan, there's nothing that can ruin today. This is my sixteenth birthday."

"I forgot. Happy birthday, darling."

The dogs were anxious to go and I rode the brake down the long chute before giving them their head and allowing them to run. When we came to a long hill I got off and ran with them. At the high altitude it was difficult to get a good breath in the thin air. I was watching the clouds of vapor rising from the dogs every time they exhaled when suddenly the radio came to life and Dan's voice boomed, "Get on the brake! Get on the brake, right now!"

I was running up a hill, pushing the sled, leg muscles burning, and here was Dan yelping at me to give up my forward momentum and get on the brake. Was he crazy? Against my better judgment I jumped onto the runners and stomped the brake. And just in the nick of time, because my leaders disappeared over the ridge and plunged downhill. It was like the sensation a parachutist must feel when he jumps from an airplane. Free falling.

"Corner, lean left!" barked Dan.

I did not have enough time to react and the sled went over. I drove my left elbow into the snow and felt something give in my shoulder. No time to worry about injury. Get the sled upright! I fought to push the sled into position, and as it came up there was a corresponding stab of pain in my shoulder. What was pain? I could deal with a little pain.

"You okay?"

I nodded.

"Only ten miles to go," called Dan.

I had been repeatedly warned that the last ten miles coming into

Lander was a bearcat, real technical, with a lot of quick downhills and random, sharp switchbacks thrown in for good measure. I had to find a way to deal with it.

"Switchback right. Quarter-mile switchback left."

I took them in stride. No problem. I kept waiting for it to get bad, but it never did. Ahead I saw the dark, boxy outline of houses. Civilization. I figure it had to be Lander since there were no other towns around.

The Wyoming television stations and the newspapers had been reporting my progress. I was the feature story and my support, especially with the kids, was growing, because I was someone they could identify with. As I drew near I heard people shouting, encouraging me. Kids, more than twenty classrooms, lined the chute and as I came into the checkpoint they broke into song, singing "Happy Birthday." They did not start together but were staggered, and so it was like a round of "Row-Row-Row-Your-Boat." I laughed and pumped my fist in the air. It was the best birthday gift any sixteen-year-old could ever hope to receive, several hundred kids coming together to sing "Happy Birthday." Wow!

And it got better. Dad was waiting for me at the truck with sixteen lit candles adorning a cheesecake, my favorite. I made a wish. Actually, three wishes: that I stay strong, that my injured shoulder not give me any problem, and that I finish the race.

"You're halfway through. You're gonna make it." Dad wrapped his arms around me.

I devoured a piece of the cheesecake, and then the television and newspaper reporters descended on me. I answered every question that was posed to me, and then I was whisked away to the mushers' banquet. There was food and lots of it. I ate four helpings and more birthday cake. When I was called onstage I told the crowd, "This is such a long race that when I started I was only fifteen years old. Now I'm sixteen."

Once again they sang "Happy Birthday" to me. After that we called it an evening.

The following day was a short twenty-eight-miler between Lander and Atlantic City. When I got to Atlantic City I asked why a town in the middle of Wyoming was called Atlantic City. I had dwelled on the absurdity of it all day. No one knew the answer.

The run from Atlantic City was to cover forty miles. I drank a lot of fluids beforehand, and as a result about twenty miles out I was in desperate need of a restroom. I knew I could never make it twenty more miles. But I held on. Finally matters reached the point where I was forced to ride the runners cross-legged. I told myself, "This is not going to work."

Dan and I had discussed this very subject, in a more or less joking fashion, and he said when I felt the urge to void—"void" was his word, not mine—I was just to drop my trousers and take care of business. For once in my life I wished I had been born a man. The technical aspects of performing this procedure would have been considerably easier.

We were on an easy section of trail and Dan had taken a break and was behind me. I called over the radio, "See an uphill anywhere soon?"

"Ahead of you about a hundred yards. Goes for a half mile or so."

"Anyone behind me?"

"Not that I see."

"Suppose you could go on ahead?"

"Why?"

"Just because."

"Because why?

"Dan, I've got to piss."

"Oh!"

I heard the whine of his snow machine as it barreled past me. And now that I was down to the act of actually undressing I had this horrible vision—falling and being dragged bare-butted across the snow. But what choice did I have? I could not waste valuable time stopping in the middle of a race. Hastily, yet cautiously, I went through the process of shucking clothes. Finally I was down to my one-piece bodysuit and then there was nothing between me and nature besides what God had given me.

I wasted no time and after the act was completed, to my great relief, I began pulling on clothes. Out of the corner of my eye I saw movement, and I turned my head in that direction in time to see a sled pass me. It topped the ridge and broke over the downhill side. I never knew whether the other musher was a man or a woman, and thankfully, whoever it was had the decency to never bring it up.

The next couple of days were long runs through the mountains. The temperature gradually warmed and the snow turned slushy and slow. Each time we came to a hill I was off and running. It was hard work, but I wanted to save my dogs the extra labor of pulling my weight across the sloppy snow.

While I was tending to chores at the third campout the cold returned and forced me to pull on extra mittens to protect my fingers. After having been frostbitten they will always be susceptible to the cold. Dan came up and told me, "Good news, sweetie. You can sleep in a shed tonight. Some of the other mushers are already setting up in there. I saved you a spot on the floor, right in front of the fireplace."

A comfy place to sleep sounded totally divine. And while I walked the dogs I was thinking about the warm hearth and the roaring fire that awaited me. When the dogs were bedded down I found Dan at the bonfire and he showed me to the shed. I laid out my gear and spread my wet clothes near the fire so they would dry. I could have called it a night right then and there and crawled into my sleeping bag, but there was another banquet to attend and another round of interviews to endure. For the fifth night in a row we were served lasagna. I love lasagna, but five nights in a row was pushing even my limit of tolerance.

After returning from the banquet I put on a headlamp, took the dogs for another walk, and massaged the ones that needed it. Dot required the most attention. When I bedded her down I piled extra straw around her. And then, finally, it was my turn. I went to the shed, stepped over the other mushers who were already asleep and snoring up a storm, and stumbled to my spot on the floor. I think I was asleep before my head hit the rolled-up pants that were my pillow.

I awoke suddenly. The fire had been reduced to a bed of lively coals. I saw a shadow near the door and for some reason assumed it was Dan and that he was going outside. I told myself that it must be 6:00 a.m. and it was time to go. But no one else was moving. *Their loss,* I thought. *Let the sleepyheads be. I'll get a jump on the day.*

I dressed, stuffed my sleeping bag, and when I gathered up my clothes I was surprised to find that most were still damp. After a night by the warm fire they should have been dry. It never occurred to me to question why. I simply pulled on dry clothes and packed the wet ones. On the way out I took special care not to wake the sleepers, silently stepping over the bodies sprawled on the floor. Outside, the air was cold. Stars sparkled in the dark sky. I used my headlamp to look for Dan. He was not near the dogs. I stored my stuff on the sled, organized things, broke the ice, and watered the dogs. They never stirred and that was a little odd, because usually in the morning they get up, stretch, and are thirsty and hungry.

There was light from the bonfire and I could hear voices. Maybe Dan was there, eating breakfast. As I drew near I was hailed, "Hey, Rachael. Come on over and sit with us awhile."

A woman got up and threw her arms around me. "I really admire you. I don't think I could do what you do. You're my hero."

"Thank you," I said, not knowing quite what else to say. I sat with the group of volunteers and race officials and we visited, but after about a half hour and no sign of Dan, I finally asked, "Say, have any of you seen Dan?"

"Not for a while."

"When did you see him last?"

"Around midnight."

And then it hit me. "What time is it?"

One of the men looked at his watch and announced, "It's twelve fifty-six."

"Excuse me." I leaped to my feet.

"Stay."

"Sit with us."

I scampered to the sled, hauled out my gear, and returned to the shed. I removed my sleeping bag, once again hung the wet stuff to dry, and stoked the fire. I tumbled back onto the floor and it seemed that about a minute later Dan was shaking me awake.

When I emerged from the warm shed I found the sky off to the east was beginning to lighten and the air was bitterly cold. But the run that day, thirty miles, was routine and my team made it seem like little more than a training run. We held our position. And then we were down to the last day, a modest twelve-mile loop. A television crew had made arrangements to follow me, and Dan had warned them to stay back and not impede my progress in any way. He said, "I don't want your snow machine scaring the dogs."

"No problem," the driver of the snow machine said.

As I was leaving the chute, the television crew swept in so close they forced my dogs to shy away and leave the trail. The crew was lunging in powder snow and I spoke to them: "They're sorry. They don't mean to scare you."

My comments, meant mostly for human ears, went unheeded by the film crew. In fact, they became even more intrusive, to the point one of my dogs jumped the gangline to get away from them. I had to set the snow hook and fix the tangle. It was at that point that I lost my patience. My temper flared and I shouted at the film crew, "Stay away!" And they did for a while, but before long they were swooping in to shoot more close footage.

My voice was nearly gone, but I tried to make myself heard, "Give me some room."

Ahead was the finish line. I was going to make it. I would become the youngest musher, and the first blind person, to ever complete a five-hundred-mile sled dog race. This was to be the culmination of everything I had worked for: the thousands of miles I had run training the dogs, the running to get myself in shape, the efforts of so many friends and supporters who had helped me along the way. This race would prove something to all the doubters who thought a blind girl could never measure up in the sport of sled dog racing.

But more than anything I was thinking about Dad. I knew how

proud he must feel at this moment. I had accomplished something that had eluded him. This was my day, sure, but this was his day, too.

The irritating camera crew swept in one last time, but I did not even mind as I drove to the finish line. The crowd lining the chute cheered my arrival. I flashed them a big smile and waved.

Then it was over. People were pounding me on the back. Dad wrapped me in a bear hug. "I'm so proud of you. I love you." And then he was gone, swallowed by the throng of people who surged around me. The host families we had stayed with offered their congratulations. Kids chanted my name. Reporters talked in a rush and shoved microphones toward me. Cameras snapped pictures. Video cameras captured all the sights and sounds.

If that is it, if I never have another victory in life where I set a goal and go out and fight to accomplish it, crossing the finish line in Wyoming will be enough to sustain me. That was as good as it could possibly get.

No, I take that back. I have my sights set on the Iditarod. I will not be satisfied until I reach Nome. Then I will be satisfied.

No, not even then will I be satisfied. Running sled dogs is my life. There is no finish line in sight. Ever.

15

ATTA BOY

The Wyoming race took more out of me than I realized at the time. After returning home to Central Oregon I suffered from the effects of exhaustion, a bad cold, and when I weighed myself I discovered I had lost fifteen pounds. Maybe I should write a new diet book based on my experiences in Wyoming. I could call it *Mush Away: From Humdrum Miles to Soreness and Fatigue.*

I continued to apply ice to both my knees. They were swollen and discolored from the numerous times the sled had tipped during the race and I had fallen. My shoulder was still sore, but it was healing. And when I went to stretch I felt stiffness on one side of my chest. I pulled up my shirt and found an angry-looking purple bruise the size of a fist. When I touched it, several ribs moved. Ribs are not supposed to move. The ribs hurt when I twisted, hurt when I took a deep breath, and hurt especially when I laughed. But to put the accumulation of aches and pains in perspective, I figured it was a small price to pay to become the youngest musher to ever finish a five-hundred-mile sled dog race.

Track season kicked off and I went into it nursing two sore knees and the sore ribs. My times in the 3000 meters and the 1500 meters were slower than I had run since my freshman year. No matter how much I pushed myself in practice, my times refused to come down.

I blamed my poor showing on the injuries but finally had to admit the obvious, that during the past year my body had changed. No longer was I the willowy girl with a pencil-thin body. I had become a young woman. My body had developed and matured; chest and hips had gotten bigger. Never again would I be that promising young runner with a world of potential. My best running days were in the past. For a competitive person that was a bitter pill to swallow.

I continued to run and train during the summer, but when cross-country season rolled around it was a rehash of my dismal showing on the track. At best I was an average runner, but I stayed with it because running was excellent training for sled dog racing. If I could run the hills I would have a distinct advantage over some of the other mushers who were content to ride the runners.

My sights were set on doing well in the inaugural Atta Boy 300 sled dog race. It was a stage race to be run at locations throughout Central Oregon. Dad was the organizer and race director. For more than twenty years he had dreamed of holding a world-class sled dog racing event in Central Oregon. With the sponsorship of American Nutrition and Atta Boy Dog Food, along with a small army of friends and dedicated volunteers, Dad had laid the groundwork to make his dream become a reality. It would be one of only six World Cup events sanctioned by the International Federation of Sleddog Sports (IFSS), and if everything went as planned, the Atta Boy 300 would attract the most famous mushers in the world and become the premier sled dog race in the Lower 48.

The race consisted of eight separate stages to be held in locations near Bend, Sisters, Prineville, LaPine, and Sunriver. Each community would welcome the mushers at public banquets, and local families had volunteered to host mushers in their homes.

Not only would the race bring diverse people together and showcase the sport of sled dog racing and the tremendous beauty of Central Oregon, but it had also been designated as the "Race for Vision" and would raise public awareness of individuals with vision impairments. I was to be the race spokesperson and help to enlist eye care professionals to provide free vision screening, eye exams, and glasses for any Central Oregon individual in need.

It was a difficult fall, having to juggle my duties as spokesperson, train dogs, and start my junior year at Redmond High School. I was relieved when the day of the ceremonial start of the first Atta Boy 300 finally arrived. The event was held at Government Camp on Mount Hood. The location, only an hour's drive from Portland, provided close access for newspaper reporters and photographers as well as representatives from Portland television stations.

The sky opened and rain poured down. In Central Oregon we do not get as much precipitation in an entire year as the mountain received in that single afternoon. But the west side media, used to the rain, took it all in stride. They slogged through slush, thrust microphones and cameras in my direction, and I tried to be upbeat and positive, even though I was getting soaked to the bone. I paid attention to how Libby Riddles, the race marshal and first woman to win the Iditarod, handled herself with the media and I tried to emulate her. She has always been a hero in my eyes, and she was a great help to me that day.

Each musher was to carry a sponsor or a dignitary in the basket for the two-mile ceremonial race. Steve Mills, vice president for marketing and sales at American Nutrition, the parent company of Atta Boy Dog Food, was my rider. Without Steve, who stepped forward with the financial commitment to have American Nutrition serve as the title sponsor, the race never would have gotten off the ground. I wanted our run to be uneventful but fun.

Matt DiFrancesca, who had been my handler the year before in Wyoming, agreed to ride a snow machine and be my visual interpreter for the race. But as I hooked up the six dogs I made the decision that I did not need Matt on the snow machine that day. Steve would serve as my eyes. It turned out to be the wrong decision.

Less than a mile into the run Steve and I missed a trail marker. We took a wrong turn and ended up on a trail where skiers suddenly began to pop into my field of vision. My sled ran over the tips of a couple of skis that happened to be fastened to a skier. "Watch out!" I yelled. In my mind it was much easier for the skiers to move than for me to maneuver six racing dogs and a sled carrying two bodies. We passed a lodge and a ski lift.

"We might have gone the wrong way," Steve offered.

No one had said anything about skiers, a lodge, or a ski lift. We definitely had gone the wrong way. I was embarrassed at my blunder and promptly set the snow hook. I directed Steve to crawl off the sled, walk to the front of the team, and physically turn them around. Even before he had a firm seat in the basket we were off and running, the dogs lunging ahead and skiers scattering like a covey of quail in front of a speeding car.

Once we reached the proper trail the dogs tried to backtrack. Again I brought out the snow hook and again Steve had to turn the team. I laughed, trying to convey that this sort of happening was fairly typical of sled dog racing, but on the inside I wondered if Steve might be considering pulling his sponsorship. He proved to be a good sport and eventually we did make it to the finish line. I was wet, tired, and mad at myself and I still faced a four-hour ride to the kickoff ceremony in Bend.

At the kickoff ceremony I sang the national anthem, but still wet and chilly, I was not capable of staying on key. The crowd helped by singing along and we labored our way to the end. After that, as the spokesperson for the "Race for Vision," I made a short speech and then stood in the cold and listened to what seemed like an endless array of speakers thanking this person and that person. All I wanted was to get out of the cold, peel off my damp clothes, and jump in a warm bed.

The first race of the inaugural Atta Boy 300 was held at Mount

Bachelor and consisted of a forty-five-mile loop that began and ended at the Nordic Center. I had a few problems to contend with, and they all revolved around the fact that in the sled dog tour business we operate at Mount Bachelor, we typically make runs of seven miles. My leaders, Gus and Abrahams, were of the mind-set that they would run seven miles and then they expected treats and a rest. I had to keep switching leaders every seven miles. It was annoying and frustrating.

And then to compound my problems, the three dogs we call the Baseball Brothers—Hank, Willie, and Mickey, named after baseball greats because as puppies they showed such great athleticism—forgot what they were trained to do: race. They reverted to a more basic animal instinct, wanting to breed Ginger, who was starting to come into heat.

"Boys, behave yourselves," I was constantly calling to them. Several times I had to stop and straighten out tangles. This was not the race I had in mind.

And then, at about the thirty-five-mile mark, Devers gave out. I had to put her in the basket on the sled. Normally she is a great dog, but not this day. The only good that came of it was that a photographer from the Bend *Bulletin* snapped a picture of Devers with just her head poking out of the bag and it made the front page of the sports section. She looked so darn cute.

It rained and the start of the forty-mile second leg near Sisters had to be moved to a higher elevation because of the lack of snow. I had not slept much that night because I was worried about Ginger and those knuckleheaded Baseball Brothers. We were able to get off the line but had not gone far before the Baseball Brothers were up to the same antics as the day before. I fought with them constantly to keep them in the race. Every few miles I had to stop and untangle dogs, and then it was every mile, and then every couple of hundred yards. At one point I had the snow hook set and was finishing up my work on the team when the hook popped free in the sloppy snow. I made a grab for the sled and just barely managed to catch hold of the handlebars and tip the sled over.

It was at this point that Melanie Shirilla, a friend and a terrific musher, passed. She called to me, "Say something positive."

She was little more than a formless blur, but I called, "You look absolutely fabulous." And then she was gone in a swirl of snow. I laughed at the irony of our encounter as I pulled myself to my feet. But maybe some good did come from Melanie's passing, because my dogs lined out and began working together as a team, even the Baseball Brothers. We flew over the next ten miles. It had been the slowest thirty miles of my life, followed by the ten fastest. Go figure.

The third leg of the Atta Boy 300 ran forty-five miles from Sisters to Mount Bachelor, passing through some of the most scenic country on the planet. The snowy summits of the Three Sisters dominate the skyline to the west, and the wilderness is interspersed with open meadows and thickets of pine and fir trees. There are quick changes in elevation as the trail crosses steep ridges and plunges into canyons.

I discussed with Dad the possibility of dropping Ginger from the team. Every musher starts with sixteen dogs and has the option of running up to twelve at a time. I had been running only ten, so I would have fresh dogs to put in my team. On one hand, Ginger was one of my best dogs, but on the other, she was a distraction for every male in my team. It was a difficult decision to make, but I left her at the truck.

We started that morning and the dogs tended to the business of racing. They were doing everything I asked of them and I knew I had made the right decision by leaving Ginger behind. I was looking forward to the run. I had barely settled into the pace when Matt called over the radio, "Hard right coming up." Duchess, an awesome dog, was my leader and I called to her, "Gee," and she turned right. I guided the sled through the tight corner. This was going to be fantastic! We were going to make up so much time. I might even go into the fourth leg in the middle of the pack, maybe even the top third. We were flying up the trail.

"Pull up and stop," Matt's voice called over the radio.

"Pull up and what? This is a race. I'm not pulling up."

"Just do it."

I put on the brake and when we slowed I set the hook. Matt was there a moment later. "This better be a real problem," I called.

When he slowed, his snow machine sputtered and died. "It's a real problem. I'm having trouble keeping this thing running."

"Fix it."

Warren Palfry reached us and slowed. He is from Yellow Knife, Northwest Territories, Canada, and knows all about temperamental snow machines. He called, "Motor's overheated. Pack snow around it to cool it."

For half an hour we stayed in one place. Matt tried to start that infernal machine while other teams passed us, and then Matt suggested, "I'll run back and get another machine."

"And lose an hour—I don't think so. Get on. We'll double up."

Matt horsed the heavy snow machine to the side of the trail, grabbed the fifty pound pack he carries, and tossed it in my sled, my racing sled that weighs a mere seventeen pounds. He balanced his 190-pound frame on the runners and reached around me to hold on to the double handlebars. I pulled the snow hook and we took off. It did not take long to determine that Matt and I could not ride the remaining forty miles to Mount Bachelor this way. So he took the left runner and I took the right runner. We balanced there like two birds attempting to perch on a telephone line during a hurricane. We fought to maintain our balance and not fall off or step on the brake. We missed a corner and went over. My snow pants were literally ripped off in exposing my jeans underneath. But I did not want the jeans to get wet if we wrecked again and so I tried holding up the ripped snow pants with one hand while clinging to the handlebars with the other. We wrecked again, and again, and again. On the uphills I ran while trying to keep up those stupid snow pants. We reached the top of one ridge and I stopped.

"This is ridiculous," I said, and tore off what remained of my snow pants. After that I gave the dogs snacks and a few treats to keep up their energy level. I knew that the next few miles held some technically challenging tight corners and steep hills.

"Get ready for some fun," I told Matt. We charged ahead, bumping into each other, lurching from side to side, and flailing about. We were like the Marx Brothers in a comedy skit and I had to laugh and Matt joined in. We were just a couple of kids riding a sled together, laughing and having fun.

We were thirty-five miles into the run when we came across a driver and his snow machine, and after we had explained our predicament to the rider he graciously gave up his machine to Matt. We were able to finish the race like we had started, with Matt on a snow machine and me alone on my sled. The gallant snow machine rider caught a ride in with a buddy and reclaimed his machine after the race.

Going into the fourth leg near Prineville at Big Summit Prairie, I was dead last. I hated having to pull on the black bib to signify that I had been the slowest racer the previous day. I would start first and I swore no one was going to pass me. This was going to be my day.

I put together my best team: Dugan, Duchess, and Vampire were my veteran leaders and Joe was an adequate backup. Vampire, a great lead dog, did not like to lead out of the starting chute. I planned to switch the four dogs throughout the run and always have fresh leaders that were eager to run. Even the Baseball Brothers co-operated, and that day the miles melted away under a blue sky.

Matt called off the mile markers. When he reached thirty I thought, *Sweet. I'm running every hill, we have a great time going, the dogs are working perfectly as a team, and no one has passed us.* We reached the summit at Pisgah. Ahead were a series of tight corners that Matt had warned me were treacherous. But we charged into them and the sled was like the tail of a snake winding this way and that with only the slightest effort from me. The last five miles were all uphill. I had vowed to run the entire way, and when we reached the bottom of the grade I was off and running.

About halfway up the hill Gwen Holdmann caught me. Though it hurt to be passed, because I was working as hard as I could, I was happy for her and resigned myself to second place. But that was not to be. I finished sixth out of twenty-four teams and yet I felt good about the run. My dogs and I had done our best and we were running in front until the last couple of miles.

As I tended the dogs, checking them over carefully, I noticed that Duchess had a swollen wrist and it seemed to be swelling more by the minute. I felt terrible about the injury and blamed myself for not noticing it sooner. The fatigue and my disappointment at not hanging on to the lead heightened my self-contempt. I started to cry and had a hard time stopping the tears.

Jacques Philip, a well-respected musher originally from France but now living in Alaska, checked Duchess's wrist. He gave me a small tube of ointment, explaining it was a super anti-inflammatory. He advised me to rub a bit of the ointment onto the injured wrist and wrap it so Duchess would not be tempted to lick it off. He promised that by morning the injury would be much better and that Duchess would be back running in the lead within a day or two.

That evening I did as Jacques had directed. I massaged the injured wrist, added another layer of the ointment, and loved Duchess with pets and caresses. The following day on the run at Newberry Crater, I left her behind. Gus and Abrahams returned to their trick of running seven miles and wanting to stop. The Baseball Brothers decided the pace was not fast enough and they got bored and tried to play with one another. As a consequence they jerked the team all over the trail. I had to fix one snarl after another. The strange part of that day came when I reached the rim of the crater and realized I had stood at that exact spot when we were at cross-country training camp.

The final run of Saturday was at Mount Bachelor and required a campout the night before. When I reached the campout I staked out the team, fed and watered them, and laid down straw so they were warm and comfortable. People came around to look at the dogs and this unnerved the Baseball Brothers, who are always skittish around strangers. I took off my Northern Outfitters coat, laid that over them, and bunched up straw around them so they were hidden away from prying eyes. I shook out my biv sack, cuddled with Duchess for a while, and went to the lodge to visit with the other mushers and eat dinner.

When I left the lodge it was dark and snowing. The conditions made it almost impossible for me to see. I hate to admit this, but I could not find my team. I stumbled across several teams, the dogs lying curled in balls with snow covering them, before I finally located my dogs and camp. After exercising my dogs I climbed in my biv sack, cozied up with Duchess, and quickly fell asleep.

The cold woke me. I had a bag that was supposed to provide protection to ten below zero, but I was freezing. I felt around and found the zipper had broken. Just my luck. Up on the mountain I could make out a few faint lights, and I assumed they were Snow-Cats grooming the runs. I got up and watered the dogs. I like to make sure my dogs are well hydrated before a run. I want them full of energy but not bloated on a heavy meal. After tending the dogs I went to the lodge, hoping it was open, so I could stand beside the roaring fire and get warm, but I found the doors were locked. All I could do was walk, and it seemed as if I walked for hours before they finally allowed me to come inside.

After breakfast I got ready for the last day of racing. The sun was out and the sky was clear. It was going to be a beautiful day. I planned to run all the hills and finish the race strong. I dressed in layers of light clothes. My plan, as the day warmed and I started exerting myself, was to peel off layers as needed.

Part of the course we would be traveling was the same trail where I learned to ride a sled. I felt as though I owned this trail. I had Duchess back in the lead. I made up my mind that we were going flat out for all thirty miles.

Three and a half miles down the trail is an open meadow. This is our turnaround spot on our tours. We reached that point and I had to sweet-talk the dogs into continuing by giving them treats. At the fifteen-mile mark the sun went behind a bank of clouds and the temperature plummeted. My hands, even though they were inside gloves, became cold and quit working efficiently. I have had that trouble ever since my episode with frostbite at the Chemult race. There is not a thing I can do about it except try to keep the blood flowing.

Several teams passed us, but that never bothered my team. My dogs were perfectly content to plod along at a leisurely pace. While they lollygagged I was off the sled, running and trying to encourage my leaders to set a good example.

"You just passed the twenty-five-mile marker," Matt called over the radio.

That announcement renewed my optimism. "Only five miles to go," I told the dogs. I could drag the sled and the team five miles if I had to. I encouraged Duchess, "Come on, girl. You can do it. Pick up the pace."

"Three miles to go," Matt's voice informed me.

Now I was smiling. "Good girl. Way to go, boys. Don't let anybody else pass us. Come on; you can do it."

We reached a place where I figured we had two miles to the finish. I passed Matt, who was sitting on his snow machine, and he yelled, "I made a mistake—this is mile twenty-five."

"What? Are you kidding me?"

"No. Five more miles to go."

My enthusiasm dissipated like a handful of snow pitched into a roaring fire. I was wet, tired, and now had been stricken with a bad case of apathy. I told myself that I really did not care if I even finished this ridiculous race. And my dogs picked up on my sour attitude. They slowed their gait even more and I fought them for every miserable yard.

"You're at mile twenty-six," Matt called pleasantly over the radio. "Four to go."

I had reached my breaking point. I did not want to hear his cheery voice. Why should he not be pleasant? He was sitting on a warm snow machine. If he wanted to move forward all he had to do was tweak the throttle and he would leap ahead as if he had a team with a hundred fresh dogs at his disposal.

"Shut up! Just shut up, Matty," I muttered under my breath.

I crossed the finish line, claiming the twenty-fourth spot out of twenty-eight teams. I tried to infuse a little cheerfulness by thinking, *Well, at least you finished.* But there really was not much solace in finishing as far back as I did.

Before the banquet that evening friends took me out shopping.

They insisted on buying me a wonderful black dress, new shoes, and all the necessary undergarments. After painting my toes and fingernails with red paint, right there in the store, they called it good and we rushed off to the banquet. The one thing I did not have time for was the thing I wanted most: a hot shower. I was all gussied up, but I smelled like a pack of dogs. I suppose that is the life of a musher.

My junior track season was a dismal failure. And I followed that performance with a senior cross-country season where I was usually the last person on the team. I ran and lifted weights with only one thought in mind—I needed to get stronger if I ever hoped to complete my sled dog qualifying races and have a chance to run the Iditarod.

Going to school cut into the time I needed to train my team. Wendy Davis had worked for Dad the previous two winters as a guide in our sled dog business, and she saved the day by agreeing to come back to help train my team. As a reward she was promised the opportunity to run a second team in the 2003 Atta Boy 300.

Wendy and I were already great friends, but as we trained together on weekends and during breaks from school we developed a special relationship. We became more like sisters, except that we never fought. In the evenings we walked the puppies. We did the chores together. We ran dogs together. Sometimes we just sat and talked for hours. We loved being together.

As the second Atta Boy 300 drew near, we enlisted two additional members to our team. Terry Silbaugh, a retired Deschutes County sheriff who had also been the head of Search and Rescue in Deschutes County for thirty years, agreed to ride a snow machine and be my visual interpreter. Wendy enlisted a friend, Ben Moon, to handle the dogs for us. We were set. All the pieces were in place and the dogs were well seasoned and ready to run.

On paper it looked as if this would be my breakout year. A high finish in the Atta Boy was going to launch me into a position where the Iditarod Trail Committee could no longer ignore my credentials or me. They would have to let me race.

The second Atta Boy 300 began with an inauspicious run. We were barely five miles into the first leg when Terry radioed me that there was a sharp hairpin corner to the right coming up. I went into it too fast, tried to pull the sled around, but brushed a tree and knocked the snow hook out of the holder. It landed at my feet. I bent over and reached for it, but it fell off the runner and set itself in hard ice. The line snapped. There I was, five miles into the race without a hook and with no way to stop my team of hard-charging dogs.

To compound my problems, Duchess was in heat. Hank, one of the infamous Baseball Brothers, decided she was beautiful and he could not wait another minute to breed her. Without a snow hook to stop the team and separate the two of them there was absolutely nothing I could do except stand on the brake and hope Hank changed his mind or Duchess refused his advances. If I tried to leave the sled the team would likely run off. And so I stood on the brake and waited for Hank to finish his business.

It was pretty much the height of embarrassment to have a steady stream of passing competitors glancing over their shoulders at my two dogs hooked together and have them call back to me, "Tough break, girl," or, "That's too bad," or, "If I find a water hose I'll send it back to you."

On the second day of the race I put Hank in the wheel dog position so that he did not have the opportunity to fall in love with any more of the girls. I kept a close watch on him. When I saw him go down I panicked, but by the time I set the snow hook and got to him he was dancing and lunging at the harness, wanting to run. I figured he had just lost his footing and I had simply overreacted.

We continued on, but less than a mile down the trail Hank dropped again. This time I did not take any chances. I pulled him from the team, took him back to the sled, and zipped him into the bag on the basket. Hank used the opportunity to stick his nose in the goody bag, and by the time I saw what was happening he had devoured most of the snacks. At the end of the run I checked with the vet and Hank had two problems: an upset stomach and sore feet. I had to drop him.

At the start of the third leg the dogs seemed totally focused. But after only three miles that harlot Duchess stopped. She was in fertile heat. She raised her tail, trying to entice one of the males to breed her. I quickly pulled her out of the lead and brought her to the back, putting Ned in the lead. But we had no sooner gotten under way when Ned decided he wanted to breed Duchess and doubled back through the team. I was forced to untangle an absolute mess of twisted harness and crazy dogs. All the males wanted Duchess.

I switched leaders, but my troubles continued. Every few hundred yards I had to stop and separate the culprits of a potential breeding. I looked at my watch and realized I had been out on the trail for three hours and had traveled less than twelve miles.

Another tangle occurred and while I was trying to sort this one out Mickey took the opportunity to breed Duchess. Then Willie bred Duchess. That made three brothers in two days. I told Duchess, "You, girl, are a tramp." I even threatened the Baseball Brothers with castration. Nothing I said fazed them.

The other mushers had passed me going out and, having completed the loop, were on their way in. One stopped and asked if there was anything he could do. At that point Willie and Duchess were hooked.

Terry Silbaugh, who had been patiently sitting on his snow machine with the engine turned off, said, "Not unless you would care to light a few candles and play a little romantic music." Only then did the musher see the situation, and he did not waste time getting down the trail.

By fits and starts I managed to coax the team as far as the Wanoga snow park. We train our dogs out of a snow park and they know that when they see vehicles the dog truck will be there along with a warm bed and treats. The team tried to turn off the trail, but I held them back and persuaded them to continue on. But after a few hundred yards they stopped and refused to go farther.

The sun was riding on the edge of the mountains. We had now been on the trail for six excruciatingly long hours. I had fed the dogs all my treats. We were twenty miles into the run with twenty-three more miles to go. I tried loving the dogs. Tried clapping. Tried getting mad. Nothing worked. They sat on their haunches or lay on the snow. They refused to budge.

Terry came up and stood beside me. "I'm willing to stay out here with you all night if that's what it takes. But I want you to know this is the only place you can pull out. If you choose to continue you'll have to finish the loop. From the way it's going I'd estimate that'll take until about noon tomorrow, if we're lucky."

"I don't want to give up," I wailed, "I've never given up on anything in my life."

"I know. But the fact of the matter is you're only allowed to be on the trail twice as long as the winner and you're already pushing that. You're probably going to be disqualified anyway."

"I know," I snapped, and then immediately apologized. "I'm sorry. This is the hardest thing I've ever had to do." I drew in a deep breath, expelled it. "Okay, we're done. I quit."

Tears spilled down my cheeks. The last thing I wanted was to quit. But it was not fair to my dogs, not fair to Terry, not fair to the judges and the volunteers. I looked around for Dad. He had always been there when I needed him, my Rock of Gibraltar. But he was not there.

When I turned the dogs around to go back to the snow park they leaped forward with genuine enthusiasm. I called out, "You knuckleheads, that's what I've been looking for all day. Where's it been?" In nothing flat we were at the snow park. I staked out the dogs and waited for Ben, Wendy, and Dad.

When they arrived I fell apart. "They wouldn't go," I wailed. "No matter what I tried, they just wouldn't go."

I expected Dad to lecture me, but I was impressed at how he handled the situation, as well as his disappointment. He wrapped his arms around me, stroked my hair, and in a voice that was both gentle and soothing consoled me. "I know how bad you must feel. A competitor never wants to quit. You're a competitor. You proved that in Wyoming. I'm sorry, sweetie-pie."

We loaded up the dogs and took them home to Alfalfa so that we had only Wendy's sixteen dogs to care for. As we traveled I tried to rationalize and justify what had happened and why I had been forced to pull out of the race. Finally Wendy put it in perspective: "It's just one race."

"Just one race," I repeated.

That night it took a long time for me to fall asleep. I fought through the depression of having had to quit. I got past blaming myself, feeling sorry that it had happened to me. I convinced myself that this was no longer about me and promised that in the morning I would awaken with a new attitude. I would dedicate the remainder of the race to Wendy and to working as her handler and helping her in any way I could. And then I fell asleep.

After the Atta Boy 300 I returned to Redmond High School to face the remaining five months of my senior year. After graduation I would be able to devote all my time and energy to preparing for the Iditarod, and judging from what had been written in newspapers and printed in the sled dog chat rooms on the Internet, I knew I would have to work to convince people that I was a capable musher. And also I would have to convince the Iditarod Trail Committee to grant me special accommodations that would allow me the opportunity to compete in the Alaskan Iditarod race.

16

THE BIG DAY

After graduating from Redmond High School on June 5, 2003, I stayed at the all-night party until midnight and went home to rest and prepare myself for what I thought, at the time, might very well be the biggest day of my life.

The Iditarod Trail Committee (ITC) board of directors was meeting on June 6 to discuss my proposal to be granted special accommodations to participate in the 2004 Iditarod Trail International Sled Dog Race. I was requesting to be allowed to use two visual interpreters riding snow machines. Two in case one machine broke down. My friend Dan MacEachen and I would be connected in a conference call to the board of directors' meeting. Dan was to be one of my visual interpreters, and Gwen Holdmann, who would be attending the meeting in person, would be the other.

The morning of the meeting I was seated in front of a large table in the conference room at the Bend *Bulletin*. The only thing on the table was a black upright speakerphone. It was facing me. Dad was seated directly behind me and several reporters as well as a crew from the local television station had taken up positions at the far end of the table.

Once the connection was made linking me to the Iditarod board meeting, I recognized President Rick Koch's voice. After a few words welcoming Dan and me to the conference call, he took care of several business items. The connection was terrible; static hissed and the voices were barely audible. I had to listen intently in order to hear what was being said.

I tried to sit still and not fidget, knowing that in a few minutes the board's attention would be directed at me; but I found myself fooling with my hair, twisting it in my fingers.

I never anticipated the board's decision to allow me to run the Iditarod was an automatic slam dunk. I knew that Rick Swenson, five-time Iditarod champion, had been very vocal against changing any of the rules to accommodate my needs. Also, from what had been reported in the newspapers and from information passed on by friends, I understood that some of the other board members had questioned my participation. And yet I never believed my proposal was something that was extremely controversial or might threaten to divide the board. After all, the Americans with Disabilities Act (ADA) virtually required that I be granted reasonable accommodations. The law was on my side. Fairness would triumph over narrow-mindedness. Common sense would prevail. Besides, having me run the race would attract more public interest. In the long run that could only benefit the Iditarod.

I expected, after a lively and thoughtful discussion, that the board would vote in favor of my proposal and allow me to participate. At last the dream I had first dared to dream when I was eight years old, the dream that had sustained me through the difficult times when other kids mocked and terrorized me, the dream that pushed me to my best in the classroom, on the track, and over the trail, would finally come true. The Iditarod would open its collective arms and welcome me into its elite family. That was the direction I saw this meeting going. I was so naive.

Rick Koch said, "Rachael has requested accommodation and entry in the 2004 Iditarod. The purpose of this discussion is to respond to that request."

Board member John Handeland fired several questions addressed to me, wanting to know if I had been accepted into any Iditarod qualifying races, if those races were going to allow special accommodations, and exactly what accommodations had been agreed upon. I fumbled with the answers. Not only was it hard to hear the questions, but I did not understand what Mr. Handeland was driving at, except to express his doubts that any Iditarod qualifying race would be willing to grant me special accommodations. Dad was whispering suggestions in my ear and scribbling notes on a sheet of yellow paper that he shoved in front of me. This added another distraction and made it nearly impossible for me to concentrate. My level of anxiety soared. When I glanced at my hands I noticed they were trembling slightly. I had never been that nervous in my life. But of course there was a lot riding on this meeting. The way I saw it, my entire future was riding on the outcome.

Gwen Holdmann interceded on my behalf, stating she had run the Iditarod, the Yukon Quest, and many other major races and not once had she been grilled about her credentials and what qualifiers she had completed. She concluded by saying, "I feel this line of questioning is totally inappropriate. No other rookie has been asked these questions. The issue here is whether or not Rachael is capable of running the Iditarod and what accommodations you might consider to compensate for her lack of vision."

Rick Koch noted that there seemed to be a significant amount of concern regarding my two visual interpreters. He repeated several comments he had heard about the snow machines being used to pace my team or break trail for me. He questioned whether my visual interpreters might feel compelled to select and prepare campsites, help with the care of the team, and perform general maintenance chores. He addressed the next question to Dan MacEachen, asking what he would do to help me in a difficult situation.

"I was her visual interpreter in the five-hundred-mile Wyoming International Pedigree Stage Stop Sled Dog Race," Dan said. "Generally she didn't want me nearby and I stayed three to five miles out in front, except in problem areas. What you have to remember is Rachael doesn't want help. In most instances she doesn't need help. She is perfectly capable of driving a dog team. What she needs is another person to serve as her eyes when she cannot see, and in dangerous situations. That's all."

Gwen offered, "I think Dan and I have proven ourselves. I think we have good reputations in the sled dog world as honest and trustworthy individuals. Like any other musher, you have to assume Rachael has integrity and would not accept outside assistance. And like any other musher, this has to be based on the honor system."

I mentioned that I planned to follow the rules every other musher lived by. I said it to assure the committee members that, except for the visual interpreters and the two snow machines, I planned to run this race on my own. I would reach the finish line, or fail, based upon my own skills and the ability of my dog team.

But my comment seemed to incite board member Rick Swenson. He snapped at me that from the tone of the voice it sounded as if I felt the Iditarod had gone out of its way to solicit my participation. "I certainly never asked you to sign up for this race," he angrily stated. "We never said we would allow you to have two snow machines. That was your proposal when you demanded special accommodations. Don't be turning things around. I don't want to be put on the defensive here."

His remarks, his annoyance, and the way he spit out "special accommodations," with so much loathing, shocked me. I did not know how to respond. So I sat and said nothing. But criticism of my proposal to be included in the race, and me personally, did not end there.

"What we are being asked to do is to change the rules of the race. It isn't one individual we're dealing with. If we grant special accommodations to this individual, we are opening the door to changing the whole event," board member Richard Burmeister said.

Board member Mike Owens added, "Do you want us to rewrite the rule book? Or maybe you want a revision of the whole event. Maybe that is how we should be looking at this. If we focus on one person, and make special accommodations to suit that person, then we have to revisit special accommodations at every request. We're being asked to compromise this race, to change the event. I don't like it."

"You might as well throw the rule book out the window," said an unidentified speaker.

Finally the remarks, the weight having built layer by layer to an intolerable level, propelled me to respond. My words came with a heated urgency: "I seriously disagree with you gentlemen. You are not throwing the rule book out the window. But you absolutely need to be prepared, and willing, to discuss any accommodations, mine or someone else's, on a case-by-case basis. At some point there will be other impaired mushers who will want to run your race. They might seek accommodations different from what I need. I can't see. I would like to be able to have sight equal to what any of you enjoy. I never will. The closest I can come is with the aid of a visual interpreter."

Gwen was much more composed and sensible than me. She said, "I know you have concerns and that you think by granting Rachael special accommodations you would be opening a can of worms. But what you are actually being asked to decide is a simple two-step process. The board has to decide whether to change the rules and allow accommodations on a case-by-case basis, and secondly you have to decide whether Rachael's request fits under that rule change."

"That's it in a nutshell," boomed Rick Koch's voice. "The guidelines for granting accommodations are based on the Americans with Disabilities Act. I'm not saying that this act does or does not apply to the Iditarod. That is a legal matter a judge would need to rule on if the question is presented in court. If the judge issues a ruling that the ADA does apply, then we are required to consider any accommodation that a disabled individual may request. It would be our decision as to whether those accommodations were reasonable or not. The ADA provides an avenue for people to participate in events and things that they would otherwise not have the opportunity to participate in. It is the law of the land, even in Alaska.

"Furthermore, there have been a number of discussions concerning how the snow machines are going to interfere with the race. Let me say this about that aspect: According to the *Anchorage Daily News* there are between two thousand and twenty-five hundred snow machines out there already between Wasilla and Skwentna gathered in places to watch the teams go by."

Board member Lee Larson broke the tension in the room. He said, "Rachael, I want to congratulate you for putting this comprehensive plan together. You have done a great deal of work preparing it and I want to thank you for bringing this important issue to the forefront and for the consideration of this board. I think it would be inappropriate for us not to recognize your previous mushing accomplishments. Personally I applaud you."

I thanked him. His remarks were the last positive thing I would hear for some time, as the more outspoken board members chose to fire questions at me concerning exactly what I could, or could not, see. Rick Swenson asked, "If you are running a twelve-dog team how many of them can you actually see?"

"I have run eighteen dogs and can tell where the leaders are. If there is a big tangle I can see that," I said.

"If there was a tree across the trail could you see that?"

"It would depend on the size of it and how far away it was." I was trying to keep my voice as emotionless as possible.

"How about a boulder?"

"The same answer. It depends on the size and distance. That is why I'm asking for a visual interpreter. Because I cannot see, I am legally blind."

Others fired silly questions at me. "What if a snow machine breaks down?" "How can you care for your dogs' feet if you can't see them?" "How can we guarantee you won't cheat and have your visual interpreters do the work for you?"

It was suggested that the board eliminate all rules and allow mushers to accept outside assistance. Someone made the inane comment: "If I'm a short basketball player does that mean the NBA is legally required to provide me with a ladder?" There was peal of laughter in response and people began talking back and forth over one another. I was only hearing a small part of what was being said.

A motion was made to table my request indefinitely. Without further discussion it passed. Rick Koch thanked me.

"What just happened?" I asked him.

"Your request was denied," Rick Koch responded.

I whispered to Dad, "What do I do?"

"Ask if you have any recourse," he whispered back.

"Do I have any recourse to that decision?"

"I suspect you might very well have recourse. But it would not be appropriate for me to advise you of the direction of recourse that you might want to consider, except to say this board might entertain the possibility of meeting with you in the future."

Rick Swenson, acting as though he had won the war, said, "How about if you sign up and run the race like anyone else. Why don't you try playing by the same rules as the rest of us mushers?"

"Don't you understand, she can't see," Rick Koch growled.

"When I take off my glasses my eyesight is worse than hers ever was. And she wants special accommodations. That's not fair."

"Who said that?" I wanted to know so that I could respond.

Someone said, "Rick Swenson."

"I am offended by that remark, Mr. Swenson. I do not have the luxury of putting on a pair of glasses to cure my disability as you have the luxury of doing. I am legally blind. I can't see." It was pretty obvious to everyone that from the way my voice was cracking I was emotional and had begun to cry.

Again Rick Koch thanked me, and he said good-bye. I think all those in attendance at the meeting assumed the teleconference call had been terminated. But I could still hear them. Bedlam had broken out in the room and yet I distinctly heard one of my supporters say, "If we were to change a few names this could be Selma, Alabama, 1965. This is nothing but bigotry."

"You're the bigot," snarled one of my most vocal detractors. "You want to screw up our race and open it up to all those kinds of people."

Only after that outburst did the line go dead. Dad leaped to his feet and shouted, "What an ass! Did you hear that? Did you?" He pounded his fist on the table and swore. I do not think I have ever seen him as mad as he was at that particular moment.

The reporters in the room asked if I planned to take the Iditarod Race Committee to court. I puffed up like a barnyard peacock and proclaimed, "If it comes to that I most certainly will take them to court. I have every right to run that race. They can't keep me from it. Not with their prejudice, not with their bigotry, not with their good-old-boy way of conducting business. You bet I'll take them to court, and I'll beat them fair and square."

It took a moment for my anger to dissipate. When I was a little more rational I realized how silly and immature I had acted. My remarks were totally tactless. I asked the reporters to please, pretty please, not print what I had said. And then I gave them a less angry and much more thoughtful response, saying that I wanted to continue to work with the ITC board of directors in the hope we could find some middle ground that would provide the accommodations I needed while maintaining the integrity of the race.

"I'm just going to keep doing what I'm doing. This fight is definitely not over. I will continue to build up my team and do some serious racing this winter. I want to prove to all those people who doubt me that they are wrong."

One musher contacted me and said, "Doesn't Rick Swenson realize the glasses he wears are his special accommodations?"

Another musher, with tongue in cheek, told me, "I didn't have any idea that Rick Swenson's eyes were so bad. I don't think we should let him run the Iditarod. What if he was on the trail and broke or lost his glasses? He could potentially pose a huge risk, not only to himself but to other mushers and his dogs, too."

I had always realized that there was that remote possibility the ITC board would turn down my request, but I thought if they did I would have a field day with the media. In the end public opinion would sway the board and they would have no choice but to reverse their decision and allow me to participate. Now I was not so sure about such an approach. Maybe it would be better if I kept quiet, allowed a little time to pass, tempers to cool, and tried again in a few months to reach a compromise.

We were bombarded with requests from the media: television, radio, magazines, and newspapers. Everyone wanted to do a story on my entry being denied and my reaction to the denial. We thanked them for calling but told each of them the same thing, that we did not want to make any comment at this time, and referred them to Paul Herschell and Dave Wise, my agents at Sports Unlimited in Portland. We felt we might be able to schedule another meeting with the ITC board and did not want to jeopardize the potential for a meeting or say anything that might offend the members.

Some of the reporters were insistent. We were as gracious with our denials as we could be. One woman told me, "If you don't give me a quote I'll just make something up and print that." I hung up on her.

Several months later we were able to negotiate a second meeting with the ITC board. This time I would attend the meeting in person. I felt it would be easier for me to defend myself and more difficult for the board to deny my request a second time if I met them face-to-face.

17

FACE-TO-FACE

That summer Jay Rowan drowned. Jay was a Redmond High School swimming champion and one of the best pole vaulters in the Intermountain Conference. He was smart and kind and an all-around great guy.

On the day of the accident Jay and a friend were inner tubing on the Deschutes River. Jay was swept over Awbrey Falls and somehow the hydraulics of the current pushed him into a lava tube. There are many lava tubes on the high desert. Thousands of years ago lava pumped through these openings and when the molten lava drained away the tubes remained. Jay was pushed into a small opening in one of these underwater tubes and maybe he hit his head or maybe he could not find a way out of the tube, but he drowned.

I was devastated by the news of his death and remembered that whenever I ran, he would leave the pole-vault pit and stand at the edge of the track shouting encouragement to me. He was there on every lap letting me know the positions of my competitors. His support always gave me confidence. It made me try a little harder to push through the pain. I wanted to show Jay what I was capable of achieving. He was an upperclassman. He was someone I looked up to. He was someone who inspired me. He was my friend.

After the funeral I approached Jay's mom, Judy, and I told her how sorry I was that such a tragedy had occurred to her family. She held my hands and quickly changed the subject, asking what was happening with my efforts to be included in the Iditarod. I told her that I had been turned down, but another meeting was scheduled and I was planning to go to Anchorage to meet the board.

"Don't let them say no," she advised. "Make them say yes. That's what Jay would have done. That's what he would want you to do."

I promised I would fight just like Jay would have fought and then, since others were waiting to express their sympathies, I stepped aside. I watched Judy for a while and I was inspired by her composure, her strength, and her grace under such trying circumstances.

The next time we had a litter of puppies I picked the best one— the biggest, strongest, smartest, best-looking, the one with a personality that could light up a black night, and I named him Jay. I hoped that one day Jay would be on my Iditarod team.

"Dad, I think I should go alone," I said, referring to my opportunity to meet with the Iditarod Trail Committee board of directors on September 19, 2003. I expected a different reaction from him than I received.

Dad smiled. "Why do you think that?"

"You know what people are saying?"

"When have we ever cared what people said?"

"I don't want the board members to think you're pushing me. I don't want to be perceived as Daddy's little girl. If I went up alone, they couldn't say that."

"Interesting concept," Dad said. He smiled again. "I've been thinking the same thing."

"You were?"

"Yeah, but I don't want you thinking it's going to be easy to let you go. Take your cell phone with you. And you have to promise you'll call me at every break, keep me posted on what's going on. Promise?"

"Promise."

Then he told me, "I'm proud of you. Proud you want to stand on your own two feet, that you're willing to fight them on this issue. You're going to win. I know you will, and you're going to run the Iditarod."

Dad drove me to the airport in Redmond, wished me well, and said his good-byes. The last thing he told me was, "Keep your cell phone on. Call when you get there. Call if you have the least bit of trouble. Call in the morning and at every break in the meeting. I want to know what's going on. I love you, hon. Have a safe flight. Kick butt."

On the plane ride to Portland, and from Portland to Seattle, I read my Bible, hoping it would give me insight and personal strength for the campaign that lay ahead. When I reached Seattle I called Dad. He asked what I had been doing.

"Reading my Bible."

"What book?" he asked.

"Genesis."

"You might want to read Matthew, Mark, and John," he suggested. "Those are the ones that talk about Jesus."

"You're probably right," I told him. And on the trip to Anchorage I actually did read a little from Matthew. Dan MacEachen was supposed to meet me, but I got in a little early and had an opportunity to explore the airport. I found the baggage claim area and located my bag. As I was wandering along I just happened to see someone out of the corner of my eye walking in the opposite direction. It looked a lot like Dan.

"Hey, Dan. You looking for me?"

In the morning I put on the outfit I had agonized over and finally selected for the meeting: flared black pants with slits up the sides, a pair of Mom's leather boots, a pink paisley top, and a dark brown blazer. When Dan and I went to the airport to pick up Gwen Holdmann she was wearing almost the exact same outfit. It was as if we had called each other to make sure we coordinated our attire.

Since the Millennium Hotel Anchorage is the official Iditarod race headquarters and was the site of our meeting, we decided to have breakfast there. Dan and Gwen ordered normal meals, but I was feeling too nervous to eat much of anything and settled for a strawberry smoothie. Over breakfast we visited about a lot of things, but mainly we talked about the Iditarod.

I have read everything ever written about the Iditarod Trail International Sled Dog Race. The basis for the modern race took place in 1925. Dr. Curtis Welch diagnosed an outbreak of diphtheria in the children of the isolated community of Nome and sent a telegraph message to the outside world pleading for antitoxin serum. Without serum delivered as quickly as possible, many of the children of Nome would die.

Only two planes were available in Alaska and they had been dismantled for winter and stored in a hangar in Fairbanks. Governor Scott C. Bone made the decision to have the serum transported by dog teams. Twenty mushers took part in a 674-mile relay from Nenana to Nome. It was Gunner Kaassen who drove his tired dog team down First Avenue in Nome and delivered the serum, saving several hundred young lives.

As we ate breakfast we discussed the spirit of the Iditarod and how if those mushers back in 1925 had believed the words "No, you can't," the serum they were transporting would never have reached Nome.

"If the ITC thinks that my two snow machines are going to ruin their race and that I'm going to throw up my hands and quit because they say, 'No, you can't,' they have another think coming. After all, isn't the spirit of the Iditarod to overcome any obstacles that are thrown in your way?" I said. I was pretty confident and full of myself.

Dan and Gwen talked about some of the mushers they had witnessed accepting outside assistance. They told about one musher who left a checkpoint in the middle of a blizzard. A video cameraman was documenting it all, as well as blazing a trail with his snow machine. Another incident they discussed was a helicopter landing and resupplying a musher between checkpoints. And they told about the time a new sled was mysteriously delivered to a musher on the trail. I wondered why the committee was making a big deal out of my two snow machines.

After breakfast we walked into the lobby of the Millennium Hotel Anchorage. I would characterize the decor as lavish while still maintaining a casual Alaskan rustic motif. I saw stuffed animals everywhere: polar bear, grizzly bear, moose, bighorn sheep, wolverine, and a wolf. There were ornate chandeliers and a fancy staircase. The carpet was either brown or gray, with random squiggly lines running through it.

We walked up a flight of stairs to a landing, through double doors, and into a big room with tables arranged in a horseshoe fashion. We assumed the board would sit around the tables, and took seats toward the back of several rows of chairs. A number of spectators were already there, including seven television crews.

Shortly after we were seated, Rick Koch came into the room. He walked directly to us. I stood, shook his hand, and thanked him for his help in arranging this meeting. He confided that after the June meeting he had gone home and written a letter of resignation, relinquishing the presidency of the Iditarod board. But according to him, "I decided not to resign and to see this thing through."

I thanked him again, this time for not resigning. He walked to the head of the tables and we sat down. Several members of the Alaska ADA Watch Group approached me and introduced themselves. Other supporters wished me well. It felt good to know there were people on my side.

The meeting began with a short introduction by Rick Koch and a statement that this meeting had been called for two reasons: The first was to discuss the applicability of the Americans with Disabilities Act to the Iditarod Trail International Sled Dog Race, and the second was to consider my request to be allowed special accommodations to participate in the race.

A motion was made to acknowledge the applicability of the ADA. Much to my surprise, it passed without discussion or fanfare. I thought, *All right, I have a chance.* But any celebration was short-lived, because almost immediately the board backtracked on the motion they had just passed.

Rick Koch invited board member Mark Moderow to recap the last meeting, where I had spoken with the board by telephone conference call. Mark said that previous discussions had centered on my request for special accommodation and he thought that discussion was premature because the board first needed to establish whether or not the laws outlined in the ADA applied to the Iditarod.

"The real question is do we have to abide by the rules imposed by the ADA? If we don't have to do it, then we have to make a separate decision—do we want to make an exception for Miss Scdoris?" Mark said.

Apparently I was not the only person confused about the logic of debating an issue that had already been accepted. Rick Koch said, "If you would like to hear from counsel and his review of the ADA, he is here today and available to address the board."

"Not at this point," Mark said. "Maybe we should discuss this and hear any public comment before we listen to the advice of counsel."

Rick Koch invited Mona McAleese, a member of the Alaska ADA Watch Group, to address the board. She was very well-spoken and pointed out that the ADA most certainly did apply to the Iditarod. She backed up this statement with facts about the Boston Marathon allowing disabled athletes to compete, and she pointed out that the Supreme Court had decided in favor of Casey Martin and against the Professional Golf Association because the accommodation that Casey Martin requested, being allowed to ride the course in a golf cart, did not fundamentally change the game of golf. She went on to say that my request for accommodations would not change the sport of sled dog racing and that twenty years from now we would look back on this meeting with mild amusement and wonder what the big deal was all about.

Further discussion centered on specific rules of the ADA. Don LaVonne, a member of the Alaska Disabled Veterans Sports Program, made a presentation. He said, "The accommodations Miss Scdoris has requested are not unreasonable, nor are they outside the scope of the law as it applies to ADA. I know that if she is allowed to meet her high goals she will become a leader of an entire generation of disabled youth. When they see what a blind athlete is able to accomplish they will know that even if they have restrictions on their physical or mental capability, they, too, can attain their personal goals in life."

At that point Mark requested a fifteen-minute recess so the board could go into executive session and hear from legal counsel. The audience slowly filed from the room. The reporters and camera crews tried to corral me but Dan intercepted them. He said, "She needs her space. Is there anything I can answer for you?"

One of the reporters asked, "Do you think the use of snow machines is an unfair advantage?"

Dan said, "I don't care how you try to sugarcoat things, being blind is never an advantage."

I smiled and thought to myself, *Good answer, Dan,* as I continued down the hallway, I called Dad, telling him briefly what had transpired. He asked how it seemed to be going. "I don't really have a handle on things. It's like trying to watch a game of Ping Pong. The ball bounces one way, then it bounces the other, and I can't tell who is scoring the points."

"Call me at the next break."

I promised I would.

The fifteen-minute executive session stretched to forty-five minutes. When we were finally allowed to return to the room Rick Koch held a chair at the end of the horseshoe and asked me to have a seat. I looked around. The spectators were behind me and the board was in front of me. I felt totally exposed, as though I had been singled out, as if I were on trial pleading for my life before this tribunal. And in a way I suppose I was. But I tried not to show any hint of anxiety.

During breakfast Gwen had coached me: "Don't play with your hair." (I have a habit of doing that, twisting strands whenever I'm nervous.) "Don't fiddle with your sunglasses. Don't bite your nails. Be strong. Don't show any signs of weakness."

I started to fiddle with my hands but stopped immediately. I waited for someone to say something. Again those fingers wanted to fiddle. I thought I might have to sit on my hands.

"Miss Scdoris, would you care to address the board?" Rick Koch asked.

I smiled. I've found that a smile is always a good way to start. It disarms people and makes you feel good. "Thank you for taking time out of your busy schedules to meet with me today. I know all of you would much rather be out training your dogs than be cooped up in this room. I know I sure would.

"I want you to know I am serious about the sport of professional sled dog racing. I was raised on a sled. I've logged thousands of miles on the trail. Being allowed the opportunity to run the Iditarod has always been a goal of mine. Ever since I was eight years old I have dreamed about the Iditarod. It is the pinnacle of sled dog racing. My proposal for two snow machines and the visual interpreters will not detract from the race. I believe my participation will heighten the public's interest in the race.

"If you decide to grant me special accommodation I don't want you to feel as though you are being forced into a corner by the law or what somebody tells you that you are required to do. I want you to see me as a fellow musher, a professional, and I would hope you allow the races I have run with visual interpreters on snow machines to count as my qualifiers. I don't want you to simply allow me in. I want to have your blessings to run the Iditarod."

I found myself fiddling with my glasses again and immediately stopped.

"Have you ever run dogs over an unfamiliar trail?" Rick Swenson asked.

"Yes, a lot of times," I answered. "The trails I train on are familiar, but most of the trails that I race on, I've never been over those trails."

"Would you ever go out alone on a trail you were unfamiliar with?" he wanted to know.

"Never."

"Why?"

"It wouldn't be safe. On a new trail I need to have another person serve as my eyes. After I'm familiar with a trail it's a different story," I said.

Rick Koch prefaced his question by saying some members of the board had voiced concerns over the safety of the dogs. "There are times when a split-second decision needs to be made to render assistance to a dog. I realize that your plan provides as much protection as possible. Our main concern is the safety of the dogs. Do you believe the risk of injury to the dogs in your team is comparable to that of your sighted competitors?"

"Like you, and all the other mushers, my main concern is always the safety of my dogs," I said. "None of us would purposely risk an injury to a dog in order to gain a higher finish. But any time we hook up dogs and race we assume a certain level of risk.

"I am not totally blind. I can see. What I see might be one-dimensional. It might be slightly out of focus. It might be limited. But I can see my dogs and lots of times I can sense things that some of you might not pick up on, when a dog is not pulling right, when a dog is tired, when a dog is about to go down. My visual interpreters warn me of obstacles coming up on the trail. I am responsible for my team."

Questions were fired at me like bullets spit rapid-fire from a machine gun. "In the races you have entered what special accommodations have been made for you? Would it work for you to run a tandem sled with a visual interpreter? Have you ever run at night? Do your visual interpreters give you advice? Are your dogs trained to follow a snow machine? The radio you carry, is it a two-way or only one-way? What will you do if your visual interpreter gets lost? What is the range of your radios and how far away will they work?

What happens when you hit the glare ice at Unalakleet? The race you ran in Wyoming, did they use reflective markers like we use? Is part of the reason you want two snow machines so you can have a film crew following you? Are they going to make a movie about you? Describe your ability to recognize the gait of a dog. Can your dogs run sixty miles a day? What about lack of sleep? How are you going to handle that?"

The questioning went on and on. A question from this side of the horseshoe, another from over there, it was making me dizzy. I tried to answer without hesitation, and I was always conscious of my hands. Mostly I kept them on my lap.

Dan and Gwen were asked to move to the front row, directly behind me, and an occasional question was tossed in their direction. "If you are going down Dalzell Gorge and there is three feet of overflow and a dog can go through it and a snow machine can't, what will you do? Are the radios reliable? Will you be wearing headsets so you can keep your hands free? At night will you run with a headlamp or with the light of the snow machine?"

A second executive session was called. The thirty minutes they requested dragged into an hour and fifteen minutes. Afterward there were more questions for me to answer. Around and around it went, the same questions phrased slightly differently, until I felt like a farmer plowing the same field time after tedious time. Yes, I felt confident I could take care of my dogs and myself. No, the visual interpreters were not going to give me an unfair advantage. No, they were not going to interfere with the other mushers. And no, they would not provide assistance to me beyond serving as my eyes.

Dogs, snow machines, visual interpreters, ADA, bending rules, establishing rules, doing away with rules. I wanted to scream at them, "Stop! Just let me run the race. I'll prove what I can do." Instead I sat there patiently answering every question, trying to remain composed, sincere, smiling at every opportunity, and injecting a little levity into the proceedings whenever possible but not being overtly flippant with my answers.

Richard Burmeister asked what I would do if I encountered a

moose. He said, "You don't look like the kind of girl who packs a .45."

This provided a perfect opportunity for me to poke a little fun at myself. I said, "I'm perfectly capable of shooting a firearm, if that's what you're asking. But my aim is not particularly good. But you know a moose is a pretty big target. And if I'm close enough I'd have to think it'd be rather difficult to miss a moose, even for a blind girl."

Everyone laughed and that seemed to break down a bit of the tension. Gradually the antagonism melted away and the questions became more sincere. The board members were curious about how I would respond to given situations I might encounter on the trail. How would the cold affect me, the lack of sleep, and how might my dogs react to the rigors of the trail? None of their questions had anything to do with my request, but I conscientiously answered every question posed to me.

Gwen interrupted the proceedings to offer something that, in my opinion, saved the day. "I think it is sad." She paused to allow that to sink in. "Sad that Rachael can never run this race like all of us have been able to do. She would much prefer to be out there alone in the wilderness with only her dogs for company. But she can't do that. She has to have someone accompanying her who can see.

"There are rules, and then there is the Iditarod spirit. If someone had told Joe Redington Sr. that he could not pull off this race he would have laughed. He was a 'can do' man. And this race is a 'can do' race, a race about overcoming adversity. Rachael is here attempting to overcome the adversity she was born with. All she asks from you is a chance. Just a chance."

After a moment Rick Koch spoke: "Have you ever considered running the race with two dog teams?"

"I'd love that," I shot back. "But practically speaking, it might prove too expensive to outfit two teams."

"Is it a simple matter of economics? Or is there a technical reason a snow machine would suit you better?" he asked.

I responded, "Part is economics and the other is that I need to have two full teams of identically matched dogs. Instead of using my best dogs I would have to compromise and settle for two average teams."

The board elected to go into executive session and the audience once again filed out of the room. I immediately called Dad.

"How's it going? How are you holding up?" he wanted to know.

"Not bad," I said. "Except I feel like I've been somersaulting down a hill for the last five hours. Rick Koch asked me whether I wanted to run the race with two dog teams."

"What did you say?"

"I said it was going to double our cost and that we didn't have two teams capable of running the Iditarod."

"Perfect answer. So what do you think? Are they going to give in and allow you to run with the snow machines?"

"Dad, I don't know. I just don't know. My head is whirling. We've been going at this for hours now. It hurts to think. What do you think?"

"I think they're going to fold. If their lawyer has given them sound advice and told them that ninety-some percent of the Iditarod is run on public lands and that if they want to have a race they have to adhere to the rules of the ADA, then they have no choice. They fold."

"And if they don't?"

"They will."

"But if they don't?"

"Then we force the issue and take them to court."

I did not want to fight the ITC in court. I wanted everyone to just get along. I was not out to wreck their race.

After an hour had passed we were called back into the room. I had pulled myself together emotionally and was feeling more confident. From the moment I entered the room I could sense a change. No longer was I at odds with the board. We were not adversaries squared off and ready to do battle. We were now part of the same team. I wondered if I was imagining these things. Were my senses that far out of whack?

The answer to my self-doubt was quickly answered when Rick Swenson made a motion to allow me to use two-way radios and instead of two snow machines he offered to substitute a qualified musher and an additional dog team. Further, he stated that the entry fee for the second dog team would be waived and that any qualifier races that I ran under these conditions would count and that if I completed the qualifiers I would be allowed to run the Iditarod. The motion passed unanimously.

I was in. I had won.

But now the challenge was for me to run the qualifying races. According to the Iditarod rules, a rookie musher "must have completed two approved qualifying races with an accumulated total of at least 500 miles, or must have completed one race of at least 800 miles within the last five racing seasons and a 300-mile race in either the current or previous racing season. A musher must complete any qualifying race and finish in the top 75 percent of the field . . ."

Bring it on.

18

RACE TO THE SKY

I started training for my initial Iditarod qualifier before the first storm brought snow to the mountains. We live on the high desert of Central Oregon and I began training the dogs on a seventeen-mile loop in the Badlands, an undeveloped area of sagebrush, rimrock, and junipers that surrounds our home. We live there surrounded by one hundred dogs, miles from the nearest neighbor, beyond the power grid, and off the beaten path. We haul our water, get by just fine on solar power and generators, and stay in touch with the outside world through cell phones that do not always work. A good dose of solitude makes a person fully appreciate nature and some of the finer things in life.

My goal was to have twenty-four dogs, two full teams, prepared to run the Race to the Sky in Montana during the second week of February 2004. I started the training process with the dogs pulling me on a 4-wheeler around the seventeen-mile loop, adding mileage the way a marathon runner will, extending the workouts by about

10 percent a week. My goal was to keep the dogs running at eleven miles an hour, a good, steady racing pace.

I brought the dogs up to the point where we were making three or four loops, camping for a few hours, and continuing on. It did not matter whether it was day or night; we kept moving as if we were running a race. Night was always more fun. The only sounds were the hum of the wheels as they spun, the soft padding of the dogs' feet coming in contact with the sand, and the rasping of their labored breathing as they gulped and expelled air. Sometimes the wind moaned through the sage and the rock outcroppings, but mostly the quiet stretched off, seemingly to infinity.

It was easier for me to see at night when the only light came from stars sprinkled across the expansive sky or when there was a partial moon that threw faint shadows across the landscape. If the moon was bright, the reflective tape on the dogs' harnesses glowed with an eerie brightness while the forms of the dogs were constantly changing shape as they ran. The most magical time was always just as the moon began to set. In those fleeting moments everything I saw became totally clear and distinct. I do not know if this was caused by the angle of the moonlight or the diminishing intensity of the light. But I know my vision was clear and it was wonderful.

Nights are cooler and better suited for the dogs. There are fewer distractions and they concentrate more on the simple act of running. Mushers have told me about some of their experiences at night with dog teams chasing after deer, elk, rabbits, and even skunks. But I never have had any problems. Once in a while a kangaroo rat or a mouse would dart through my dog team and I might catch a fleeting glimpse of motion, but that was about the extent of it.

Constantly running the same loop can get boring and at times my mind played tricks on me. My cell phone rang, but I did not have it with me, I saw a tree where there was no tree, I had a strange feeling of being watched, and to reassure myself I glanced over my shoulder to make sure no one was behind me. Little things like that forced me to pray for snow in the mountains so we would have new trails to run.

Training is about routine and trying to duplicate actual race conditions we would be facing in the two Iditarod qualifying races I had chosen, the Race to the Sky and the Beargrease. In both these qualifiers, unlike the stage races, the race is basically from the start to the finish, with campouts and mandatory layovers.

When the weather turned cold I layered up and pulled on my Arctic mittens. The colder it got the better, because usually the sky cleared and the stars became more vibrant and intense. If it rained or snowed it settled the dust, always a problem on the desert because dust gets in the dogs' eyes and lungs. They do not like dust. But they do like puddles. They splashed through puddles and sometimes we stopped and I allowed the dogs to drink at what I perceived to be a particularly friendly puddle.

Usually I am alone on the desert with my dogs. At times Dad runs a second team, but we will be miles apart. Except for actually participating in a race, training is my favorite part of having sled dogs. But coming in from a long run, having a hearty meal and a long, hot shower is hard to beat, too.

I was running the Race to the Sky as an Iditarod qualifying race according to the rules and conditions established by the Iditarod board of directors. I was allowed to use two-way radios, and my visual interpreter, Dan MacEachen, would ride a second sled. Dad would be my handler, and Becki Thuson, a family friend, would handle for Dan.

In the dark of early morning we loaded twenty-four dogs, two full teams, into the dog box on the truck. We pulled away at 5:00 a.m. heading east. I had the entire backseat to myself and stretched out. For a while I listened to Dad and Becki talk politics. Dad is a moderate and Becki is a die-hard conservative. I am somewhere in the middle, a little more conservative than Dad but not as extreme as Becki. After a while I got bored, put on my headphones, turned on my CD player, and listened to music. I like artists like Jewell, Evanescence, and Verticle Worship. Really, I like anything with a good, strong beat.

The sun was creeping over the Blue Mountains when we stopped for a break. Every few hours the dogs need to stretch, drink water, and have a snack. That gives them something to look forward to on a long trip and helps keep their muscles loose. We hopscotched our way across a corner of Washington and the panhandle of Idaho to reach Montana. Along the way we saw several moose. Or rather, I never actually saw them, but Dad and Becki swore they were there. I had to believe them.

Montana was cold, way colder than Oregon. We rented a cabin and went to the airport to pick up Dan. Returning to the cabin, I introduced Dan to the dogs and went over the little idiosyncrasies and quirks of each—pointing out where Tinker was a little sore, saying that Joe was kind of a bad eater and occasionally liked to goof off rather than race, showing where King was a little tender on the point of the shoulder. One by one we went through the dogs, dividing them up so we had two evenly matched teams.

The following day was set aside for festivities and the introduction of the twenty-two registered mushers and their teams. I entered a lead dog competition with one of my favorites, Duchess, the same girl that had caused me so much trouble in the Atta Boy when she bred with all three of the Baseball Brothers. She had a wonderful litter of puppies and I love her. Duchess and I ran an obstacle course and won third place. I was awarded a candy bar and Duchess received a dog treat.

That evening at the banquet the public had the opportunity to bid for rides with their favorite musher at the kickoff ceremony. The winning bidder would ride a tandem sled hooked behind the musher's sled for the first five miles of the race. A rodeo bull rider purchased a ride with me and I was looking forward to the event because he was kind of cute. Maybe he partied a little too hard that night, because in the morning he was a no-show.

Instead Dad rode the tandem sled behind me. Becki rode with Dan. However, none of us recognized the drop-off point and Dan and I carried our riders several extra miles before a fellow on a snow machine caught up to us and shouted that we were supposed to have dropped our riders "a fair ways back." He offered to tow the tandem sleds and the riders back to the drop-off site.

The Race to the Sky is a 350-mile race that weaves through the rugged peaks on the eastern slope of the Rocky Mountains, climbing above the tree line and tumbling down steep slopes. The high elevation and rugged trail conditions offer the mushers and dog teams some of the greatest challenges to be found in the Lower 48.

The first forty miles were a technical nightmare but fun, with narrow trails and steep turns and littered with windfalls and boulders barely covered with snow. We reached a road crossing and my two leaders insisted they wanted to go down the open road instead of sticking to the trail, a narrow chute up a vertical bank. They ran for a ways before I could get them stopped and turned around. And when I finally was able to turn them onto the trail they were wild, plunging through the snow and trying to catch up to Dan's team. I stood on the brake, but it did very little to slow the dogs. We went over a bump, I lost my balance, and my foot was somehow trapped under the drag brake. I was completely helpless, and if we had hit a rock or a windfall hidden under the snow my leg bone would have snapped like a chicken wing. I managed to free my leg and get my feet back on the runners where they belonged.

When we reached Dan two of his dogs, Eddy and Jovi, decide to settle an old argument. Since I was right beside them when the fight broke out, I waded in, pried them apart, and admonished them both, and we continued on. After a few miles Dan's team suddenly concluded they did not want to pull anymore. Teams passed us. Nothing was going our way.

Eventually the dogs decided they wanted to be sled dogs again and we stumbled into the first checkpoint at Cain Ridge West, forty miles into the race. It seemed as though we had lurched from one catastrophe to the next, and now Eddy was limping from his disagreement with Jovi. Dan was afraid he might have to drop Eddy, but the vet took a look at the injured wrist and pronounced him fit to run. I went to the warming hut and had a bowl of really good soup. It revived me. I returned to the cold and told Dan, "Time's wasting; let's get this show on the road."

At the next opportunity my leaders, Angel and Lisa—because of an unfortunate series of circumstances I would soon rename them Brain-dead and Wrong-way—turned away from the trail and followed a road.

"Stop? You missed it. You're going the wrong way," Dan's voice yelled at me over the radio.

The road had recently been plowed, but luckily I found a chunk of ice and was able to set my snow hook there. I leaped off the sled, sprinted to the front, and spun the leaders. I knew that as soon as they reached the end of the snow hook line the hook would automatically release and the dogs would be off and running. I plopped myself down on the gangline and the dogs rolled me over and around like a load of clothes on spin cycle. I was getting banged up and scratched, but if I gave up and turned loose, the dogs and my sled were as good as gone. I swam my way through the dogs toward the sled; grabbing tugline, gangline, harness, tugline, gangline . . . and finally the sled. With a clumsy lunge I swung onto the runners. I was afraid my inglorious moment had been videoed and would be shown on *America's Funniest Home Videos*. The viewers would think it was hilarious, but for me, at that particular moment, there was nothing the least bit humorous about it.

Dan was somewhere ahead of me. He radioed he could see me and was waiting at the top of a ridge. Wrong-way and Brain-dead saw him and decided the shortest route between two points was a straight line, even though this straight line led up an almost perpendicular ridge face. The snow was so powdery there was no way to slow them with the brake and the snow hook refused to hold. Come hell or high water, we were going up that face.

The dogs high-centered on a stump. I waded through the hip-deep snow and pulled them free. They showed their appreciation by going over the top of me. I fought them, but it was difficult, because they were light enough to stay on top of the snow, while I plunged through. Dan later told me that from his vantage my little escapade had looked like a three-fall grudge match on The Wrestling Channel.

By the time I reached the top of the ridge I had expended so much energy I could barely move. I was sick to my stomach and vomited the soup. When the soup ran out, my stomach tried to turn itself inside out.

"Are you okay?" Dan asked, coming to stand near me.

I retched a couple more times, backhanded my mouth, and lied, "Fine. I'm fine. Let's keep going."

We passed a number of other mushers who had set camp, and when we got to the top of a long pull we finally called it a day. We put down straw for the dogs' bedding and fed and watered them. Since we were going to be there for only an hour or two I did not think it was worth getting into my sleeping bag. I pulled out Dad's big down coat and curled up on the straw with Zack, pulling the coat over the two of us. Zack is part English pointer and does not have a heavy coat. He enjoyed having me to snuggle with and I wanted to reward him because he had been a sweet dog and the hardest worker in my team that day.

I slept fitfully and awoke shivering because Zack had stolen the coat. Dan was already up. I wanted to get warm and said, "We might as well go." After I dispensed a few special treats to my dogs, we rushed off into the darkness, running with the light from our headlamps. We ran all night and reached the White Tail Ranch checkpoint, 112 miles into the race, at 6:00 a.m., making up for the time we had lost on the first leg. We tied the dogs down on a snub line, warmed up food for them in the alcohol cooker, and made sure they were content and bedded down before we went to the lodge for breakfast. I tried to sleep, but with the sun up and more mushers arriving all the time I was anxious to keep moving.

The run from White Tail Ranch to Seeley Lake is fifty-four miles. About halfway there I hit the proverbial wall and crashed. I had not been eating and had slept only one hour out of the last thirty-some hours. I was out on my feet. And then the strangest thing happened. I saw a girl about my age, wearing Levi's and a cute summer blouse, appear in the middle of the trail just in front of my dogs. I saw her clearly. She was there. But when the leaders reached the point where she was standing she fell backward like a cardboard cutout. When the sled passed over where the apparition had stood I looked down, fearing we actually had run over the girl, but nothing more than white snow stared back at me.

That same thing happened several more times. People, no one I ever recognized, stood in the trail and fell over backward when we reached them. I knew from past experience and other mushers' stories that I was hallucinating. I thought if I ate something it might help. I loaded up on Snickers bars, Pop-Tarts, and Gummi Bears. I had learned in high school track and cross-country that all three are good sources of quick energy. I drank some water, too, and that seemed to do the trick. The hallucinations stopped.

At Seeley Lake I dropped Spud and Dan dropped Eddy. Both the teams were tired and so were Dan and I. We elected to take a twelve-hour layover. Our objective was to finish the race and finish in the top three-quarters. We did not have to burn ourselves out trying to win.

I had a great sleep, but the layover put us behind the field. I was committed to making up time on the next leg to the turnaround at Holland Lake Lodge. We reached the lodge, took the six-hour mandatory layover, and got busy trying to catch the field of mushers who were in front of us. Before we left Holland Lake, the Trail Boss caught up to us and said, "I just wanted to warn you about what's up ahead."

Dan told him, "There's nothing you can throw at this girl that she can't get through. She's one hell of a musher."

"Hold it just a minute," I said. "You're throwing compliments around. Do you remember that girl who couldn't seem to keep her dogs on the trail? The girl who crab-walked up a ridge and then got on her hands and knees and puked? The girl who flipped out and saw things that weren't there? That girl?"

Dan laughed. "That same girl."

"I just wanted to make sure you take the cutoff to Owl Creek," warned the Trail Boss. "Otherwise you end up on a major highway, and there's no telling how bad that could be."

When we reached the Owl Creek cutoff it was night and I was in the lead. I missed it, flat out missed it. Dan yelled at me to stop. But my dogs were sprinting down a plowed road and there was no place to set the snow hook. I leaned as far as I could to the side, trying to jam the hook into the bank, but the rope was not long enough. Within a few minutes I began to see the headlights of cars on the highway.

Oh shyster! I thought. *I'm in big trouble here.*

I visualized my team bolting onto the busy highway. I imagined cars and semitrucks slamming on their brakes and, in their futile effort to keep from hitting a dog team and a screaming girl, careening into a massive pileup. I never gave up trying to jam my snow hook onto the road, but there was nothing but a thin layer of ice over asphalt. It refused to set. I even tried tipping the sled, hoping the friction of the sled on ice might slow the team, but we were going so fast I could not get the necessary leverage. We were speeding straight into the jaws of disaster and there was absolutely nothing I could do to prevent it.

The helplessness I felt, the hopelessness that seemed ready to gobble me up and swallow me whole, was only heightened by the ominous sight of headlights, the bright red of taillights, and the frightening noises I began to hear: trucks downshifting, exhausts blaring, and the loud blew of tires skating on ice. I was terrified. How many of my dogs would die! Common sense screamed at me to bail off my sled and save myself. But I could never abandon my dogs. Would I die or be seriously injured? "God, it's in your hands," I shouted into the wind. I continued to slam the snow hook into the ice.

And then a miracle occurred—the snow hook caught and stopped the dogs just short of the highway. I sprang off the sled, sprinted to the leaders, spun them, the hook popped free, and I swam my way back through the dogs to the sled. If I were to practice that entire maneuver I would fail ninety-nine times out of a hundred. But this time it worked. We raced away from danger and the menacing sounds of traffic receded behind me. I uttered a prayer of thanks.

I was feeling lucky to still be alive, and on the run to Seeley Lake I drank in the beauty of the countryside, a lush forest of evergreens with the moon sliding in and out of clouds. We topped out on the summit and I gazed down over the serene white surface of the lake bathed in the glow of the moon.

Dad was waiting for me at the checkpoint. I balked at having to take another six-hour mandatory layover. "I need to keep going. If I don't finish in the top three-quarters this isn't going to count as an Iditarod qualifier," I said. "And I'll be sunk."

"No, you're in great shape," he assured me. "The trail has been so tough that seven teams dropped out. All you have to do is finish and you automatically qualify."

That information certainly buoyed my spirits. I even managed to get a few hours of sleep before we started the last seventy-seven miles. Having dropped Zack and Pat at Seeley Lake, I was down to nine dogs. The dogs were tired and I was tired, but we got back on the trail. To keep from falling asleep I munched on candy bars and quick-energy snacks and drank plenty of water.

With only eighteen miles to go the sun dropped below the horizon and the dogs slowed to a walk. I pulled up and we rested for a little more than an hour and then, afraid we might be overtaken, I rallied the dogs, and we continued. Darkness settled in and we ran with headlamps. The moon came out and the snow was absolutely perfect, smooth as glass. The moonlight turned the ice crystals to glitter and a barrage of shooting stars made skinny streaks across the sky.

At the ten-mile marker the trail began a slow, steady ascent. We went up and up and up. I was off the sled and running. But suddenly I felt a jabbing stab of pain in my lower back, so intense it momentarily stole my wind and I had to step on the runners to keep from falling. I thought to myself, *Here we are, less than ten miles from the finish, and I prove to be the weak link.* I gritted my teeth against the pain, rode the runners, and pushed off as much as I could.

By the time we reached the summit the night sky had clouded over and it was snowing hard. Off to the side was a sheer drop, hundreds of feet down, and I prayed that Brain-dead and Wrong-way would not choose this moment to self-destruct. They remained focused, or maybe they were too tired for any sort of nonsense. I encouraged them, telling them how good they were and how pretty they looked running in the snow.

The trail dropped down and started back up again. The snow turned to rain and the trail became a quagmire of slush. I caught a glimpse of the lights of Lincoln and knew we must be getting close. The trail emptied onto a road covered with deep, sloppy snow. The lights disappeared as we descended once again, but we were near enough to town that the clouds were illuminated with a strange fluorescent glow. Again we climbed.

Dan was stopped at the top of the last hill. "Go ahead."

"Where do I go?"

"Straight ahead."

When I crossed the finish line Dad rushed up to me and excitedly told me, "You finished eleventh—out of twenty-two teams. Way to go, girl. Great job. One qualifier down, one to go."

19

JOHN BEARGREASE

John Patten, Dad's former sled dog partner in Bend, Oregon, founded the John Beargrease Mid-Distance Marathon. It is a four-hundred-mile sled dog race that follows along the shore and over the ice of Lake Superior. It is named for John Beargrease, a legendary Chippewa Indian who delivered mail along the North Shore of Lake Superior by sled dog team. He was known for his dependability and predictability and the bells on his dogs' collars, worn both to scare off the wolves and to alert people at the scattered homesteads and settlements that the mail was coming. For many of the isolated inhabitants of the North Shore, John Beargrease provided their only link to the outside world.

The Beargrease is considered to be one of the most difficult qualifying races for the Iditarod. That was exactly the reason I chose to run it. I did not want anyone to say I had sneaked in the back door with easy races. I wanted to break the door down by running not only the Race to the Sky but also the John Beargrease.

Mark Stamm of Riverside, Washington, had agreed to serve as my visual interpreter. Mark, an established musher who has been racing for more than thirty years, is a longtime family friend. He had finished the Yukon Quest, the UP 200, the Wyoming Stage Stop, the Seeley Lake 100, and the Atta Boy 300, and he completed the Race to the Sky ten times. He lives to race dogs and I was honored when he agreed to serve as my "eyes" for the Beargrease.

Mark has an excellent dog team; they are hard workers and well behaved. With Mark using his own team I was able to choose my very best dogs rather than dilute the best dogs by dividing them into two teams as I had done at the Race to the Sky.

Mark and I share a lot of common interests besides dogs. One of those interests is our mutual love for music. Mark names all his puppies after famous musicians. When out on the trail Mark is very focused and does not believe in useless talk. I like that. I want to hear my dogs and the sound of nature, not a lot of jibber-jabber.

The first week of March 2004 we left home together bound for Duluth, Minnesota. Both teams rode in the dog box on the back of our crew-cab pickup. They were doubled up because they could stay warmer with two dogs to a compartment. Dad had fixed a bed in the alleyway between the dog boxes and we took turns going back there. It was the best. I could stretch out and sleep for a couple hours until we stopped to exercise the dogs and switch so someone else could catch some sleep. Along the way we listened to a lot of Mark's music, mostly classic rock and roll like the Stones, Led Zeppelin, Styx, Lynyrd Skynyrd, the Eagles, Dire Straits, and Pink Floyd.

The Beargrease begins at Lester Park in Duluth and follows the North Shore of Lake Superior over rolling hills carved by glaciers. At the town of Tofte the trail doubles back, following the same course on the return leg. Mark, who had run the race before, told me what to expect, and we worked out our race strategy. We would maintain a steady pace, taking as few rest breaks as possible, for the first two hundred miles. We would run every uphill and brake on the downhill. Most injuries to the dogs' shoulders and wrists occur on the downhill, when the weight of the sled and rider pushes them too fast. By braking we would avoid the likelihood of injury. There were two mandatory six-hour layovers, and mushers and their dogs were required to have an additional twenty hours of rest, at the mushers' discretion, along the way. We would run while our dogs were fresh and rest them in the later stages of the race, when they needed it the most. That was our race strategy.

Another last-minute decision we made was that I would take one of Mark's lead dogs, Marley, named after the legendary Jamaican reggae singer Bob Marley. "He's a great dog and I know he'll follow me anywhere," Mark assured me.

On the day of the race, with the sun hidden behind a bank of sodden clouds, the light was perfect for me. Spectators lined the streets of Duluth and cheered as we passed. Soon we were in the hill country surrounded by the quiet, except for those occasions when we were overtaken by mushers and their exuberant teams. Each time we were passed my competitive juices kicked in and I had to remind myself that "The race goes to the one who maintains a steady pace. Be the tortoise, not the hare."

We passed the first checkpoint, Billy's Supper Club, to the shouts of a few well-wishers and then we were alone again. We passed thick stands of birch and maple, their bare branches pointing like long, skinny fingers against the steel gray sky. In the open areas small spruce trees poked a few dark branches out of the snow. We traveled at eleven miles an hour, a good, solid pace.

We ran all that day, with a few short breaks, and when the sun set we turned on our headlamps and put lights on our dogs so they could be seen by the occasional snow machine operator who traveled the trail. My dogs had small blinking lights like bicycle riders use at night, but one team passed us with her dogs wearing so many lights it looked as if we were being overtaken by a Christmas tree.

The second checkpoint was at Highway 2, sixty miles into the race. We stopped to rest the dogs for a couple hours and I grabbed a short nap. Then we were off to the town of Finland, the third checkpoint. Running at night, the temperature was much colder, the snow firmer, and the runners glided over the trail better than when the sun was melting the snow. We kept a close eye on our dogs' feet, making sure they were waxed so that the snow, which had begun to crystallize, did not accumulate between their toes and cause problems. A couple of the dogs needed the extra protection of booties.

It was bright daylight when we arrived in Finland. We took care of the dogs and I massaged Seth's front left wrist. He was starting to favor it a little. Mark showed me how to put a Ziploc bag around the wrist and then put a wrap over it. It was a neat trick that prevented the wrap from cutting off the circulation and still kept the affected area warm. Every musher has a bag of tricks and it was good to add something new to mine. When the dogs were bedded down Mark and I went inside for hot chocolate and a hamburger, followed by a short nap.

The fourth checkpoint, at Sawbill, was 133 miles into the race and required a six-hour layover. I set up the alcohol cooker to warm food for the dogs. The sun was bright and it seemed to take me forever to open the fuel, pour it in, and light it. The fire burns with a hot blue flame and the only way I knew that it was going was by the heat it threw off. I stood near the cooker, enjoying the warmth. As the snow in the pot melted I added more, and without knowing how big the flame was, because I could not see it, the sleeve of my coat accidentally caught on fire. I patted the flames with my gloved hand to put the fire out before it burned me.

Later I went to the warming hut, where food was available for the mushers. I took another look at my sleeve and was lamenting my mistake when Blake Freking walked over to me and said, "Stood a little too close to your cooker, aye? You're lucky; happened to me last year in the Iditarod, got a little too close to my cooker, and set my pants on fire."

We laughed and I told him, "Thanks; now I don't feel quite so blond."

The town of Tofte was the halfway point of the race. On the way there we crossed a section of Lake Superior ice. The wind blew and the cold settled in, but the flatness of the ice made a fast and easy run. Dad was waiting for us. He said he thought I was in sixth place, although it was hard for him to calculate because of the dissimilar layovers the various mushers had taken.

I slept a couple hours and on the way back to the starting line I realized I had left my race bib at the truck. I had to have Dad stand on the brake while I ran up the hill to get the bib, pulled it on, and sprinted back to my sled. All the way I was kicking myself for making such a rookie mistake.

As we departed Tofte an enormous full moon rose directly behind us, immersing the countryside in dazzling whiteness and causing the shadows of the dogs, the sled, and me to be weirdly deformed, warping and twisting in ghostlike images. I waved and my elongated shadow waved. I ducked down and only the shadows of the dogs and the sled were visible. It was as though I had disappeared off the face of the earth.

The dogs were moving a little slower now, but the race was half-over; we were on the downhill slide. I drank in the loveliness of this evening, the bigness of this wilderness, the solitude and wonder of this place, and I thanked God.

We made a layover at Sawbill and continued on to Finland, and somewhere during that run all the incredible facets of the race, which I had appreciated so much, were replaced by boredom, monotony, and fatigue. The dogs were bushed, too. We pulled in at the checkpoint at Finland.

"You have a choice to make," Dad said as he pulled me aside. "It's entirely up to you. Do whatever you think is best. Either way I'll support you one hundred percent.

"Here's the choice: You have one hundred and eight miles to go to finish the race. You can rest here for six hours. If you do, your dogs will be rested, you will be almost guaranteed to finish, and you will qualify for the Iditarod. Or you can take a short break and go out. Most likely you'll finish in the top six. But by going out early you run the risk of having your dogs quit and not finishing at all. You know what that feels like. It happened to me, too. Think about it. The choice is yours to make."

I tried to feed my dogs, but they were not very interested in eating. They did go for raw meat mixed in with their water, and that gave them something of substance. I tested each dog, lifting the skin around the neck and releasing it. If it snapped back it indicated they were hydrated. All the dogs were in good shape except for three. Mandy was having a problem with her left hind leg. Angel was, too. And King's shoulders and one wrist were bothering him. I decided to drop all three. I was down to only nine dogs.

After the dogs were cared for I moved away from everybody to do some soul-searching. I prayed a lot and pondered whether I should take it easy and just finish or risk it all. I thought about my dogs quitting me in the Atta Boy 300. And I thought about Wyoming, and Dad hooking himself into the lead and pulling the sled for thirty miles, until he could pull no more and fell facedown in the snow. I thought about each of my dogs, what they had given me to get us to this point, and attempted to gauge how much they had left to give. I imagined how each of them would vote, if given an opportunity.

"What are you going to do?" Dad asked as I approached where he was standing.

I drew a long breath and expelled it. I stood up straight, looked him in the eye, and said, "I didn't come here to run dogs. I came here to race dogs. Let's race."

On the way to the sled I said a short prayer: "God, let this be the right decision."

John Patten was there and he gave me a quick pep talk: "Don't think about the distance. Divide it up into small bites, five or ten miles, and before you know it you're crossing the finish line. Good luck."

As we pulled away into the darkness I was thinking about all those nights when I was eight years old, sitting up with John and listening to him tell those fantastic stories about running dogs and racing in the Iditarod. That was where my dream began, from John's stories. And now all that separated me from my dream of running the Iditarod was 108 miles.

"You can do it," I told myself. "Ten miles down the trail and you'll be under a hundred. Click the miles off. Keep going."

We ran for twenty miles or so and then Marley, who up until that point had faithfully followed Mark, decided he wanted to try a

different trail. Before I realized what was happening we were crossing a train track and when the sled hit the rail it tipped over. I
stopped the dogs, muscled the sled upright, turned the team around,
and fought to get back on the proper trail. This took time and
robbed all of us of needed energy.

Coming out of the Highway 2 checkpoint, I calculated that fifty-
five miles remained in the race. The sun was beginning to lighten the
day, and the thick clouds opened up and poured rain. During the
night a warm front had moved in and the balmy temperature, along
with the deluge, turned the snow to the consistency of mush.
Patches of gravel and mud appeared on the trail. I ran every uphill
and pumped on the downhill. The dogs were tired. They shuffled
along.

We passed a road where a man standing beside his pickup
hollered, "You've got eighteen miles."

"To where?" I called.

"In the race. You only have eighteen miles to go in the race.
Good show!"

"Yeah, all right," I shouted, and told the dogs, "You're doing
great. Keep it up. Eighteen miles, you can do it."

I had been putting a lot of pressure on Marley, relying on him to
lead the team. But with fifteen miles remaining he stepped off the
trail and into a patch of small trees and lay down.

"No! No! I yelled at him. "Keep going. Get up, Marley. Let's
go."

Marley was having none of it. He demanded a rest and the other
dogs gleefully joined the mutiny and plopped themselves on the
snow. If we were to keep going, my only choice was to resort to
bribery. I broke out the chicken and beef sticks and hot dogs. I
passed them out with impunity, along with large doses of admira-
tion for all the hard work the dogs had given me. I told them I was
proud of them and encouraged them not to quit, that we had a
measly fifteen miles to go.

"That's less than one time around the loop at home." But at that
moment the Badlands had never seemed farther away.

After spending twenty minutes as a cheerleader and switching

dogs around, I went back to the sled and announced, with all the enthusiasm I could muster, "Hike!" And to my amazement the dogs
rose and began moving forward. It was a slow pace, granted, but it
was a pace. We caught up to Mark, who had stopped to rest his
tired dogs.

"I was worried about you," he said.

"No big deal," I assured him. "We were just taking a little
siesta."

Mark led the way to a road crossing. Apparently one of the
teams ahead of us had stopped there and snacked, because my dogs
smelled meat, stopped, and demanded treats. I broke out everything
I had and fed it to them. By then it was raining even harder and I
was soaked to the bone.

A man riding a snow machine arrived with the announcement:
"I just came from Highway 2 and you've got four teams closing in
on you, maybe a half hour back."

I refused to let this news rattle me. I continued massaging the
dogs that needed it, petting every one, dispensing affection and in-
spiring them not to fail me now. I promised them shelter when we
got back to the truck. I promised to rub them down with a towel. I
promised to give them special treats.

I switched Marley to a double lead alongside Cletus. And when I
told them to move out they did and I jogged along beside the sled,
telling the dogs how wonderful they were and imploring them to
keep moving.

I sang to them, every worship and gospel song I ever learned in
church: the "Happy Song," "God's Romance," "Better One Day,"
"Overwhelmed," "Gonna Sing like the Saved," "Worthy to Be
Praised," and "He Never Failed Me Yet." I thought "He Never
Failed Me Yet" was particularly appropriate in this situation, and I
sang it several times to inspire the dogs. They continued to shuffle
along, not because they particularly wanted to race, but I think it
was more an effort on their part to get away from my singing.

I recognized a hill we had climbed leaving Duluth and a chain-
link fence where people were gathered offering their encourage-

ment. We went through an intersection. I knew we were getting close to the finish line at Lester Park. I was wet, cold, exhausted. But I kept jogging to one side of my sled.

Mark pulled to a stop to allow me to finish ahead of him. Dad was there. The race was over. Out of twenty-eight teams that started the race I had taken sixth place and traversed the four hundred miles in seventy-five hours. I was thrilled that I had taken a gambler's chance and my dogs had made it pay off.

Within a few minutes of my finish four other mushers came in, one right after the other. I concentrated on my dogs and started to work making sure that I kept each and every promise I had made to them out on the trail.

20

AIMING FOR IDITAROD

The Iditarod Trail Sled Dog Race covers a distance of more than eleven hundred miles as it crosses the backbone of the Alaska Range and traverses the vast interior of our forty-ninth state. But the race itself is like the tiny tip of an iceberg. Submerged below the surface is all the work involved as the Iditarod musher prepares, plans, trains, and raises the necessary sponsorship to actually run "The Last Great Race."

For me, the quest to follow my dream and participate in the Iditarod began years ago. Dad and I have worked to develop a breeding program in our kennel that produces dogs with speed, stamina, desire, and heart. If a breeder happens to get one or two puppies from a litter with those qualities, she is extremely lucky. Dogs not making the grade are weeded out and given away to loving homes.

Training my 2005 Iditarod race team began in a fenced enclosure on our property that we call the playground. The playground is about the size of a football field and typical of the High Desert landscape with lava rock, sagebrush, and juniper. The dogs run and play. I run and play with them, and it is quickly evident to me which dogs are true athletes. My attention is always drawn to those competitors that are eager to play, will leap off the ground in wild exuberance, and never seem to tire. Those are the dogs I want on my team.

Our play helps to build a base of physical endurance in my dogs. Any time a group of dogs grows weary of chasing one another I simply turn loose another dog and the race renews with all the dogs chasing the newcomer. I get some of my physical conditioning playing with my dogs. I also run and visit the gym as often as I can. That is not always easy. I have to adjust my schedule to whatever Dad is doing so he can drive me the twenty-plus miles to town.

The first official event on the Iditarod calendar is the Iditarod Volunteer Picnic and Sign-Up held in June at Iditarod headquarters in Wasilla, Alaska. Dad and I decided to attend so I could register in person, pay my entry fee for the 2005 Iditarod, and get the ball rolling. By attending the picnic I would be eligible to be in the top one-third of the draw for a starting position and have the opportunity to meet some of the other mushers.

The *Anchorage Daily News* had printed several stories critical of my entry into the race and the Internet sled dog chat rooms were buzzing over the blind girl from Oregon who was attempting to crash the party. They questioned whether I actually would have the nerve to follow through. By attending the picnic I could show everyone I was serious about running the Iditarod.

We flew to Anchorage, rented a car, and drove to Wasilla. On the way Dad and I talked about the type of reception I was likely to face. I worried that some of my most vocal critics might take this opportunity to blast me with public statements. But Dad, trying to lessen my nervousness, said, "I really don't think it's going to be as bad as you think. Sure, not everyone is going to welcome you with open arms, but I don't think they're going to snub you, either. You've run the qualifiers, two really demanding races. You've played by their rules. You're one of them. You're a musher. Just be friendly and outgoing like you typically are, everything will be fine."

That helped ease my mind. Yet as we parked at Iditarod head-quarters, I was hesitant, perhaps concerned about the possibility of a confrontation—or maybe it finally hit me what a huge commitment I was making. Dad immediately left me. He met some old friends and they walked away. That was fine with me. I wanted to have a look at the Iditarod headquarters, a log building housing the history of the race. I moved in that direction, but stopped to read a Joe Redington memorial plaque. The sun was bright, and I was wearing my sunglasses. Of course, I had to get real close to the plaque and practically drag my nose across the print to read the words.

"Nobody's eyes are that bad," said a man's voice behind me. I turned around. The man gasped. "Oh, no! You're Rachael Scdoris, aren't you? I am so sorry."

"Don't think anything about it." I laughed. "That sort of thing happens to me all the time, no big deal."

I have found that people do not generally make insensitive re-marks to be hurtful, and I never take such a comment personally. But this man continued to fall all over himself. "Forgive me. I'm such a fool. I don't know what I was thinking. Obviously I wasn't thinking."

"No problem," I said. I stuck my hand out. The man introduced himself, and I recognized him as a musher, not one of the perennial leaders but one from the pack, where I would likely be running during my rookie race. We spoke for a few minutes, and he told me that after I saw the headquarters to be sure to take a look at the little log cache built on stilts. He explained such structures were used in the bush to keep food beyond the reach of bears.

That encounter seemed to break the ice for me. After touring headquarters I wandered to the picnic area and Ramie Redington, the son of legendary Joe Redington Sr., the father of the Iditarod, came up to me. I had met him before. He wished me well in the race, saying, "You're going to do just fine. You'll get through the rough spots and wonder where the rough spots were. How bad can it be? Dad ran the race at age eighty."

I saw a number of other mushers I was acquainted with—Mike Williams, Ken Anderson, Ramy Brooks, Aliy Zirkle, Jessie Royer, and John Baker. Everyone was friendly. They wished me well and told me the Iditarod was going to be a terrific experience. I sat with John Baker at one of the tables. Other people were sitting there, but I could not tell who they were until John leaned toward me and said, "Would you like to meet the Seavey boys?"

John introduced me to the Seaveys. I felt a little intimidated and in awe because the Seaveys have one of the biggest names in the sport of sled dog racing. Dan Seavey Sr. ran the first Iditarod back in 1973. His son Mitch was the reigning Iditarod champion, having won in 2004. When I was introduced to Mitch, I said, "I know you've heard this a million times, but congratulations on your victory."

"I never get tired of hearing it, thanks," he said.

Mitch and his wife, Jeanine, have three boys about my age who are accomplished mushers. Danny is the oldest, two years older than I. Next is Tyrell. Both have run the Iditarod. Then there is Dallas, who would turn eighteen the day before the start of the Iditarod and therefore be eligible to run the 2005 race as a rookie. The youngest was eight-year-old Conway.

I didn't know where I stood with the Seaveys, if they were for or against me. In the beginning Dan Senior had fought against allowing me to use a visual interpreter on a snow machine. He had made that point perfectly clear at Iditarod board meetings. But he had also gone out of his way to make me feel welcome when I met with the Iditarod board in Anchorage. I had a sense he might have helped forge the compromise allowing me to race using a visual interpreter mushing a second dog team.

After a while Mitch, Jeanine, and Dan Senior wandered away. But the Seavey boys and I stayed and visited. I had a great time. They were about the only people at the picnic who were my age. We hit it off.

Tyrell said that when he heard a legally blind musher was petitioning to be included in the race he thought blind meant blind, that

I could not see anything. But he said that after watching me he realized there are degrees of blindness. We talked about limited vision, and I described what I could see and what I could not see. He seemed interested in what I had to say.

When it came time for the grand-prize drawing, the use of a Dodge pickup truck during the Iditarod, I told the Seavey brothers I was incredibly lucky and predicted I would win. They laughed. But when the winning name was drawn, the announcer hemmed and hawed and said a second name had to be drawn. I knew I had won. I thought the reason they were thinking about refusing to give it to me was because I was blind and obviously could not drive. It turned out that indeed I had won, but the reason they did not automatically announce me as the winner was that, for insurance purposes, the truck could not leave Alaska. I explained we were coming to Alaska six weeks before the race and we really could use the Dodge pickup. And they gave it to us.

After the drawings a number of kids' prizes remained and the Seavey boys and I scooped them up and turned the stuffed animals into our lead dogs and used water bottles for our sleds. We played Iditarod. We were just kids having fun.

Dad and I returned home to Oregon. Several weeks passed and then one day Tyrell called on Dad's phone. Dad talked for a few minutes and then handed the phone to me, saying, "It's for you." He did not bother to tell me who was on the line.

"Hey, Rachael, this is Tyrell Seavey."

I was shocked that he had called to talk to me, but I managed to carry on a conversation with him. He asked about my team, and I said they were starting to come together. Tyrell talked about his team. His father was running the Seavey A-team and Tyrell had the B-team. Mostly we talked about dogs and training. I mentioned I was planning to come to Alaska in the middle of January so I could get my dogs acclimated to the colder weather.

"Are you going to run any of the qualifiers?" he asked.

I then suffered a serious blond moment. I had entered, and been accepted to run, the Tustumena 200. My mind went blank. I told him, "I'm going to run in the . . . that race on the Kenai Peninsula, the two-hundred-miler . . . oh, it starts with a T . . ."

"Tustumena two hundred?"

"That's the one," I said, feeling like an idiot.

"Oh, yeah, I was thinking about running the Tustumena two hundred," Tyrell said. "I don't want to put my dogs in a competitive situation. It would strictly be a training run."

"I totally understand," I said.

He told me he usually spent January training at Lake Louise, northeast of Anchorage, and invited me to go on a few training runs with him when I got to Alaska. He added, "In fact, if you don't already have someone lined up, I'd be glad to be your visual interpreter in the Tustumena two hundred. That is, if you're interested?"

Like a fool I turned him down. But we exchanged phone numbers and e-mail addresses and over the course of the next couple of days I thought about his offer. Then I called him and said, "I really did want to jump at the opportunity to run dogs with you, but to be perfectly honest, not everyone is thrilled about my coming up there to race. You might be setting yourself up for a lot of criticism."

He laughed. "I think I can handle it. The offer stands."

"Well, let's do it," I said without any further hesitation. And it was set. I would run the Tustumena 200 with Tyrell Seavey as my visual interpreter. I could not have been happier.

Going into fall training, which began at the end of August, I felt we had sixty dogs with the potential to make my Iditarod team. The others were too young or too old for consideration. Within two weeks that number was down to forty dogs. There are sixteen dogs on an Iditarod team, but we usually bring a field of over twenty.

I was very strict about the type of dog I was looking for. I wanted dogs with great attitudes, dogs that were eager to run even when they were tired, dogs not prone to injury, dogs with a lot of heart. If a dog was physically fit, but had three bad runs in a row, it was out. One of those dogs was Dugan. But in the past he had been a great racer so I decided to give him another chance. This time he got his act together and worked hard to make my team.

We started training dogs on a three-mile loop, watering the trail before we ran to settle the dust. Finally in late September the rains came, and we were able to move up and run the fifteen-mile loop on the desert. The dogs pulled me on a 4-wheeler, an all-terrain vehicle, over dirt roads. Then we stepped up to twenty-one miles, and after I solved the problem of passing over cattle guards—metal bars with spaces in between that keep cattle from crossing—I was able to run a big fifty-five-mile loop. Every time we came to a cattle guard, I laid out a length of carpet so the dogs could cross safely. Then I rolled up the carpet and carried it with me to the next crossing. As we traveled I stopped often, making sure the dogs drank and were hydrated. I trained at a steady ten miles per hour and when a dog goofed off I became the boogeyman. But when the dogs worked as a team I let them know what good boys and girls they were. I lavished them with praise. That is my training philosophy: praise the dogs when they do well and in return they will work hard to keep you happy.

There were some mornings when I awoke and wondered why I was doing this ridiculously boring exercise of running dogs. I wanted to stay in bed. But then it would hit me that my dogs were going to guide me across eleven hundred miles of Alaska's back country, and to do that they had to be in peak condition. The only way to achieve that level of conditioning was to put in the work now. With that incentive feeding me I pried myself out from under the covers, got dressed, and stepped outside. The dogs were always happy to see me, and sensing it was time to play they leaped in the air. "Choose me! Choose me!" they seemed to be howling.

In December I traveled to Anchorage for the Iditarod rookie meeting. I was accompanied by Becki Timson, my friend, dog handler, and, in this instance, my note taker. Every rookie is required to attend this meeting. Iditarod veterans dispense a lot of good advice about what rookies should expect during the race. Jeff King talked about perfecting our skills at the checkpoints. Basically, he said to develop a system and stick to it: Take care of the dogs first; the musher's needs are always secondary. Then he said to grab sleep, even if it came in a few stolen minutes here or there, wherever we could. He said to refrain from running dogs during the heat of the day and to avoid running from midnight to 6:00 a.m. because that is the dogs' natural sleep cycle. But more than anything he stressed hydration, saying we should carry a fresh supply of water and when we ran low, stop to melt snow in our cookers for the dogs as well as ourselves.

Mitch Seavey gave us tips on training and dog care. He concluded his remarks by saying there was nothing we could do to prepare ourselves to run the Iditarod, except to run the Iditarod. "Each time you run the Iditarod you come away with hundreds of ideas on ways you can improve yourself and your team, and lower your time. Wait and see, after you finish this race you'll know exactly what I mean."

The rookies visited Martin Buser's dog yard. He had won the Iditarod four times and holds the Iditarod record of eight days and twenty-three hours. I was not quite sure what kind of a reaction I would get from him because he had made some disparaging remarks about me, saying I should not be afforded any accommodations because of my blindness, and something to the effect that if the school bus driver were blind you would certainly not allow your kids to ride on that bus. Such a statement seemed ludicrous to me, but I suppose everyone is entitled to his or her opinion. At the end of the afternoon I made a point of thanking Mr. Buser for allowing us to visit his dog yard and for all the advice he so freely shared with us. He wished me good luck.

The week after the rookie meeting I flew to New York City by myself to visit Emmy Rossum. She is an actress I had met when I was in New York accepting an award as one of the top one hundred female athletes in America. We had hit it off and she'd invited me to be her guest at the premiere of her movie *The Phantom of the Opera*, and I was quick to accept.

Mom helped me pick out the perfect outfit, and I flew to New York City. Emmy's mother, Cheryl, met me at the airport, and a limousine whisked us to the Regency, one of the fanciest hotels in the city. My room was on the fourteenth floor. Emmy and her mother had a suite on the twentieth floor. Emmy's hair stylist did my hair, and her makeup artist added just the right touch of makeup. I put on my new outfit and felt pampered and pretty for such a special occasion.

At the premiere Emmy walked the red carpet. She was stunning, and I watched from a few feet away as she struck poses for photographers and talked to television personalities. We were escorted to our seats—Emmy was to my left, on the aisle, and Cheryl was on my right. I was introduced to the phantom, Gerard Butler, and when I went to shake his hand I dropped my head because I have never been good about eye contact and, besides, I was in awe of actually getting to meet the phantom. I have been a huge fan of *The Phantom of the Opera* since I was about six years old. Touching Gerard Butler's hand was over the top. In his adorable Scottish accent he said, "Darlin', are ya' never plannin' ta raise up your pretty eyes?"

I realized what I was doing, snapped my head up quickly, and looked at him. He was smiling.

After experiencing a gala New York City premiere, a fancy hotel, room service, the red-carpet treatment, and limousine service, I returned home and woke up the following morning to Dad saying, "Get up, princess. Chores need to be done." And before the hour was out I was in the dog yard scooping poop, a million miles away from the glamorous movie-star life Emmy was leading in New York City.

21

THE TEAM

The lineage of the dogs in our Oregon Trail of Dreams Kennel can be traced to three basic ancestors. One of these is the Alaskan malamute, a breed named for the Malmuit Eskimos of Alaska's northwest coast. These are large dogs weighing up to one hundred pounds and capable of pulling heavy freight sleds for many miles. They are large and cumbersome, and very little of the malamute can be recognized in our dogs.

The second progenitor is the Siberian husky, introduced by the Russian traders who came to Alaska as early as the 1700s. This breed is smaller than the malamute and has a tendency toward a multicolored coat and blue eyes. Leonhard Seppala made the Siberian husky famous during his leg of the 1925 diphtheria serum run to Nome. Newspapers around the world showed photographs of his Siberians and they became the model for the Alaskan sled dog. Back in the 1970s, when Dad first started running dogs, his team was comprised of Alaskan and Siberian huskies.

The third ancestor of our bloodlines comes from a mix of the Indian dog of the Alaska interior and a mix of breeds, from hounds to bird dogs to outcasts, strays, mutts, and perhaps even wolves somewhere in the distant past. Our average dog weighs forty to fifty pounds. They can have brown eyes, blue eyes, or light-colored eyes. Their coats range in color from black, to white, to brown, red, and every hue or combination in between. We look for puppies that are born with sound confirmation, tough feet, athletic talent, speed, endurance, determination, good dispositions, and the willingness to obey commands. We like our dogs to be like thoroughbred racehorses, with solid chests and shoulders, narrow waists, and well-muscled haunches.

By raising our own dogs, except for a few outside dogs that we buy or lease for a particular race, we end up with animals that fit our personalities. Dad and I want our dogs to have a "can do" attitude. We want dogs we can trust. Troublemakers and fighters need not apply. We want skilled athletes that love to run.

We do all of our own training. That way we are able to weed out the inferior puppies and save those that are going to be the true competitors. I can play with a puppy and think he has real promise, but I never know what type of a sled dog he will be until, at about six months old, I slip a harness over his head. By including several puppies with an experienced team it is quickly obvious to the trained eye which of the puppies will adapt to the team concept.

A puppy has to have a natural running style that matches the team. A trainer cannot change the natural gait of a dog. Either they fit in or they do not. If the team moves forward on my command, and a puppy jumps ahead and his back line is smooth when he comes down and the tugline does not jerk or slacken, then the puppy has reached his natural gait and it matches the gait and rhythm of the team. Becoming a competitive canine requires the mind-set of a champion. A champion is the dog that has a hidden reserve to dip into and can be counted on to always pull out the victory.

On a run I watch for a dog that constantly looks off to the side, or one that allows slack in the tugline, or a dog that leans into the dog running beside him. Any of these are signs that the dog is losing interest or becoming discouraged. When my team is running a race like the Iditarod, there is no room for disinterest, weakness, or a defeatist attitude. I want dogs on my team that want to be there. I get rid of those with physical or mental weaknesses, and they live out the rest of their days as someone's pet.

The heart and soul of any dog team are the leaders. Susan Butcher, four-time winner of the Iditarod, tells a story about her great leader, Tekla. Susan was on a training run with her team and three times she tried to urge them to cross an ice bridge over a river. It appeared safe but Tekla refused to step onto the ice bridge. Susan was trying to figure out what to do next when the ice bridge suddenly collapsed into the river. If they had been crossing, Susan and her team might very well have been swept under the ice to their deaths. But Tekla had that incredible sixth sense of danger.

That is the type of dog I want as my leader. The lead dog sets the pace. The lead dog is the engine that drives the team. The lead dog carries out my commands. And sometimes, as in the story of Tekla, the leader has to be more savvy than the musher.

In building my Iditarod team I started by selecting my main leaders, going with veteran dogs that had a history with me in other big races, dogs I could trust with my life. My best dog is Angel. Dutchess is right up there. Brick is only two years old, and I was not totally sure what she could give me, but she definitely had tremendous potential. And I knew I could count on Lim, Jewl, Tick, Glory, Walker, McGraw, Otter, Seth, and Willie. They are champions, and they do whatever I ask of them. So dog by dog I built my Iditarod team.

22

ON TO ALASKA

The month leading up to our departure for Alaska was a whirlwind of activities and distractions. I felt as though I were continually being pulled away from my main objective—getting my team ready to run the Iditarod. Each new day brought another barrage of interview requests from the media. The easiest part of my schedule, and the time I relished the most, were the hours I could escape from my obligations in the public arena and run my dogs.

The Atta Boy 300 added several more layers of confusion and disruption this year because the Atta Boy was hosting two separate world championship mid-distance races. The first two days of the competition were devoted to the six-dog class. Six international mushers stayed with us, and we furnished dog teams and sleds so they could represent their countries in the world championships.

I was so busy making sure our guests had everything they needed that I delayed getting ready for my own race in the twelve-dog class. In fact, I had to skip the musher's banquet to load the truck and my sled and get everything I would need for the three-hundred-mile stage race.

I had trained my team—some of the same dogs I planned to run in the Iditarod—to keep a consistent ten miles per hour pace, which is great for a long-distance race like the Iditarod but too slow to be competitive in a stage race like the Atta Boy 300. A stage race meant you race in stages, with a new start and finish line every day, unlike the Iditarod, which is continual. We finished in 18th place, the middle of the pack, with three really good days where the dogs kept their pace and worked hard, a couple of days that were so-so, and one terrible day when the dogs were not the least bit interested in running a race. I was pleased with the overall effort, not that my dogs were in Iditarod form—not yet—but they were progressing in the right direction. I was convinced we would be ready for the big race when the time came.

The day after the Atta Boy race finished I flew to Denver to give a talk to a national group of sales executives from Standard Insurance Company, one of my sponsors. I returned home for a last-minute round of media interviews, packed my personal things for Alaska, helped load our new dog trailer, said good-bye to friends and family, and then it was time to leave.

We pulled away from home carrying twenty-five dogs and with five sleds lashed to the top of the trailer. The back two seats of the Suburban were made into a giant bed with a comfortable mattress, sleeping bags, pillows, coolers, and junk food galore. As we headed north I lounged in back talking to my friend Becki, napping, listening to music, and letting the miles roll along. For once my blindness was an advantage because no one ever asked me to drive.

When we reached the crossing into Canada, the lady customs official wanted to know what those things were on top of the trailer. Dad told her, "Dog sleds." Then she wanted to know what we were hauling in all the little compartments. Dad told her, "Dogs."

"You mean there are dogs in all those compartments? That's a lot of dogs. What are you going to do with all those dogs?"

"My daughter is running the Iditarod," Dad told her.

"I don't know what you're talking about. Go on through," said the lady.

After all the media attention I had been receiving, and just when I thought everyone in the world must know my story, we ran into someone far removed from the sport of sled dog racing. Welcome to Canada.

As we traveled across British Columbia I was amazed by the vast distance between places. Flying to Alaska at thirty thousand feet you do not appreciate how big the country is as you do down on the ground and how many wild animals roam across the landscape. Along the way we saw wolves, lynx cats, caribou, moose, and bison. The only animals *I* actually saw were the bison. They were standing on the road, and we had to honk the horn before they reluctantly parted so we could squeeze past them. They were gigantic animals! I said a quick prayer asking that I never encounter one on the Iditarod trail.

After five long days of driving we finally pulled off the ice-glazed highway and turned down the road leading to Lake Louise, where we would meet Tyrell Seavey. We planned to have a couple of training runs before heading to the Tustumena 200. That morning the sun was especially bright. The trees were thick with hoarfrost. It was picture-postcard beautiful.

When we arrived at the lodge and found Tyrell, I suddenly got a little bashful. I think Tyrell felt as uncomfortable as I did. I do not know why—we had talked on the phone and emailed each other for several months. His hair was longer than I remembered, and I told him I thought it looked good. Some men can wear their hair a little longer, some cannot. Tyrell said he thought we should wait a few hours for the temperature to warm up before we ran dogs. He did not get any complaints from me. It was thirty-five degrees below zero. We had breakfast and chitchatted like we had done at the picnic. I was getting over my bashfulness.

When we finally got ready to go outside I layered up against the cold. I gooped my dogs' feet and bootied the team. In Alaska dogs need to wear booties most of the time because coarse snow and ice will tear their pads and snow will ball up between their toes. I did not want to take the chance of injuring a dog.

On the drive north we had stopped and dropped the dogs every few hours, but they had had only limited opportunity to exercise. When we finally started our run they were high-spirited. I stood on the brake, but on the lake ice it had little effect and we literally flew across the lake. It felt wonderful to be on the runners and I was every bit as thrilled as my dogs. How could I not be thrilled? Here I was, running a dog team in Alaska with the grandson of one of the co-founders of the Iditarod. How great is that!

Two days later Tyrell and I were ready to start the Tustumena 200. I told him, "I want to warn you—at some point during this race I'll probably cry. And when that happens, it won't be your fault. That's just me. At times on the trail I tend to get a little emotional."

"You'll be fine. This is a training run, nothing to get upset about," Tyrell said. His advice was to start at a slow pace. His theory was that, no matter what conditions you hit, if you are going slowly, you have more time to react. As a result I started the race riding the brake, but my hard-charging team ignored my efforts. Tyrell yelled at me, "Slow down."

"This is my slow speed," I barked right back at him. We tore up the trail, and I managed to make a quick ninety-degree left turn onto Sterling Highway, followed by a right turn and a quick dip. No wrecks. It was exhilarating. It always is when you can keep the sled right side up.

The hard-packed trail soon gave way to softer snow with deep holes and a lot of ups and downs, but nothing I could not handle. We climbed steadily, weaving through the trees, and when it got dark we broke out our headlamps and kept going, dropping down onto a frozen lake and out onto glare ice. I was not sure how my dogs would handle running on glare ice because most of them had never experienced it. They did fine. What seemed odd to me was the way the light from my headlamp reflected off the smooth ice and danced through the trees along the edge of the lake. The sky was alive with stars. It was a marvelous night, and I found myself thinking ahead to what the Iditarod would be like, envisioning it to be a string of nights just as perfect as this one. We stopped at the checkpoints to sign in and kept moving, taking our mandatory four-hour break at Lost Creek.

Coming out of the Lost Creek Lodge checkpoint we climbed a series of hills. Tyrell shouted back, "Hard left, take it wide as you can."

I was close enough to him that I saw him jump off his sled and sprint around to the outside, dragging his sled away from the tight corner. Then he disappeared.

"Well, this is going to be interesting," I thought and tried to take the corner wide, but my dogs were on a tight line, crowding the inside corner. Zack, my wheel dog, brushed a tree, and my sled smacked the same tree and became wedged against it. The only way to free the sled was for me to jump off, tip the sled on its side, and drag it away from the tree. As soon as the dogs felt slack in the gangline they lunged forward. All I could do was jump on top of my sled, dig in with my toes to try to slow us, and ride it out.

Tyrell was waiting for me at the bottom of the hill. My sled smacked into his sled so hard it spun completely around and our dogs got tangled. We laughed the whole time as we went about separating them.

Approaching the checkpoint at Clam Shell, the midpoint turn-around for the race, Tyrell and I were exhausted. In fact, we were so tired we were falling asleep standing on the runners. Dan Senior and Danny Seavey and Dad and Becki were waiting for us at the lodge. We said our hellos, and then Tyrell and I fed our teams and bedded them down before we went inside. It was crowded with other mushers. DeeDee Jonrowe and Jeff King formally introduced themselves, and I was a bit starstruck meeting two legends of the sport. Dinner was waiting for us, but Tyrell and I were too tired to eat much. We picked at our food and then found a room where we could lie down on the floor and sleep for a few hours.

People kept waking us to say there were beds in the next room, but I did not care. I was too tired to care. The floor was fine. I started out with my down jacket as a pillow and my light jacket as my cover, but it was cold in the room and after a while I threw the downy jacket over me and used my forearm as a pillow. I slept fitfully. When I woke, Tyrell was stirring, and we went outside to take care of our dogs. I wandered around for a while looking for the washroom, where I had gotten hot water the night before, but in the daylight everything looked different. Finally I saw Tyrell carrying a bucket and followed him.

We were required to remain at Clam Shell for a mandatory six-hour layover. We were there exactly six hours. Before leaving I dropped Cletus because he had a sore wrist. When we got on the trail Hank lay down on me, and I was hoping he had just stumbled. I got him up on his feet, and we kept going. But he lay down again, and I remembered the same thing had happened in the Atta Boy a couple of years before and that time his feet were sore. I checked his feet and they were fine. He had just quit. I did not want a quitter on my team. I pulled him and put him in the bag on the sled. At the next checkpoint I dropped Hank, and Tyrell dropped Attila.

I think Hank's bad attitude infected my team because as the day became sunny and the temperature warmed they became lackadaisical. I sang to them and that seemed to revive their spirits a little. We kept pushing forward, putting the miles behind us, until late in the afternoon when we reached an open creek. Angel and Mandy were in the lead and they refused to go into the water. I finally coaxed them over the crossing, and a couple of hundred yards downstream Tyrell pulled up and suggested we set camp and give the dogs an extended rest.

We tried to start a fire, but the wood was wet. We didn't have much luck until we fed the flames with some chemical Heet, the alcohol-based fuel from our cookers. Then we huddled around our miserable little fire and tried to stay warm. A couple of teams passed us, and we let them go. The night got colder and colder and we pulled on our parkas and finally got into our sleeping bags and lay under the stars. We talked about our families, dogs, music, and movies. Tyrell liked pretty much everything I liked. He could even quote lines from my favorite movie, *Best in Show*—"I used to be able to name every nut, and that used to drive my mother crazy because she used to say, 'Harlan Pepper, if you don't stop naming nuts . . .' I'd say peanut, walnut, macadamia nut . . ."

At one point Tyrell checked his watch and said we had been camped three hours. We thought we would give it another hour and just kept talking. After four hours, and again after five hours, we gave it one more hour. We finally broke camp after six hours.

After the extended rest my dogs were ready to go. We ran with headlamps and had been on the trail for maybe an hour when Tyrell shouted back to me, "Happy Birthday!"

It was after midnight, officially my birthday. I was twenty—no longer a teenager. I was surprised Tyrell knew and called ahead, "Thank you." I thought back to the Wyoming Stage Stop, when I turned sixteen on the trail. That had seemed the perfect birthday, but this one was even better.

We passed two teams on the way in, crossed the finish line at about 3:00 a.m., and were met by a delegation from the media, both television and newspapers. After the interviews were concluded, Dad asked me, "Where have you guys been? We were expecting you hours ago."

I shrugged my shoulders. "Camped out." And when I asked why he had not just wished me a happy birthday, he informed me I was a day early. My birthday was the following day. I guess Tyrell and I had not realized January has thirty-one days. Oh well.

I thanked Tyrell and told him this was the first race I had ever run where I did not cry. "I had a lot of fun," I told him.

"Me, too," he said. "Don't we have a warped idea of what fun should be?"

We went our separate ways. As soon as I got to the motel I took a hot shower. The water felt so good, and I was so tired, that I sat down on the shower floor and promptly fell asleep. After that I went to bed and did not wake up until two in afternoon.

At the banquet Tyrell was recognized for giving up his race to be my visual interpreter and was presented with the sportsmanship award and two hundred dollars. But I was criticized in the *Anchorage Daily News*. The reporter wrote: "[Scdoris], who has never won a major sled dog race, has temporarily stolen the spotlight from the best long-distance mushers in the world with her saga of triumph over personal adversity."

The story went on to say that I would either be forced to scratch early because of the rough Alaska trails or that I would move from checkpoint to checkpoint until the novelty of having a blind girl in the race wore off and the media lost interest. The reporter concluded, "Until that happens, however, the race contenders will continue to be caught in the shadows. . . . On March 5 along Fourth Avenue in downtown Anchorage, look for Scdoris in the spotlight, but recognize that the spotlight will eventually swing away."

23

CEREMONIAL START

With my birthday and the Tustumena 200 behind us, we drove up the Kenai Peninsula, through Anchorage, and continued ninety miles to the home of John and Mari Wood near Willow. They are fellow mushers and were gracious enough to allow us to stay with them for a month while we trained for the Iditarod. Nearly everyone in that area has a dog yard, so it was no big deal to have another couple dozen dogs in the neighborhood. At night, when a moose or some other visitor wandered through, several hundred dogs would raise their noses in the air, smell the intruder, and howl. It was like surround sound, and the colder the night, the more the intriguing range of voices was amplified.

Word sifted through the grapevine that one or two of the local mushers were not particularly happy to be sharing their trails with an outsider, but I was not concerned about a confrontation because my visual interpreter, who would be training with me and running the Iditarod, was none other than former professional wrestler, national weight-lifting champion, and world-record-holding weight lifter Paul Ellering. Paul is one man who can definitely take care of things. Known as "Precious Paul," manager of World Wrestling Entertainment's "Legion of Doom," Paul wrestled professionally for twenty years and loved every minute of it. He got into mushing on a wrestling trip to Alaska in the early 1990s. Eventually he bought fifteen dogs and competed in the 2000 Iditarod, finishing in 54th place.

I met Paul when he ran the Atta Boy 300 in 2002. I also raced against him at the John Beargrease, where he finished one place ahead of me. He agreed to be my visual interpreter in the 2005 Iditarod. In his musher's biography he wrote: *"Funny how we are all given talents in life, some get many, some get few, but what we do with what we have is the bottom line. For someone so young, Rachael has the ability to see the invisible, to believe the incredible, and in the end to never think the impossible. As competitors we put our name on the line, only for the chance, understanding full well that the Iditarod is its own taskmaster. I thank you, Rachael, the Iditarod, and all who stand on the runners for this chance. I've never been more alive than today."*

Paul was my hero. Not only had he verbalized his feelings so succinctly, but he had also realized that by giving of his time and skill as a musher to be my visual interpreter he might help change a lot of peoples' opinions on what someone with an impairment could achieve if given a chance. I looked forward to Paul's arrival and the beginning of our training.

Paul drove from his home in Minnesota with his team of dogs in a trailer, and almost the minute after his arrival at the Woods' place, he clapped his hands together and declared, "Let's go to the gym and work out."

At the gym in Wasilla it quickly became evident that Paul had a different idea about working out than I did. I enjoy getting my heart rate up and extending myself, up to the point of actual physical pain. But Paul was like a drill sergeant, moving through repetitions of squats, curls, step-ups, sit-ups, push-ups, and military presses.

Paul seemed to enjoy the pain. We did so many squats my quads became the consistency of Jell-O. I was seriously afraid my knees might bend backward if I ever straightened them all the way.

The next day I could hardly move, but Paul was raring to go. We hooked twenty-four dogs to the pickup, and they pulled us up and down the back roads around Willow. Every time there was a tangle, Dad and Paul sat in the pickup and I was expected to jump out, run up, and fix whatever problem there was. I think the two of them did it just to watch the way I lurched this way and that from my sore muscles, like a drunk trying to perform a field sobriety test. After about six hours of this nonsense I told the two of them, "I'm not doing this anymore. Tomorrow we start running dogs with the sleds." And then, for good measure, I added, "Paul, I'll continue to work out with you. But you do your thing and I'll do mine."

I said those things because I was tired, my muscles were sore, and because I thought it was important to establish that this was my race. I had plans about how I wanted to do things. But as it turned out, over the course of the next month leading up to the ceremonial start of the Iditarod, I had less and less control over my life. The media descended, and it seemed as though there was a feeding frenzy to interview me. Paul got his share of requests, too. We both thought it was important to accommodate the media, but that often cut short our training runs.

Another time stealer was preparing our drops for the Iditarod. It would be impossible to carry all the food and necessary supplies for the entire race on a sled, so each musher divides up what he thinks he will need into drop bags. The Iditarod distributes these bags to the nineteen checkpoints scattered across the Iditarod trail. Since Paul had already run the race, I relied on his expertise as we measured dog food, beef fat, and salmon for the dogs. Each dog would require between eight thousand and twelve thousand calories a day.

Becki, bless her, took over her brother and sister-in-law's kitchen in Anchorage and fixed all the human food we would need, sealing each meal in a Ziploc bag and freezing it. On the trail we would just toss a bag in the cooker when we heated water so we would have hot food. Some of the checkpoints would have hot water for us and a few actually had microwave ovens, but generally the mushers had to dip water out of a hole in the ice or melt snow.

We worked on the drops for three straight days, and when we finished there were eighty bags lining both sides of the Woods' driveway—nearly a ton of food and supplies. We delivered them to Anchorage, where the Iditarod crew took over, arranging the bags according to the proper checkpoints: native villages, ghost towns, and sometimes only a tent set up on a frozen lake.

It was a big relief to have the drops finished. I am sure John and Mari appreciated being able to park in their driveway once again. But if I thought life was going to become easier I was wrong. Every day there were more and more requests for interviews from television stations, both local and network, and newspapers and magazines. I tried to accommodate each and every request because I realized my participation was good for the sport of dog sledding and it had the potential to bring a new interest to mushing and the mushing way of life. I did get tired of being "Rachael Scdoris, the blind sled dog racer," but the reality is that my blindness is a big part of my story.

Paul was great with the media. From all his years in the spotlight as a professional wrestler and promoter, he knew how to conduct himself during an interview. He used terminology straight out of wrestling hype to describe our partnership. When asked what he thought about being my visual interpreter, he would run his big, rough hands over the top of his bald head, glare like a professional wrestler, and say, "So, you want to talk about the Beauty and the Beast. . . ."

Though Paul had brought his own team of dogs from Minnesota, they were not evenly matched to mine. So I gave him six of my best dogs: Gimpy, Cletus, Walker, McGraw, Otter, and Willie. We ran forty dogs through the pre-race vet check, and all the dogs passed their EKG and blood-work tests. Each dog was fitted with an identifying microchip, and Paul and I would each choose sixteen dogs to use on our respective teams.

Two days before the Ceremonial Start, the mushers' meeting

was held at the Anchorage Millennium Hotel. That evening we attended the Iditarod banquet, where two thousand people packed the giant auditorium for dinner and the chance to meet their favorite mushers. A steady parade of Iditarod fans stopped by our table to wish me well and have me sign posters. When my name was called I made my way between the tables to the stage and said a few words into the microphone about what an honor it was to be standing there, how much I was looking forward to the race, and thanking my sponsors for their support. I drew my starting position: number 10.

Later, there was a drawing for door prizes, and I said to those at my table, "I wonder what I'll win." Some of the people—those who did not know how lucky I am—thought I was joking. One even said, "Look around. With all the people here you'd have to be awful darn lucky to win."

The first prize was a one-thousand-dollar spending spree at Cabela's, a company that sells outdoor gear and is one of the chief sponsors of the Iditarod. My name was drawn, and as I made my way to the stage to claim my gift certificate people cheered. After that I signed more autographs and had the opportunity to meet Vi Redington, widow of Joe Redington Sr., and Norman Vaughn, a lively ninety-nine-year-old who had been a member of Admiral Byrd's 1928 expedition to Antarctica. His hair was white as snow and his eyes sparkled. He had a smile that seemed to light up the whole auditorium.

That night we stayed at the Hilton Hotel. The dogs were outside in the trailer, parked in a lot adjacent to the hotel. This made the late-night drop convenient for us, and the dogs had the opportunity to stretch, drink water, and take care of their business without being rushed. Beginning early the following morning, and all that day, I was in the media spotlight. All I really wanted was to tend to last-minute details and love my dogs, but that was out of the question. It reached the point where I felt I was being crushed with all the attention and I had to escape to my room, where I rested while Dad picked up the slack for me.

We ate a late dinner and before going to bed, I walked to Fourth

Avenue and watched the work crews bringing in snow. That seemed odd to me, to be in Alaska and having to truck in snow, dump it on the street, and spread it with road graders. Another group of dedicated and efficient workers was busy erecting a snow fence, stretching it between parking meters, separating the sidewalk from the street.

Watching them lay down the snow for the ceremonial start brought the reality of the race home to me. It ignited many small fears, not that my fears were much different from any other musher. Every rookie wonders if he or she will measure up to all the unknowns the trail can throw at you. Questions roll through your mind: What if the weather gets nasty and the temperature drops to fifty or sixty or even seventy below? What do you do if you encounter a moose or a bison? What happens if an ice bridge collapses, or the wind pins you down, or a snowstorm traps you for days? But it is all the unknowns that make the race such an adventure. It is just like Mitch Seavey said: You cannot know about the Iditarod until you run the Iditarod.

My greatest fear was to encounter an enraged moose, or a bison, on the trail. I had read about the moose attacking Susan Butcher's team, killing two of her dogs and injuring eleven more. And I will never forget Dad telling the story of Jeffrey Mann in the Yukon Quest killing a moose with his hatchet.

A moose attack is a very real danger in the Alaskan bush. Paul would have a gun. I would not. I'm a terrible shot. Paul said the last thing he wanted was for me to be behind him with a loaded weapon. Other than Paul—if he happened to be close when a moose attacked—my only protection would be my ax. I planned to keep that ax at the ready. If it came down to defending my team, I knew I would not hesitate, I would wade in swinging my ax against a ton of bad attitude and sharp hooves. I said a prayer, asking God to please never put me in such a scary situation.

My second concern was how I would handle the sleep deprivation. Once the race began, the best I could hope for would be quick catnaps. I am a person who enjoys her sleep. In previous races lack

of sleep had caused me to become groggy, slowed down my thinking and reaction time, and made me hallucinate. How would I react
over twelve or thirteen days?

And of course, like a lot of rookies, I was concerned about the
tough places on the trail—for instance, the Happy River Steps, a
dangerous series of three quick drops where sleds can shatter and
mushers can suffer injuries that force them to scratch from the race.
Following that there is the climb up and over Rainy Pass and then
the wild ride through Dalzell Gorge, a narrow passage that drops a
thousand feet in five miles with nasty side hills to contend with,
open water, and the real possibility of moose and buffalo in the
trail. It is a very technical and intimidating stretch, and no place to
make a mistake. After that comes the Buffalo Tunnels, followed by
Farewell Burn, a desolate landscape punctuated by downed timber
and a trail where the snow often is blown away to bare dirt. And all
those dangers come within the first two hundred miles of the race.
Beyond that . . . I did not even want to think about the frozen lakes,
the vast expanse of tundra, the ice of the Yukon River, and crossing
the Bering Sea.

I took a deep breath of the fresh Alaska air, exhaled, and
watched a grader push snow across the street. I could feel the tense-
ness in my shoulders. I told myself to relax, and then I smiled, because tomorrow would be the biggest day of my life. And every day
after that, for as long as I was on the Iditarod trail, was going to be
the biggest day of my life. I went back to the Hilton, took a long, hot
bath, went to bed, and slept as if I did not have a care in the world.

In the morning a parade of dog trucks passed on the street in
front of the Hilton. Some were new, with fancy letters painted on
the dog boxes advertising the mushers and their sponsors. Other rigs
were thrown-together outfits, mushers operating on a shoestring
and counting on a decent payday at Iditarod to carry them through
the year. Dogs' noses peeked out of the round holes in the doors,
testing the wind and smelling the other dogs as well as the growing
sense of anticipation and excitement that rode the air currents.

The winter sun struggled to come up and break free of the

jagged outline of the Chugach Mountains. I squinted in the bright light, put on my sunglasses, and stepped into the street where the snow that had been brought in last night was deep and slushy. Dad had moved our rig to the corner of Fourth Avenue and H Street, pulled out the metal struts, and was attaching the heavy chains onto which we snapped the dogs' collars. I went to give him a hand, but was intercepted by a television crew. A microphone boom was thrust in my direction. Video cameras pointed at me. I did my best to answer questions while also concentrating on the work that needed to be accomplished.

Opening one of the doors on the dog box I reached in for Dutchess. She had been my most consistent leader and had led in every big race I had entered since I was fourteen years old. Out on the trail she instinctively knows what I want her to do. She stays on the trail and takes commands. She is a born athlete and loves to run. The Dutch is mostly black with a little white and what I call liver color on her muzzle and throat. Whenever I go out into the dog yard Dutchess always rolls over onto her back and wants me to rub and pat her belly. She loves that. But Dutch is eight years old, getting old for a race dog, and she has a wrist that tends to become sore over the course of a race. I would never think of running the Iditarod without Dutch, but after that I planned to retire her. This would be her last run. And what a way to end a fabulous career, finishing the Iditarod and arriving in Nome.

The next dog I dropped was my other main leader, Angel. She is blond with a white mark on her forehead between her eyes. I can honestly say she is the cutest dog in our kennel. When she was a year old I put her in harness and there was only one place in the team where she was comfortable, and that was at lead. She was born to lead. She has a great attitude, and even though I renamed her Wrong-way for a time during the Race to the Sky she is usually perfect with commands and she has the heart of a lion. In fact, during the Tustumena 200 the dog that impressed Tyrell the most was Angel. Ever since she was a puppy she has been my sweetheart.

Next I pulled Ned to the ground. He is my wheel dog extraordinaire. Big and strong, Ned works his tail off to protect the sled. Nothing ever bothers him; he is tireless, and if he falls or gets bumped he shakes it off and hardly ever breaks stride. He is seven years old.

Seth is eight years old and an amazing worker, a totally sweet dog. I do not think I have ever seen slack in that boy's line. I tried to retire Seth, telling him he was getting old and I had all these young dogs coming up, but he was so animated in training, keeping up with all the other younger dogs, that I pulled him out of retirement. He would be a team dog, but he was also my ace in the hole and could fill in if I found myself in need of a strong, dependable leader.

I went down the line pulling dogs and snapping them on the drop chain. The next dog was Eyes, an eight-year-old I was leasing from Dean Osmar for this race. She had run the Iditarod four times, and one of those times was only ten days after winning the five-hundred-mile Yukon Quest with Dean's son Tim.

Lisa is four years old, blond with overtones of brown, perky ears, and pretty brown eyes. In a lot of ways she is a younger Dutchess. She can be a strong and determined leader or a good team dog. Sometimes she lacks enthusiasm, but out on the trail she will put her head down and run forever.

Jovi is a three-year-old. During fall training he kept trying to pass the leaders, so I put him in lead and discovered: Wow, this puppy can really lead. I focused on developing him as leader, and he picked up on it incredibly fast. He has a good lead of his own, and in the Atta Boy proved to be a strong leader. But sometimes Jovi can be timid, and once in a great while he becomes afraid of own shadow. Another year and he could be a great one.

Dugan is six years old and was named after Libby Riddles's famous leader. In his prime he was a great leader, but now he is a team dog with a solid attitude. He is a workhorse. Athens is five. I bought her last summer from Mike Hutchins in Michigan. She is a bundle of pure energy, has an incredible passion for racing and responds well to verbal commands.

Dad had dropped dogs on the opposite side, and I worked my

way down the line giving each dog a love. There was Kitty, Karelan, Possum, Pia, and Mandy. All of them are reliable team dogs and can serve as leaders in a pinch. Bernard was probably the hardest worker on the team. Brick, as a two-year-old, was the youngest. She has a great attitude, has never been injured, and I am confident she is a star on the rise.

We put out the metal dishes and watered each dog. I paid attention, making sure each dog drank. When I looked up there were more television cameras aimed in my direction and the boom mike was still following me. I tried to complete my chores, but I was continually interrupted by questions from the media and spectators.

"How are you feeling right now?"

"Do you think you have a chance to reach Nome?"

"Are you nervous?"

"How are you going to feel if you have to scratch?"

"Are you scared?"

"What can you see?"

No matter how ridiculous the question, I tried to be pleasant and answer to the best of my ability. I realized I was not only answering for myself, but I had also become a spokesperson for the Iditarod. I did not want to offend anyone. I wanted to be personable and accommodating and I wanted everyone to like me.

The snow fence that lined the street was having a minimal effect holding back the spectators. As many people crowded the street as stayed behind the barricade. People were everywhere. Some were wearing fur hats and fur coats. One fellow appeared to have been swallowed by a wolf with only his face sticking out of the wolf's mouth. This was the biggest show in all of Alaska, a grand spectacle dedicated to elevating the final frontier to the height of myth. And for the moment all of this seemed to swirl around me, so close that it was hard to catch my breath. I was at the center of a whirlwind of microphones, cameras, questions, people requesting autographs, people so close I could not make a move in any direction without running into someone.

Then Tyrell stepped into this maelstrom, and, mercifully, the media took a collective step back and allowed us a little breathing room. The crowd formed a circle around us. I felt like a fish in an aquarium. Tyrell took a nervous glance around and asked, "How you doing?"

"A little overwhelmed at the moment."

"No kidding. It's a circus. How do you manage to keep smiling?"

"Do I have a choice?"

Cameras clicked. We knew our every move was being recorded and that tongues would wag. Tyrell leaned close to my ear and said, "Don't worry, once you get out on the trail, they can't follow."

"Great," I replied.

"Well, good luck. Have fun. See you tomorrow." Tyrell stepped back, and the crowd pressed in like water rushing to fill a low spot. I could hardly move, but I was able to make my way to Angel. I gave her a kiss on her forehead, lifted a front leg, and slipped a bootie over her paw, tightening the Velcro strap so the bootie would stay in place. After Angel I moved on to Dutchess and then to Ned and Lisa. As I worked I was distinctly aware of the crowd. They were slowly crushing me with their attention. I looked up once, toward the snow fence, and I could see it had bowed out from people leaning against it trying to take my photograph. The pressure was intense and consuming. I could not draw a full breath, only little gulps of air that sustained me for a few seconds at a time. I was starting to hyperventilate.

And then Libby Riddles was there. She put an arm around me and pushed everyone away. Her voice boomed, "Stand back. Move aside. This is my musher. Give us some room."

She led me to the Suburban, opened the door, and pushed me inside. And then she crawled in with me and slammed the door shut. It was relatively quiet. I could breath again. The first tear rolled down my cheek, followed by a mini deluge. I felt as though I was melting, but with Libby you can cry and laugh at the same time. I threw my arms around her and told her, "Only you could get away with something like that."

"I did pull it off, didn't I?" said Libby proudly.

I inhaled and exhaled several times then declared, "Peace and quiet. Thank you." I knew that Libby, having been the first woman to win the Iditarod, knew better than anyone what I was feeling. "It must have been like this when you reached Nome."

"Every bit as bad," said Libby. "Maybe even more so because I had spent so many days on the trail, then coming up off the sea ice onto Front Street and facing all those people lining the street, everyone shouting and waving. My heart was pounding so hard I could feel it thumping against my ribs. The crowd fell in behind me, sweeping us up the street, and when we stopped under the arch I was asked, 'How do you feel, Libby?' And I didn't know what to say because there weren't any words that could explain how I felt."

"That must have been something." I tried to envision the scene, the commotion of that moment.

"This is just the eye of the hurricane," Libby warned. "As soon as you step outside it's going to hit you all over again."

"I can handle it," I assured her. "I just needed a little break, to get away from it for a minute. That's all."

Dad opened the door and slid onto the seat beside me. He hugged me and asked, "Are we having fun yet?"

I wiped at a few wayward tears and smiled. "You bet I am. Let's get this show on the road."

When I emerged from the Suburban, the loudspeaker down the street was booming the names of mushers and counting down the seconds to their send-off. Passing in front of us were teams of dogs barking, yipping, yowling, and lunging. Mushers and handlers were trying to maintain control as they slogged their way through the ankle-deep snow leading to the chute. The noise level was amped to a level of delirious insanity.

My sled, along with a tag sled Dad would ride, was fastened to the trailer, and the gangline was stretched across the snow, pointing toward the starting line. I directed my handlers to begin moving dogs up and fastening them to the gangline. I pulled on my Iditarod racing bib and grinned at the cameras because it was the first time I had worn it. Dad handed me a cap advertising Standard Insurance

Company, and I put it on my head. My Iditarider, Molly Murphy, a twelve-year-old girl from Solana Beach, California, took her seat in the basket of my sled. Her parents, who had paid $2,200 to win the bid to have her ride with me on the eleven-mile run, were taking pictures. The Iditarider program allows fans to bid for a ride with their favorite musher during the ceremonial start. All the money raised goes into the race prize pool.

"Move up," an official directed.

The anticipation and tension were at a fever pitch. My dogs were going wild. The handlers, mostly friends, had leashes to each tandem of dogs and were trying to control them as best they could, avoiding tangles and trying not to tromp on a dog's foot in the process. I stepped on the runners of my racing sled, looked back at Dad on the tag sled, and nodded. He kicked loose the quick release, and we were off, headed up the chute.

My handlers maneuvered the team through the deep snow up Fourth Avenue to where a large banner proclaimed, IDITAROD TRAIL RACE—START. I motioned for the handlers to step away. A voice over the loudspeaker blared a quick introduction, saying my name and that I was one of the twenty-eight rookies competing in the thirty-third running of the Iditarod. Then the countdown began. "Ten . . . nine . . ."

Like flipping through a photo album, I saw images and quick impressions—the faces of those who had told me I could not do something because I was just a little blind girl, kids who had terrorized me at school, but also friends who had helped me along the way, images of my dogs on training runs and in races, Dad and Mom, Dr. Weleber and Marla Runyan.

Jay Rowan called encouragement, "You can do it." I felt a surge of pride, the same feeling I had had on the day Dad first allowed me to take the dogs on that one-mile run. And I felt a satisfaction in overcoming the bitter disappointment I had felt after the first time I had spoken with the Iditarod Trail Committee. So much had been invested by so many to reach this one moment in my life. And now I was not quite sure what I should feel or how I was supposed to react.

"Five . . . four . . . three . . ." The sun found a hole in the clouds, and I had to squint even though I was wearing sunglasses. I became aware of the crowd and its muffled roar surrounding me. Photographers knelt in the snow to snap my picture. Television cameras panned the scene and locked on me. Out in front was an open trail to run, and in the distance I thought I could distinguish the white outline of snowcapped mountains. I was at the starting line of the Iditarod, about to tackle the biggest adventure of my life. I had won.

"Two . . . One . . . Go!"

My dogs surged forward, jerking the sled and creating the momentum to carry us on an exhilarating ride down Fourth Avenue. The crowd leaned into the snow fence, clapping, cheering, and shouting words of encouragement.

"Good luck!"

"Get 'em, girl!"

"Show 'em what you're made of!"

"We love you, Rachael!"

"See you down the trail!"

"Go, Rachael, go!"

I rode the brake and tried to acknowledge everyone as well as drink in all that my senses could take in so I would never forget a precious second. At the same time I intently watched my dogs because this was not the place to have a tangle or a wreck. Not here. I glanced behind me at Dad, and he had a smile plastered across his face that could have melted a glacier. I was sure those were tears of joy making his cheeks wet and shiny, and knew he must be experiencing the same flood of emotions I was. I felt happy that the two of us could share such a special moment.

I thought we would eventually run out of spectators, but we never did. People were scattered over the entire eleven-mile course. One group cheered extra loud for me, calling out my name, and as we swept past I turned and shouted, "See you in Nome." They went nuts.

24

THE RACE

We spent the night at John and Mari Wood's place, but when it came time to go to bed I was full of nervous energy, and it took a long time for me to fall asleep. In the morning I indulged in a long, hot—very hot—shower. I knew it would be nearly a week until we reached the checkpoint at Takotna, where I would have the chance for another shower.

Because of the lack of snow at Wasilla, the traditional starting point, the restart of the Iditarod Trail Sled Dog Race was moved thirty miles to Willow Lake. We were directed onto the lake ice to the stake with my number 10 where we got busy dropping dogs. When they were fed and watered we took my racing sled down from the trailer. Dave Sims built it for me and promised it was "bullet proof" and would withstand anything the Iditarod could throw at it. I started sorting through the gear I was taking. The rules require mushers to carry all the equipment necessary for a musher and his dogs to survive under severe winter conditions.

A sled always steers best with the weight low and toward the back. From the many times I had practiced this procedure I knew where everything was supposed to go, and I started packing my red sled bag mounted to the sled. The heavy cooler full of dog food went at the bottom, in the back. The cooker to heat water, the dog pans, and the dipper for ladling dog food are light so I put those items near the front. My big Arctic sleeping bag followed by gloves, mittens, snacks, headlamps, goggles, sunglasses, and face shields—a necessity if the weather turned so cold that no skin could be exposed without suffering frostbite—were stowed, as were packages of dog food and dog treats. Lots of dog treats—salmon, hot dogs, and beef fat. I tied the ax in its leather sheath where I could reach it easily and made sure other essential items were packed: dog booties, dog medicine and foot goop, spare lines and harness, cables for tying dropped dogs, tools for sled repair, a camera, CD player, CDs of some of my favorite music, and extra batteries. I puttered, taking my time, doing one thing and then stopping to be interviewed by the media or to give my dogs a love.

Mark Nordman, Iditarod race marshal, had requested that Paul and I give up the positions we drew and start at the back of the pack to avoid complications and criticism. There are a number of disadvantages for a musher in last place. The trail is horrible, torn up by all the traffic, dog teams, sleds, and snow machines. And, since every other team already passed that way, if any dog in front is sick with a stomach bug or a virus there is a good chance the last team will pick up the germs and become sick later in the race. And even though I could not leave until the other seventy-eight mushers had departed, my time would begin when the number 10 musher was scheduled to depart: I would lose more than two hours before I ever left the starting line.

Everything I needed to do could have been done in an hour. But with six hours to kill, I puttered. I stretched and massaged the dogs, greased their feet and put booties on them. I checked out the wireless radio headsets that the K-9 unit of the Anchorage Police Department had loaned us. Having a wireless system, with a button

Paul and I could keep inside our gloves, was certainly going to be an advantage over shouting. Members of the media stopped by for interviews, friends came to wish me well. I waited for my turn to go to the starting line.

I was surprisingly calm but could still feel the nervous tickle in the pit of my stomach, the way I used to feel before a big race in track. I think I was generally relaxed, though, because I knew I had done everything possible to prepare myself and my dogs. We were as ready as we were ever going to be.

The loudspeaker announced that Tyrell Seavey was the next musher to go and that he was one of five Seaveys to compete in the Iditarod. I ran to the chute, arriving as he was pulling to the starting line. I wished him well and on a whim gave him a good-luck kiss on the cheek. And then I stepped out of the way and he was off. I knew he had a good team and would be among the front-runners. The next time I would see him would be in Nome.

WILLOW TO YENTNA—45 MILES

One by one the mushers near us began to leave, and as each departed my dogs got more restless and eager to run. I did not want them waiting too long in harness expending useless energy in their excitement, and I delayed until the last minute before giving the go-ahead to have my team harnessed and hooked to the gangline. From that point forward everything in my world became a blur of motion and activity. Paul and his crew were just as busy.

Paul pulled forward, and my dogs, knowing they would soon get their chance to run, were wild in their excitement. My handlers did a fine job, petting the dogs and trying to keep them distracted. We pulled into the chute, and Paul sprinted toward me. He threw his arms around me in a quick embrace, reassured me we would reach Nome, ran back to his sled, hopped on the runners, and away he went. I moved forward until the brushbow of my sled was poised under the Iditarod banner. In front of me was a long chute lined with people, and beyond was the trail leading off into the unknown.

I said a quick prayer, asking God to please take care of my dogs and me, and then I asked Him for one specific favor, "Please, God, don't let me crash on the first corner."

The handlers stepped away. The countdown happened quickly. I barely had time to hug Dad and clasp hands with Libby. She shouted over the roar of the crowd, "Show 'em what you can do, girl."

And then we were under way and the crowd, held back by a banner-lined snow fence, cheered as my sixteen racing huskies charged ahead, powering into the big sweeping right-handed corner. Paul was somewhere out in front. I could not see him. As we circled the frozen lake we began to close the gap, and I caught him at the point the trail turned off the lake ice and led up onto the first rolling hill.

We topped the ridge and the commotion so familiar in my world fell away. Ahead was eleven hundred miles of wilderness. I was ecstatic to leave behind the media, the crush of people, the noise, the confusion, and the schedule of scripted activities. From now on my world would be simple and basic. It would be about the dogs and our race to Nome. I let out a huge sigh of relief.

A group of people gathered around a campfire yahooed, and I realized I was far from alone. We passed other groups along the trail, and friendly voices called my name and wished me well. As we were going up a steep hill a woman ran over and handed me a necklace, telling me they were good-luck beads.

"How are you doing?" Paul's voice spoke over my radio.

I depressed the finger button. "Couldn't be better."

The Outdoor Life Network helicopter hovered overhead, following every twist and turn as my dogs snaked through the trees and up and over the hills. The sun dropped into a bank of clouds, and the helicopter departed. As the light faded and darkness crept over the land, I thought that now, finally, I would be alone in the night, but we dropped down on the flat plain of the frozen Susitna River and every mile or so snow machines would be pulled into a circle like covered wagons, where bonfires would be roaring, and people would be partying and having a good time. Paul and I were running with headlamps, and as soon as the revelers saw us coming they would shout encouragement at us, and as we swept past they called out, asking if anyone was behind us. When we let them know we were the last two racers, they whooped and hollered some more and went back to their party.

This social scene lasted all the way to the checkpoint at Yentna. As we arrived, a host of other teams were resting beside the trail. We were directed to an open area, and Paul and I pulled in side by side. The soft snow made it difficult to set a snow hook to stake out the team. So I used my ax as an anchor, and to keep it from pulling out I set a bale of straw over the line. I took care of my dogs and tried to curl up on the straw and sleep with them, but I was still too excited to sleep. I walked inside a building where a nice woman said she was rooting for me and insisted I eat a plate of spaghetti. I did not have much of an appetite.

"Take my bed," she offered.

"Thank you, but I can't do that." I explained, "I'm not allowed to have anything special. If you offer your bed to me you have to offer it to every other musher."

I found a place to sleep under a table and curled up there, but woke up when the woman placed a sheet over me. Then a man woke me because he was leaving and needed his stuff sack that I had been using as a pillow. Other people stepped over me and on me. I finally gave up and went out into the night, looked after my dogs, and got ready to hit the trail.

YENTNA TO SKWENTNA—34 MILES

We left Yentna in the dark and ran all night with headlamps. Once in a while Paul called to me on the radio or I caught a glimpse of his headlamp, but mostly it was wonderful to feel alone in the big Alaskan night. The trail was rough, chewed up by mushers in front of us riding their brakes on the downhill stretches and leaving deep furrows. But my dogs took the winding trail smoothly. I passed some teams and moved up to 65th place. If everything went according to plan, I thought I had a chance to finish in the middle of the pack. That would be almost like a victory. But deep inside I knew my thinking at this early point of the race was rash, and that on the Iditarod trail good things and bad things had a way of happening when you least expected them.

When the sun came up, harsh light fell on the white peaks of the Alaska Range, looming ahead of us like an impenetrable barrier. Two of my dogs tangled, and I stopped to fix the problem. Lisa's right hind leg was caught in her tugline, but it appeared to be a rope burn, nothing more. When we arrived at the Skwentna checkpoint I treated the rope burn with Algyval—an anti-inflammatory medication—rubbed some antibiotic ointment on it, and gave the leg a massage. The injury was not swollen, and she did not favor the leg.

Paul and I had planned a conservative race. Our schedule called for a six-hour layover in Skwentna. After the dogs were fed, Paul and I grabbed a bite to eat. Paul told me the vets wanted him to drop Cletus. He was one of the dogs I had given to Paul for the race to make our teams equal. In the Tustumena I had had to drop Cletus because of an inflammation in the tendon in his left leg. But it had seemed fine in our training leading up to the Iditarod.

"Is it his tendon?" I asked.

"No. He has a respiratory problem," Paul said.

As a pup Cletus had gotten dust in his lungs, and every once in a while, if the temperature was warm and he was working hard, he had an occasional problem with coughing. I did not think the condition would bother him in Alaska, but the weather was unseasonably warm, hovering around or slightly above the freezing mark.

The veterinarian crew took Cletus to the landing strip to fly him back to Anchorage, where Dad would pick him up and care for him. A half hour later a man on a snow machine roared up and said, "Your dog got loose and they can't catch him. Jump on the sled and I'll run you out there. Maybe he'll come to you."

I got on the sled attached to the snow machine, and the driver roared off. I held on with both hands and tried not to get bounced out. When we reached the makeshift airstrip I asked a fellow leaning against a plane, "Did they catch the dog?"

He shrugged. "Don't guess so."

"Do you know where he is?"

He seemed totally disinterested. "He went running off. A couple of the vets chased after him."

I thought, *Oh, that's great because Cletus is afraid of his own shadow.* I knew that nobody was going to be able to chase down a sled dog on foot. "What direction were they headed?"

"Don't know. Wasn't paying no attention."

The man on the snow machine took me through the woods until we found two men chasing a dog. I got off and called Cletus. He immediately came to me. I put Cletus on the sled, and we rode back to the airstrip, where I loaded Cletus onto the plane.

After that the fellow on the snow machine asked me a series of questions about what I could or could not see, how the race was going, and if I had any reservations about the upcoming trail through the Alaska Range. Finally I told him, "I'm running a race. I've got to get back to my team."

As it turned out, the fellow on the snow machine was Craig Medred, outdoor editor of the *Anchorage Daily News*. He had written a number of critical stories about me and my quest to run the Iditarod. He once referred to me as: "An eighteen-year-old musher pushed into the race by her boosterish father," and declared there was no way I could ever drive my dog team over the Alaska Range. In his latest story he would point out that I had enough visual ability to catch my dog after it got loose, leash it, and walk around a Cessna 185 without bumping into the propeller or the strut beneath the wing. He added, "But when she returned to checkpoint headquarters, after having been there once before, she mistook the cabin of Joe and Norma Delia for the checkpoint cabin. Although the buildings have some similarities, they are quite different and located in distinct settings."

If I ever run into Mr. Medred again I will ask him why he did not feel an obligation, or have the common courtesy, to introduce himself to me before he interviewed me, and I suppose I should apologize for having too much sight for a blind person.

SKWENTNA TO FINGER LAKE—45 MILES

Paul and I departed Skwentna at three in the afternoon and traveled through a sparse spruce forest on winding trails that dropped down onto frozen lakes and swamps and passed through thickets of cottonwoods. The trail here was broken apart and churned into loose snow and deep moguls by the other teams as well as a small army of snow machines that had passed that way. My dogs, trained in the desert and on groomed trails, had difficulty in the soft snow and deep wallows. At first Paul called back on the radio and warned me about the deeper holes, but there were so many, and they came with such rapid-fire frequency, that he only warned me when it was something totally extreme.

When we hit a hole I tried to swing the team to the edge, but generally the sled slid to the bottom anyway. Finally I figured out the best way to hit the holes was straight on. The mushers in front of me had ridden their steel brakes and created a groove to follow. If I followed in their tracks, I simply dipped down and popped back up without sliding and dragging my dogs sideways. This helped to avoid jarring them in their harnesses and possibly injuring one of them.

We ran the last few miles into Finger Lake with headlamps. There, the only available water was through a hole cut in the ice. I dipped water, set up my cooker, and fed my dogs. The veterinarian looked at Lisa's leg and gave me some white goop, an antibiotic ointment, and zinc oxide, which causes the medicine to be absorbed into the bloodstream. I wrapped her injury, but there was no swelling and she was not favoring the leg.

The only place to sleep was a wall tent without heat. Several mushers were there, snoring away. To escape the serenade I shook out my sleeping bag and slept with my dogs, managing to get in three good hours before hitting the trail.

FINGER LAKE TO RAINY PASS—30 MILES

The next thirty miles would be a crucial test because we would climb into the mountains and plunge through the Happy River

Steps, a dangerous section of the trail that other mushers had warned me about. Joe Runyan, a past Iditarod champion and friend, described the Steps as "a half-mile descent that comes in three distinct drops and borders on an out-of-control free fall." If I could make it through the Steps, it would feed my confidence for the challenges ahead in Dalzell Gorge and the rugged section of the trail coming out of Rohn.

The sun came up and the wind stirred to life. The trail turned from bad to horrible. The holes were as big as semis. I could get a pretty good idea of just how bad they were going to be if, when Paul tried to warn me on the radio, I heard him grunt like someone punched him in the stomach. Then I knew it was going to be a pretty serious bump. I tried to bend my knees and get low on the runners to absorb some of the shock. Several times I crashed and turned the sled on its side, but I held on and managed to right it without much problem. Wrecks are part of mushing. You either get used to wrecking or you take up a less strenuous sport like pool, or bowling, or golf.

We were on a narrow trail zigzagging through a dense forest. The trail rose steeply and dropped off fast through a long series of violent bumps. With my feet perched on the runners it was like trying to stand on the back of a wildly bucking bronc. I knew we had to be getting close to the Steps, but I did not want to radio ahead to Paul like a scaredy-cat and ask, "Where are we? Are we getting close to the Steps, Where are?" He was out of sight several hundred yards in front of me, and I figured he would either warn me when we approached the Steps or have me tackle them without warning. I was hoping for the latter.

Some mushers call the Happy River descent Kamikaze Hill, but from the television programs I had watched it looked more like the Suicide Race at the Omak Stampede, where the Indian cowboys ride their horses off the top of a rimrock and down a nearly vertical face to the roundup grounds. I was thinking about how crazy they were when Paul's voice barked at me over the radio.

"Drop off. Drop off. Drop off. Hairpin left. Get ready!"

I barely had time to tromp down on the steel brake, jamming it into the snow with all my weight, before my dogs began to disappear, a pair at a time. And then it was my turn. The sled tipped on end, and we started down. I felt weightless. Free-falling. I rode the brake so I would not run over my dogs, muscling the sled to keep it heading straight down the hill and hoping for the best.

The deep ruts made by the other sleds actually helped because all I had to do was stay in the trench. And then the first drop was over. There was a short reprieve and then the second, followed in quick succession by the third. Ned stumbled, and I was forced to ride my brake to keep from running over him. A sled has very little maneuverability with the brake digging into the snow. My inside runner caught and my sled went into a violent, twisting somersault. One second I was vertical and moving forward and the next I was horizontal and stuck in deep powder snow. Miraculously I had managed to hold on to my sled. I lay faceup in the deep powder laughing because it was such an outrageous position for an Iditarod musher to find herself in. I had made it down Happy River Steps and fell at the bottom only because I had ridden the brake instead of popping it a time or two.

At least I thought this must be the Steps. Maybe this was not the Steps after all but merely another bad section of the trail. What if the Steps were still ahead? How bad were they?

"Congratulations," Paul's calm voice came over my radio. "You just passed the first test on the Iditarod. You successfully made it down Happy River Steps."

"Yes," I said as I jumped to my feet and dusted off the snow. I righted my sled, pushed the button on my radio, and told Paul, "Thank goodness, because if that wasn't the Steps I'd hate to see how much worse they could be."

After that wild ride, the trail resumed in a steady, deliberate rise, up a steep drainage, and into the Alaska Range. My team was in good spirits, still leaning into their harnesses and trotting at a steady pace. But I was feeling fatigued and a little dizzy from a combination of lack of sleep, dehydration, a lackluster diet, and probably a little bit of relief at having made it through my initial test.

As soon as we reached the checkpoint at Puntilla Lake, the dogs bedded down on straw from a previous musher. I hiked to a hole that had been cut through three feet of ice on Puntilla Lake and dipped water into my cooler to carry back to camp. After heating up food for the dogs, I tossed the Ziploc bag containing the tri-tip steak that Becki had prepared into the remaining hot water, waited until it was warm, and then opened the package and devoured the meat. Afterward I wanted to just lie with my dogs and feel wonderfully content, but there were too many chores to complete. In addition, members of the media were persistent, wanting to know how I had handled the Steps and what I thought about the race so far.

The checkpoint was behind a series of low hills that protected us from the heavy winds. Rainy Pass was a few miles up the trail. This was the checkpoint where Libby Riddles and the other mushers in the 1985 race had been forced to lay over and wait out a snowstorm that paralyzed the race for three days.

I checked Lisa, and her leg was swollen. The veterinarian examined her and gave me more of the white goop. I wrapped the wrist and hoped for a miracle, that the swelling would go down and Lisa would be able to continue.

Then more bad news. Jacques Philip, a friend who had also been staying with the Wood family in Willow, showed me his hand. It was swollen and at least one finger was broken. He said he had caught it between the handlebar and a tree. He was dropping out of the race. I felt terrible because Jacques had a top ten team and I hated to see him have to scratch.

The bad news just kept piling up. I noticed Dutchess and Karelan had picked up a bug and now had runny diarrhea. The veterinarian gave me medication and told me to try to get more fat into their systems. I had a bottle of liquid soybean oil, high in fat, that I mixed with both dogs' food and they ate it all. I thought they would be over the virus in a day or two.

As I was completing my chores, the crew from Outdoor Life Network asked if they could mount a camera on my sled. They promised to land their helicopter on top of Rainy Pass and retrieve the camera and battery pack before we started down the west side into Dalzell Gorge. I was not thrilled to have my dogs pack the extra weight, but it would be only a short distance. I thought it was important to cooperate for the sake of the sport of sled dog mushing because OLN was planning a series on the Iditarod, and I wanted to help them get the footage they needed. The camera was mounted on my brush-bow and was aimed backward, giving them a bird's-eye view of me.

I checked on Lisa one last time, and the swelling in her leg had not gone down. I would never want to run on a swollen leg like that. My decision was easy. I dropped her. In mushing circles it is said that races are won on the backs of the dogs you leave behind.

The last thing I did before we departed was to put on what I called my body armor. Actually it was motocross protective gear. There were two big plastic plates across my chest, a plate over my stomach, two hard shoulder pads, elbow and forearm guards, and a plastic plate across my back. It was bulky and stiff, hard to move in, but I thought it might protect me if I crashed passing through Dalzell Gorge. I felt like a turtle, but it was worth it if it might save my life.

RAINY PASS TO ROHN—48 MILES

The afternoon sun elongated the shadows as we left the valley and pulled the long grade toward Rainy Pass. The bluish-tinged mountain peaks closed in around us and we continued up, and up some more. At last we reached the top of the Rainy Pass. At 3,160 feet above sea level this barren landscape is the highest point on the Iditarod trail. The wind howled and sent veiled curlicues of snow off the tops of snowbanks like spindrifts off a wave. Chaotic weather can intimidate a team, but Dutchess and Brick knifed through the wind. I trusted their judgment. One thing I knew for sure: In these whiteout conditions the OLN helicopter was not going to be able to land at Rainy Pass. I would have to carry the camera and battery pack through Dalzell Gorge, and it would record my run, frame by frame. If I wrecked, or suffered a blond moment, it would all be captured on film.

As we started down the west side of the Alaska Range, the sun dropped below the horizon. I had insisted we run Dalzell Gorge in the dark. I was adamant about it because I thought I could see better at night; at least I was hoping I could stay close enough to Paul to follow his headlamp.

I pulled on my hockey helmet with the face guard, and we started the slow descent toward Dalzell Gorge. Each time the trail dropped a little faster I thought, "Oh, no, here we go," but every time we leveled off.

I had seen television footage of teams approaching Dalzell Gorge, and on the topside, brush sticks up out of the snow shortly before the trail begins to drop away. I saw the brush and turned on my headlamp, even though I did not need it quite yet. I knew that soon I would be too busy to turn it on.

"God, please help us pass safely through the next few miles," Paul's voice crackled over the radio.

"Amen," I said.

"Help me through this section. And please help Rachael."

"Amen," I said again.

"God, we are placing our lives in your hands. Please deliver us from all danger."

I had time to utter one last "Amen" and we were started down, dropping fast. From the footage I had seen, I recognized a rock wall on my left, another to the right. These rocky cliffs mark the true beginning of the gorge. I was no longer aware of the wind or anything but the trail in front of me, and the occasional glimpse I had of Paul's headlamp piercing the gloomy evening. The trail narrowed and angled downward. We crossed a sidehill where I had to ride the uphill runner and fight to keep the sled tracking straight instead of sliding down the hazardous incline.

Darkness covered us. All I cared about was the tunnel of light and my running dogs. Dutchess and Brick were perfect, taking the corners wide and leading the team between trees and boulders. I could feel my heart beat strong and my breathing coming faster.

"Sweeping turn, right. Pull hard or you're going to end up in the creek," barked Paul's voice.

I let off on the brake, but it was already too late. We swept into the turn and began sliding. My left runner hit something under the snow, and the sled flipped and launched into a twisting barrel roll. The sled skated out of control down the sharp embankment, and all I could do was hold on to the handlebar as we slid toward open water. It seemed as though I was on an unerring path—like a torpedo aimed at the hull of a doomed ship—and when I reached the creek my helmet hit the rocks with a sickening thud. Water splashed around me.

If I had not been wearing my helmet, my attempt at running the Iditarod might very well have ended in Dalzell Creek. It saved me. I immediately rolled to my feet, righted the sled, and told the dogs to move up. They pulled us back onto the trail, and I took a quick inventory. I was fine, except for a wet head and shoulders. The creek had been only a couple of inches deep. My only injury was my hand. It had smashed between the handlebar and a rock in the creek on my wild slide, the same type of injury that had broken Jacques's hand. I was lucky, and though my hand hurt like the dickens, no bones were broken.

After the accident I was even more focused, wanting to make sure I did not crash and burn again. I realized I could not always rely on my luck to pull me through. The trail wound through timber and rock outcroppings, and on the tightest corners I dragged the sled to the outside to avoid injuring a wheel dog or wedging the sled against a tree. It was tough going but at the same time it was exhilarating. I figured this was about as tough as the trail could dish out, and I was able to handle it.

Several times we crossed side creeks on ice bridges. The rushing water under the sled gurgled and hissed, and then we swept past the danger and were again swallowed up by the dark, silent night.

A nagging fear rode with me every mile of the gorge. I was aware that most encounters with moose and bison on the Iditarod trail occurred within the narrow confines of the gorge. I felt for my ax to make sure it was still there.

Dutchess and Brick were flawless leaders. When we popped out of the switchbacks and got back into the deep holes, they never missed a beat, until we hit a particularly deep wallow and something happened. One of the dogs stopped, and the gangline wrapped around Brick's hind leg. I stopped immediately, set the snow hook, got rid of my gloves, and went up the line to fix the problem. Maybe I was tired, or my reflexes were a tad slow, or bad luck finally caught up with me, but after I managed to pull slack in the gangline and free Brick, the dogs suddenly moved up and a loop off the gangline wrapped around three of my fingers. I jerked my hand free, except for the tip of my middle finger, and the line popped it off as if it had been sliced with a knife. Blood spurted and, oh my gosh, it hurt something fierce. I stuck the finger in the snow and that made it sting even worse. When the cold finally slowed the bleeding I wrapped up the wound with the athletic tape I kept in my pocket for just such an emergency.

Coincidentally, a couple of days before the start of the Iditarod, Martin Buser had cut off parts of three fingers on a table saw, but he was running the race, and staying with the leaders. As we traveled, my finger throbbing with pain, I wondered how he could possibly be handling it. I had respected him before, but now I respected him all the more for running the race with such a painful injury.

The trail settled down to something a little more manageable, and we ran hard and fast until the black night was suddenly blazing with a wild display of electric lights formed in an arch. It was as unexpected as coming off the Nevada desert and finding the Las Vegas strip. As we crossed under the brilliant arch someone hollered, "Welcome to Rohn."

We were directed to a spot where Paul and I could park side by side, joining a number of teams and mushers already settled in at the checkpoint. I checked my watch. We had crossed Rainy Pass and passed through Dalzell Gorge in a respectable six hours. I was tired but felt wonderful. Ahead were the Buffalo Tunnels, Farewell Burn, and plenty of other perils, but I was not even going to think about anything but my accomplishment of surviving the gnarly Dalzell Gorge.

The dogs were hungry, and as soon as they wolfed down their meal they curled up on their beds of straw and slept. I was concerned about Dutchess and Karelan. Their diarrhea had not improved, and I could tell they were not as healthy as at the start of the race. Although they drank as much as the other dogs they were becoming dehydrated. If the medication did not kick in, they would begin to lose weight and the physical strain of running would take them down even faster. I was concerned enough that I called the veterinarian's attention to it. He gave me more medication. After that I showed him my injured finger, and he cleaned the wound, swabbed it with alcohol, applied ointment, and re-taped it.

The crew from OLN came around and wanted a short interview. I flashed my light on their camera, which was no longer pointed at the handlebar, but was askew and loose. I said, "Sorry, boys, but your camera's toast."

I told them about my wreck into Dalzell Creek, and catching my finger in the gangline. They asked what I thought about Dalzell Gorge and I replied, "Without question, that was the craziest run of my life. To try to put it into words I would say it was steep, narrow, intimidating, downright scary, and totally exhilarating. We were moving fast. Right now it's all pretty much a blur."

After the interview I hiked up the hill to a one-room log cabin, where mushers could warm up, have a bite to eat, and dry out wet clothes. But there was not enough room for mushers to sleep there. A warm fire blazed in a squatty barrel stove. A rope clothesline angled back and forth over the stove and clothes were hung drying. I found a few open nails driven into the logs, so I stripped off my body armor and several layers of wet clothing and hung my things up to dry. I set my boot liners beside the other liners arranged on the floor near the stove.

At the other end of the room was a stove with a couple of pots of hot water, and beside the stove were a picnic table and a few chairs. I heated my bag of enchiladas with jalapeño and wolfed down the meal like one of my dogs. It warmed me from the inside out and I caught myself falling asleep at the table. I went outside into the cool night, unrolled my sleeping bag on the straw, and slept with my dogs. After three hours I returned to the cabin, retrieved my clothes, and discovered that many of the other mushers had already departed. My things were mostly dry, and it was heaven to put on warm, dry clothes. My feet especially appreciated the treat.

ROHN TO NIKOLAI—80 MILES

After an eight-hour layover in Rohn I put on my body armor and we departed, shortly after sunrise, for the long run to Nikolai. I had slipped to 72nd place, but all that mattered was to keep moving forward.

The trail out from Rohn sliced through a spruce forest and dropped down onto the ice of the South Fork of the Kuskokwim River, where my sled had a tendency to slide and it was hard to keep it on a steady course. My muscles ached, my hand hurt, and I was banged up from my battles the previous night in Dalzell Gorge. I was tired and wanted the going to be easier than it was. But it only got worse as we left the river and cut through the trees on a narrow trail where, it seemed, the sled bounced like a pinball from tree to tree. Banging against immovable objects and having tree branches slap at you is never much fun for the dogs or the musher. We fought our way through this section of the trail only to emerge onto an area known to Iditarod mushers as the Waterfall, a steep hillside covered with a sheet of ice. I had heard the stories of spills in this section, sleds overturning and mushers watching or axes and other equipment or of skittering across the ice to the drop-off below. We cautiously traversed this perilous section. I rode the uphill runner, staying low and keeping a steady tension on the edge of the runner so it bit into the ice like the blade of an ice skate. After inching our way across the Waterfall we began a slow descent from the mountains.

Even though my eyes did not allow me a clear view, I knew that from this high vantage a sighted person would be able to see the broad panorama of Alaska's wild interior with unending forests, tundra and frozen lakes, swamps, rivers, and creeks. Behind us were the jagged white mountains of the Alaska Range, rising straight up into a cloudless sky. I was thankful those mountains were behind us.

The trail ahead alternated between rolling hills, open meadows, and thick spruce forests. We ran fast, so the dogs would use up their rambunctious energy before we reached the Buffalo Tunnels. Over the course of several miles the complexion of the forest began to change as it became dominated by skinny alder trees and willows that were crowded together into deep, nearly impenetrable thickets. I pulled on my helmet with the face shield.

Through these thickets the bison—massive animals weighing over a thousand pounds and standing up to five feet tall—had cleared a narrow trail known in mushing circles as the Buffalo Tunnels. Above the five-foot mark the trail was overgrown with trees and branches leaning over the trail and creating a ceiling of sorts. I was glad I had on my armor plating and helmet because I was constantly being walloped by head-knockers and face-slappers. It reminded me of when I was a kid and had a ball tossed in my direction. I rarely saw the trees and branches coming, not until they were within a few feet of my face. Sometimes I could duck, or at least move my head so as not to absorb the entire blow, but sometimes I could not, and they would very nearly knock me off the sled. Paul could not begin to warn me of the many dangers; there were simply too many. I was on my own.

Not knowing how far ahead Paul might be, and fearing his passing might have riled a bison or a moose, I was constantly on guard against meeting an animal in the narrow confines of the trail. I do not know what I would have done if we had met a bison or a moose because there was barely room for the sled to pass and certainly not enough room for me to swing an ax, if it ever came to that.

I tried to calm myself, recalling stories I had been told about bison. I knew they had been relocated to the area back in 1965. They were curious animals, and even though there had been standoffs between mushers and bison, there had never been any serious problems caused by bison during the Iditarod. In fact, farther on, out on the Farewell Burn, mushers had reported waking from a nap to find a bison licking their face. I laughed at the thought of a kiss from a bison.

Moose were not going to be handing out kisses. They were mean and ornery. I did not want to encounter a moose, and fear continued to grip me as we pounded through deep wallows, slid around sharp turns, and were smacked by those infernal overhanging trees and branches. So many times was I hit, knocked off the runners, and dragged behind my overturned sled until I could right it, that I was afraid my entire body was going to be one massive black-and-blue bruise.

We plummeted off one particular hill, dipped into a wallow, hit a rock or something, and my snow hook, which I kept on the crossbar under my handlebar, jarred loose, fell, and set itself in the crotch of a windfall. Immediately my sled went from a hard charging fifteen miles per hour to absolute zero. I was thrown off the sled, flew through the air, and slammed into a tree, hitting my left side below my rib cage and above my hip bone, an area not protected by my body armor. The violent collision knocked the wind out of me. The pain was so intense I wanted to scream, but all I could do was gasp and groan. I was afraid I was seriously injured. I tried to think what organs were located in that area—kidney, liver, spleen. It hurt so badly I knew I must have ruptured something.

Finally I was able to draw a breath. I looked around. I was miles from any sort of aid. I would have to tough it out and ride my sled to Nikolai. I sure as heck was not about to go back to Rohn. I told myself to sit up. After I managed that I tried to stand, but was forced to take a knee for a moment before I fought through the pain and slowly rose to my feet. I did not pull back my clothing. Why look? I knew it was a mass of broken blood vessels. I could feel that.

What was I doing out here in the middle of nowhere? Why had I felt so compelled to run this darn race? I was crazy to have taken on such an enormous challenge. What had I been thinking? I never found a single answer. Tears spilled down my cheeks, not so much because of the pain in my side but because I felt so overwhelmed.

My dogs looked at me with quizzical expressions on their faces. I realized I had a race to run. Pain, I could deal with pain. I had to keep moving. I asked my dogs, "You guys okay? You ready to go?"

I pulled the snow hook from the crotch of the windfall. "Okay, let's go."

Once we were moving the pain in my side became less intense, more of an uncomfortable ache. It seemed like the Buffalo Tunnels would continue forever but gradually, after ten miles or so, the thickets became less of a tangled mass of confusion and slapping branches and began to thin and change back to a forest interspersed with open meadows.

The sun slid across the sky, warming the day, and the trail pitched up and down with climbs that lasted for half a mile or more. I was still wearing my body armor and when I got off the sled to run, to save the dogs from having to pull my weight on the hills, I felt like a turkey roasting inside an oven. But I continued to wear the armor because I had promised Dad I would until I reached Farewell Burn. Then I could get rid of it. And when I reached Nikolai I would mail it home, along with the cumbersome helmet.

We broke out on a hill overlooking a frozen lake and descended to run across the flat, mirrored surface of glare ice. I could look straight down through several feet of ice and see water. It was a deep blue. At least, I think it was blue. Paul was ahead, moving slowly, and we caught him where a small creek emptied onto the ice. We ran through several inches of overflow water, and I allowed the dogs to drink before we moved on.

"Getting close to the midway point," Paul remarked.

I did not reply, but for some reason Paul's remark irritated me. It seemed as if we had come so far from Rohn, and here he was telling me we were only halfway to Nikolai. I knew I was being irrational, but I did not care. My side hurt and my finger hurt and now I was beginning to get a headache that made it feel as though the top of my scalp was being peeled back.

Within a few miles Paul found the perfect camp, and I was thankful we were stopping. There were trees on either side so we had a clear view of the trail. There were teams behind us, and I wanted to see anyone who passed. There was plenty of deep snow so I set up my cooker, lit it, and started melting snow. I left the dogs' booties on them. Our plan was to rest for three or four hours and be on our way. I fed my team. Dutchess and Karelan nibbled at their food. Since Kitty had developed a serious case of diarrhea I gave her special attention. Athens was tired and close to giving up. I did everything I could to cheer her up, but she remained in a terrible funk.

I stripped off my body armor and a few layers of clothing and set them out to dry in the warm sun. My annoyance had passed, and Paul and I flopped down on top of our sleds and talked about everything we had accomplished—crossing the Alaska Range, passing through Dalzell Gorge, and surviving the Buffalo Tunnels. We had miles left to go and a lot of tough trail, but we had fought our way through the worst topography the Iditarod could throw at us. I had plenty of bumps and bruises, nicks and cuts, and sore muscles and ouches to prove it. But we had met the challenges and that ted my confidence, giving me the strength and determination to face the next forty-five miles to Nikolai. The Iditarod teaches each musher some valuable lessons. Right now I was getting a serious lesson in dedication, patience, and perseverance. And with such profound thoughts, as well as concern for my sick dogs running through my tired brain, I fell asleep.

By the time we got back on the trail the heat of the day had subsided. We traveled a few miles, came down a long hill, and reached a large camp with several wall tents, a number of parked snow machines, and a roaring fire. Several Alaskan Natives, their children, and a couple of Caucasian men greeted us. They announced we had reached "Buffalo Camp" and explained that every year they came out to hunt moose and to make a camp available to the mushers. It was evident from the piles of straw scattered around that a number of the mushers had availed themselves of the group's hospitality. We were offered hot soup, but explained to our hosts that we had eaten not long before and planned to continue on.

Two boys held out notebooks and one of them asked, "Rachael, would you please sign your name?" They knew Paul, too, and asked him what it was like to be a professional wrestler. We enjoyed visiting but after about ten minutes we cut the conversation short.

"Trail's flat all the way to Nikolai. You'll love it," one of the men called as we departed. I waved to them as we swept around a corner.

Just as the man promised, the trail was flat and easy, but it seemed as though someone was continually rolling out more and more trail. The view never changed as we crossed the treeless expanse of Farewell Burn. The wind had scoured away most of the snow, leaving dirt and rocks exposed that tore and ground at the thin plastic skins protecting the metal runners. Back in 1977 a fire had swept through this area burning off nearly four hundred thousand acres. In the early years of the Iditarod this was a nightmare for the racers who had to scramble over windfalls and bare ground, but in 1984 the Bureau of Land Management cleared a twenty-five-foot trail across the burn.

The trail and the sun were on a collision course until the sun mercifully set and the western horizon burned gold, orange, and red. I had never, not in my entire life, seen such an enormous sky, a sky so alive with color. Even though I still had a headache and my side and my lower back were aching, I found enough joy in the evening to sing to my dogs. They appreciated the diversion and picked up their pace.

As night descended the heavens opened and the stars in the Milky Way shone with such intensity I turned off my headlamp. From time to time I caught a faint flicker from Paul's headlamp, but he was way out in front and that was fine. I wanted to be alone in this big, fantastic night, mushing my dogs down the Iditarod trail. Those dreams from my childhood had finally become reality. But even in my dreams I had never imagined a night like this. The snow glistened under the stars, and the sky seemed to wrap itself around me in a tight embrace. If this moment were to last forever, I would be comfortable in the hereafter. I would never tire of a night so grand and glorious.

The first inkling that the night sky was about to change came as a tiny sparkle in the blue-blackness. This point of light expanded into a thin patina of radiance that shimmered. Soon the Northern Lights began to sweep back and forth like broad curtains. Lights winked on and off, stretched, swept, lingered, faded, and then returned with even more brilliance. The sky was alive.

It reminded me of when I was six years old and sitting in that huge leather chair in Dr. Weleber's office. I had seen a spectacle of light that day but it paled in comparison to what God had created for me this night. I believed He was putting on this amazing display strictly for my benefit, and I might have been the only person in the universe who saw it. Out there, on that treeless plain of snow and ice, I was alone with God and felt as close to Him as I have ever felt.

Eventually the magnificent light show ended, and we ran on into the night. The distance we traveled was so great without seeming to get anywhere that I became discouraged. I was dehydrated and began to act like my dogs, taking snow from snowbanks as we passed and eating it. My lower back ached, my stomach cramped, and my headache lingered. At first I thought these symptoms might be related to the pain in my side—internal injuries—but I came to realize what was happening was every woman's nightmare. I was starting my period out in the wilds of Alaska, and as we neared Nikolai, the pain in my back and the cramping became so severe I was sometimes forced to ride the runners on my knees.

All the lights in Nikolai blazed as we pulled the long hill toward town. It was the first real settlement we had come to since leaving Willow four days before. Even though it was after midnight a delegation met us shouting, "Welcome to Nikolai." How great it was to be in Nikolai because after one more checkpoint, in McGrath, we would reach Takotna and my twenty-four-hour layover, and I could take a hot shower and get a good night's sleep. It was only forty-eight miles from Nikolai to McGrath and another twenty three more to Takotna. I could do that.

Volunteers directed us to a parking spot in front of the school. As I fed the dogs the veterinarians looked at them. Dutchess, Karelan, and Kitty still suffered from diarrhea and a couple of others had sore wrists, which I massaged and treated with Algyval before wrapping them so they would not swell. I administered a round of anti-diarrhea medication and that was all I could do.

After crossing the exposed rocks and dirt of Farewell Burn I knew I needed to replace the plastic skins on the runners of my sled, but I was feeling sick and dizzy and could hardly keep my eyes open. I decided to put it off until the morning. I promised myself I would get up an hour early. I went inside and used a microwave to heat my dinner.

Perry Solmonson, a fellow musher, came up while I was eating and introduced himself. "The past couple of days you've come through on a trail as tough as I've ever seen. I'm absolutely impressed with what you've done. A lot of people thought you could never do this. You've proven them wrong. I was one of them. You've definitely earned my respect."

It took a lot of courage for him to come over and tell me that. I thanked him but really could not say much else because I was so tired I was out of it. As soon as I finished eating I hung a few clothes to dry, collapsed on a pad in the gym, and slept four solid hours. When I awoke I felt worse than when I lay down. I went to the bathroom and finally checked my side, where I found an angry discolored bruise bigger than my fist. I felt woozy, sick to my stomach, and I hurt all over. I was a physical wreck, and my mental state was not a whole lot better.

My first chore was to change the plastic skins. I had to cut them with my knife and peel the old skins off before I could put new skins on. And then, when I got my body armor, helmet, and other things together to mail home, I could not find the post office. Finally, one of the locals offered to take my bag and promised to mail it for me. I thanked him profusely. All that took precious time.

While I was getting my dogs ready a woman photographer insisted on helping me. She told me what to do, and if I did not respond immediately she jumped in and tried to do it for me.

"Thank you, but I have everything under control," I said, trying to be gentle with my words and tone of voice.

Generally when I stop I unsnap the tuglines but not the necklines, so the dogs have a little freedom to move around and sleep comfortably. This woman tried to fasten the tuglines for me. I had to be firm with her. "According to the rules I cannot accept any outside assistance." Even that did not get through and finally I had to be rude. "Stop. You can't help me. You can't coach me." This propelled her to launch into a long diatribe about free speech and her rights under the Constitution to say, and do, whatever she pleased. I did not have time for any of it. I just ignored her and went about my work.

NIKOLAI TO McGRATH—48 MILES

The morning sun was turning the trail into the consistency of mush as we departed Nikolai. A local called, "Easy going from here. Flat and fast all the way to McGrath."

The trail dropped onto the Kuskokwim River. Wherever the river made a big looping bend, the trail made shortcut portages through willow swamps and over small hills. My dogs began to wilt in the heat. I listened to Emmy Rossum sing *The Phantom of the Opera* on my CD player, and I sang along with her. I love every song on the album, but my favorite is "The Point of No Return." This revived some of my dogs, but Athens and Kitty were too tired to do much of anything except trot along with slack tuglines.

The OLN helicopter followed me, hovering in the blue sky, the popping noise of its spinning rotors washing out and spreading over the land. When it finally went away quietness rushed back in. I thought about home and what I was missing on the High Desert in March—the trill of the red-winged blackbird, the lilting melody of meadowlarks, the cooing of mourning doves, the chatter of Canada geese, and the whistle of swans as they headed north. Back home the sage was in bloom, the grasses were greening, and yellow buttercups and little pink flowers were adding color to the outcroppings of black lava rock. I compared my memory to the stark, quiet solitude of the Far North.

Paul interrupted my daydreams, his voice bellowing over the radio, "Moose on the trail, hold up!"

I stepped on the brake and set the snow hook. After a tense five minutes Paul radioed that the coast was clear and to move forward.

As we hit the plowed road leading to McGrath, something big and dark lay in the road. As we approached I realized it was a dead moose—most likely hit by a vehicle—and I called to my dogs, "On by." They passed without a sidelong glance. But I was awestruck by the sheer size of the critter, and it reignited my fear of meeting a moose on the trail.

McGrath was a small village with houses scattered over a hillside above the Kuskokwim River. I was running right behind Paul. A car drove alongside us. The driver rolled down her window and shouted, "You went the wrong way. You'll have to turn around. Follow me." The driver led us to the checkpoint and we parked our teams.

McGrath has an airfield and is easily accessible to the outside. As I went about my chores a large number of people from the media descended on me and proceeded to shoot video and snap photographs and fire questions. How was I doing? Had I encountered any surprises on the trail? Had I seen a moose? How was my team holding up? Had I had any problems?

Dad had sent my finishing sled to McGrath. It was lighter and more maneuverable than the sled Dave Sims had built for me. My friend and fellow musher Melanie Shirilla, who was taking her twenty-four-hour mandatory layover in McGrath, hiked up with me to retrieve it. It was a wooden basket sled made by Jack Backstrum and weighed a mere twenty-seven pounds. I pushed it to where I was camped and stripped my sled bag from my old sled. But when I tried to put it on the new sled it did not fit. I kicked myself for not checking that little detail before we left home. And then I could not find my Leatherman tool. Adding to my woes was the fact that the bungee cord intended to hold up the brake was broken. Dad had just used that sled in the ceremonial start a few days before and it was fine, but now it was broken.

"No problem," said Mel. "They have a hardware store up the street. We'll just walk up there and you can get what you need."

It turned out to be a mile hike. I bought two bungee cords and a new Leatherman. I soon discovered the bungee cords were too small. I was running out of time and ended up tossing everything back in my old sled rather than risking a lighter sled with a brake that did not function properly.

The veterinarian expressed her concern about the virus sweeping through my team. She said I needed to keep a close watch on Dutchess and Karelan, but since they still had good appetites she thought they might get over the sickness in a day or two. The condition of Athens and Kitty was more critical. Kitty was dehydrated, losing weight, and weak. Athens did not have the strength or attitude to continue. She was tired and had given up. I dropped both dogs. Before they were led away I gave Athens and Kitty a love, thanked them for their hard work, and told them I would miss them. I was down to thirteen dogs. Paul had dropped a dog at each of the four last checkpoints and had twelve dogs. But we still had plenty of dog power.

We planned to be in McGrath for three hours, but as I was getting my team ready for the short run to Takotna a film crew from ABC News approached and said that Peter Jennings was naming me Person of the Week on national television. They asked for five minutes of my time to ask a few questions and shoot video footage of me with my team. Of course I agreed. An honor like that does not happen every day.

To the question "Is it especially difficult for you trying to navigate the trail when you are blind?" I smiled and answered, "There are times when I'm out there and I think, 'Man, I wish I could see what's going on around here.' But I don't know anything different, and this is what I have, so I'm going to use it."

The question "Do you consider what you do to be courageous?" caught me off guard, and I said, "I'm really not that brave. I'm actually kind of a chicken, but this is something that I've grown up doing."

"What other senses do you use to make up for your lack of vision?"

"The main sense that I use, besides my vision, would be just the feel of things. If we suddenly speed up, I've got a pretty good idea that we're going downhill. If there is a certain tension in the sled, I know that someone's not doing his job."

And then I made a trivial mistake, not anywhere nearly as bad as Forrest Gump pulling down his pants to show President Lyndon Johnson the scar on his buttocks from being shot in Vietnam. I only showed the bruise on my side and said, "I had a nice little encounter with a tree. The tree won."

The filming took way more than five minutes and ended only when the fading light called it to a halt. I was thankful when it was over because I was a little disoriented and definitely not myself. But as for showing my bruise on national television, maybe that was not a mistake at all. I would have done that even if I had all my faculties. It was a totally awesome bruise.

MCGRATH TO TAKOTNA—18 MILES

Takotna, for a number of reasons, was my first choice as the location to take my mandatory twenty-four-hour layover. Foremost was the fact that the press stayed in McGrath because there were no accommodations for them in Takotna. I could do my chores, relax, and sleep without constantly being interrupted. Also, this was the last checkpoint for several hundred miles where I could rest inside a warm building and dry my gear. But more than anything, the reason I chose it was because Takotna had a shower.

On the short run from McGrath to Takotna, that shower was the only thing I thought about. It was an obsession. The luxury of hot water running over my bare skin and to actually be able to wash with soap—heavenly.

Reaching Takotna reminded me of that Motel 6 tagline: "We'll leave the light on for you." It appeared everyone in Takotna had left lights on for us. The town was ablaze, and the citizens—probably fifty people—greeted us as we arrived at the stroke of midnight. A number of other dog teams were already parked, but we were diverted away so as not to disturb them. In turn they would not disturb us when they departed.

Takotna was strangely quiet considering one hundred to one hundred and fifty out-of-town dogs had taken up residence there. Mushers train their dogs to have respect for silence and to bark only at feeding time, hitching-up time, and for alarms, such as a loose puppy, a wild animal, or an unfamiliar human visitor. Nothing is more irritating than a dog that barks just to bark. There were no offending hounds in Takotna.

I fed the dogs a warm meal, and as soon as they had eaten they arranged their beds in the straw and settled themselves. I pulled their booties and rubbed their sore muscles. They licked their feet dry, nibbling on small ice that had formed around their guard hairs, and licked their paws clean. After tucking in my team I gathered my damp gear, which was pretty much everything I owned, and made my way to headquarters.

As I stepped through the doorway, the warm air and the tantalizing smell of food hit my senses like a sweeper tree, nearly knocking me to the floor. I felt dazed, and my face flushed as I made my way across the room.

The cook stepped to the counter and said, "Sweetheart, as long as I've got it I'll fix you anything your heart desires."

My head was full of mush. I could not think. And even if I could think of something I am not sure I could have verbalized my desire.

"How about steak and eggs?"

"Sure," I stammered.

"How do you like your eggs?"

"Over easy," I said, but I thought *scrambled*—that was how my brain was feeling, all scrambled.

The cook set the plate of food in front of me, and I was aware of the delicious aroma wafting up to tempt my taste buds. I was hungry. I wanted to eat. I even took a couple of bites and then the warm air and the heavy narcotic pull of sleep got the best of me. With fork in hand, my head hunched over my plate, I fell asleep.

I jerked awake and was glad I had saved myself the embarrassment of performing a face plant onto my plate. I mumbled something complimentary about the food, but it came out garbled and nonsensical.

A volunteer led me across the road to an old log church. It was warm inside but not too warm. I shrugged out of several layers of clothes, sat on the floor, and peeled off my boots. I draped my gear over chairs so it would dry, found a pew in a corner of the room, laid out my sleeping bag, and promptly fell asleep.

At six in the morning I suddenly sat upright thinking I had to get ready to leave. Then it hit me—this was the layover and I could sleep in. I fell back onto the pew and slept three more hours. I awoke clearheaded, hungry, and ready to get on with the day. I went out to check my dogs.

It had been dark when we arrived, and now the sun was up. I had not thought to grab my sunglasses and I stumbled around. Nothing looked familiar. I could not find my team. Finally I had to approach one of the volunteers.

"Could you tell me where my team is?"

"So you've lost your team?" The volunteer chuckled.

"Not so much lost them," I countered, "just momentarily misplaced them."

We had a good laugh about that. My dogs were happy to see me, and I gave them plenty of affection. I noticed several more dogs had slight cases of diarrhea. Possum, Bernard, and Ned had joined Dutchess and Karelan. It seemed that my team was skinnier than I remembered. I put jackets on every dog, so they would not have to burn extra calories staying warm. After soaking the dogs' food— lamb, chicken, and Atta Boy—in fat and dispensing the diarrhea medication, I hiked to the headquarters building to grab a bite to eat and finally to take that shower I had been anticipating for so long.

I ate a piece of apple pie and then grabbed a towel and headed to the building that was a combination laundry room and shower. As I was putting a few of my clothes in a dryer a man came out of the shower addition and advised me to take the first shower. There were two. He said the first was cleaner and the meter gave more time for a quarter than the second shower.

I took off my boots. The floor was heated, and I wiggled my toes. Then I skinnied-down, put in a handful of quarters, and stood with the hot water pounding against my skin. I scrubbed myself and washed my hair as best I could. Becki had braided my hair into a French braid before the start of the race, and I did not want to take it out and deal with putting it up again. I rubbed a little shampoo on the top of my head and on the end of the braid, and even that little bit made me feel clean and refreshed.

I looked at my hands, arms, legs, and the bruise on my side that was now turning a sickly yellow around the edges of the dark purple. I had nicks and cuts and abrasions from dogs and ropes and collisions with the ground, ice, rocks, and trees. My severed fingertip was scabbing over. Every mark was an account of some serious, interesting, or humorous incident. Added together they told the story of my rookie run at the Iditarod. I laughed because judging from the amount of damage on my body I had quite a story to tell.

After that, until my time ran out, I stood under the showerhead and was perfectly content to allow the hot water to flow over me. I think a lot of Americans take the comforts they have for granted. But at home we live off the power grid. I am one girl who appreciates the little things in life—a warm room, electricity, and a hot shower. In Takotna I spoiled myself, luxuriating under that wonderful cascade of hot water until I ran out of quarters and time.

With my body scrubbed, and my hair somewhat shampooed, I realized I was ravenously hungry. This time I was able to eat half a stack of pancakes. Dallas Seavey was there and he filled me in on all the news. Robert Sorlie was leading and Mitch was running with him. Tyrell was only a few spots behind.

"By the way, congratulations," said Dallas. "You made it farther than Rick Swenson."

"What happened to Swenson?"

"He scratched in McGrath."

Dallas went through the names of others who had scratched, nine in all. Besides Swenson the list included Gary McKellar, Sonny Lindner, Jacques Philip, Judy Merritt, and G. B. Jones. I was in 71st place and had a good chance to pick off a few teams over the next few checkpoints and move up in the standings.

I felt bad for Rick Swenson and all the mushers who had been forced to scratch from the race, and yet the news buoyed my self-confidence because I was still going strong. I had a few sick dogs, but I was sure they would snap out of it and be fine. I was going to finish this race. I was going to be one of the elite few who earn the right to stand under the arch in Nome with their team of dogs strung out in front of them.

As Dallas and I visited I recognized a head of short blond hair as it came bebopping past me. I squinted and tried to bring the person into focus. I called out, "Becki, is that you?"

"It's me," she said and rushed over and gave me a hug.

"What are you doing here? How did you get here?"

"I wanted to see you. I caught a flight to McGrath, then jumped in a bush plane, and here I am."

It was so fantastic to see Becki. She brought along a note from Dad saying he was proud of me and loved me. There was also a note from Libby Riddles. She told me, "Way to go, girl." Becki had a handful of newspaper articles about the race. The one that caught my attention had a photograph of Tyrell and a lengthy article in which he was quoted as saying how impressed he was with my success navigating Dalzell Gorge. He stated, "I spent five hours manhandling a sled with all the strength I had. There were places where I just thanked my lucky stars I lived." He also said I could get dragged behind my sled, but it wasn't going to hurt me any more than it would any other musher. He thought the remainder of the race should be easier for me. That was good to hear.

Dallas completed his twenty-four-hour layover and rejoined the race. I checked my team. They were about the same. At least the virus had not struck any more dogs and the ones that were sick were eating and resting. I returned to my comfortable pew in the church and napped a few more hours.

TAKOTNA TO OPHIR—38 MILES

I said good-bye to Becki and at two o'clock in the morning Paul and I departed from the comparative luxury of Takotna. The trail began a steady climb. I was feeling well-rested and in good spirits. But my team did not seem to have the same enthusiasm, so I tried to set a good example by getting off and running the long uphill.

At daybreak we reached the summit, where we met Paul, waiting and resting his dogs. He told me from this high vantage point he could see over the Kuskokwim River valley to Farewell Burn and all the way back to the Alaska Range. He could even see the low dip where we had crossed at Rainy Pass. At that moment I wished I could see what he saw.

We broke over the top and started down the far side. I began to grasp the incredible distance we had yet to travel, more than seven hundred miles. But I tried not to allow myself to think in those terms. John Patten had coached me to visualize a race from checkpoint to checkpoint. He said small bites were a lot easier to swallow than trying to gulp the whole distance at once.

The next checkpoint was Ophir and after that was Iditarod, the settlement that had given the race its name. This was gold-mining country. I had seen photographs of the miners from the early days making their way into the diggings. Some harnessed themselves to sleds and pulled their gear to the mines. Others came on snowshoes, packing their supplies on their backs. These miners must have either been tough beyond belief or, as Robert Service had written in his poems about the North, "clean mad for the muck called gold."

I tried to overlook sore muscles and the tenderness on my side, now a palate of black and blue, yellow and green. Every time I swiveled my hips, which was pretty much any time I moved on the runners, I felt the pain. But I was almost used to it. We had reached a compromise, the pain and me. If it did not give me a jolt all at once, I would not cry out or wince. Pain was a dull ache that rode with me like an unwelcome hitchhiker.

I wanted this new day to be full of promise, but watching my dogs I saw they were not nearly as strong as they had been. The stomach virus was robbing them of their strength, and they were losing weight. Back in Takotna I almost dropped Karelan because he had become so skinny. But he still had his appetite and I thought he might recover and finish the race.

My team was definitely not at their best. They ambled along, and I snacked them often. The slow pace was discouraging, and the first tiny doubts—like bubbles rising in simmering liquid—began to materialize, and I began to wonder if my team had the physical strength to push on to Nome.

OPHIR TO IDITAROD—90 MILES

Ophir had been the center of a placer mining region, but only a handful of miners remained to actively work the old claims. Other than a few buildings, very little was left to indicate this village had ever been of any significance. We stayed at Ophir for only three hours and then set out on one of the longest—and loneliest—runs of the entire race. The sun was up and already the temperature was above freezing.

A few miles west of Ophir the Iditarod Trail separates into the northern and southern routes. On odd years the route takes the southern loop and on even years the mushers swing north. This is done to accommodate the villages along the Yukon who asked to be included on the Iditarod Trail. We swung south and began the long run to Iditarod in the heat of the day, slicing through a forest of spruce and birch. Snow machines and other mushers had beaten the trail into a deep quagmire that made for slow going. After ten miles the country opened onto a broad tundra plain and the wind picked up and blew in our faces.

A competitive musher will run his dogs in a rhythm of six to eight hours and rest six to eight hours. After the long layover at Takotna we thought the dogs would be rested and rejuvenated, but the combination of a bad trail, warm temperatures, and diarrhea had robbed them of strength. To compound matters wet snow began sticking to the runners and the burden became even heavier for the dogs to pull. Traveling slow, like we were, takes all the fun out of a race, and monotony and boredom began to pull me down. I could feel my energy seeping away, replaced by discouragement and depression. Dogs can totally read a human. If I ever allowed my rising frustration to become obvious to the dogs, they would pick up on it in a heartbeat. Anyone who has ever had a dog for a pet knows how it reacts to an owner's bad mood or a harsh word.

"You're a great bunch of dogs," I lied. "You're running so well," I lied some more. "Keep going. Good boy, Jovi. Way to go, Mandy. Angel, you look fabulous."

My dogs run to please me and because it is fun for them. They are bred to run, but when running becomes a struggle they lose interest in a hurry. To motivate them I stopped often, gave them loves, and tried to pump a little enthusiasm back into their tired bodies. I let them know that, much like a long-distance runner on the track, they could push through this pain, and once they had their second wind everything would be better. I was animated and expressive in my gestures and with my words. I switched leaders often so unnecessary stress was not put on any one or two dogs. We were a team, and as a team we would get through this trying stretch of trail together. I handed out salmon treats, hot dogs, and beef fat.

Tyrell had warned me about the long run from Ophir to Iditarod. He said it could prove an unpleasant experience for my dogs. However, once they made it through that stretch, they would gain confidence and begin to believe in themselves. He had said a few doubts might even creep into my thinking, and I might have concerns about whether my team was strong enough, physically and mentally, to reach the finish line.

We were hoping to reach a cabin that is used by travelers on the Iditarod trail called Don's Cabin, but due to the heat we were forced to take a long break. We rested five hours, then the sun went down, cooler air moved in, and we were able to get back on the trail. After Don's Cabin the miles slowly passed under the runners, and I told myself that even though we were moving slowly, at least we were moving.

In the darkness Paul called back, "Ice Bridge! Open water ahead!"

Paul was having trouble coaxing his dogs over the ice bridge that extended only partway over a stream, leaving a gap of several feet. After a moment's hesitation his lead dogs leaped the opening, and the other dogs had no choice but to follow, pulling the sled, and Paul, across to the far side. And then it was my turn.

Something told me to switch leaders and put Eyes up front. She was not afraid of open water. But we had spent so much time on the trail I decided the leaders I had could handle it. But Jovi, one of my leaders, was afraid of open water and refused to jump across the span. I ventured out onto the ice bridge and picked up Jovi to toss him across. The ice bridge began to sink beneath me.

"Toss me a line," called Paul.

I sloshed my way back to my sled, pulled out a line, tied off to Jovi's neckline, and tossed Paul the other end. Again I returned to my sled, stepped on the runners, pulled the snow hook, and went for it. With Paul pulling on the line the dogs made it to the opposite side. When the sled reached the ice bridge it collapsed, my feet came off the runners, and I was dunked in the icy water. The only part of me that did not get drenched was the top of my head.

If this had been a typical winter, with temperatures twenty or thirty degrees below zero, this could have been a critical situation and we would have had to stop to build a fire so I could warm up and dry out. But again, if this had been a typical winter the ice bridge would have held.

I shrugged off several layers of clothes and stripped the liners from my boots, dumping out the water and putting in new liners that were soaked within a few minutes. Then we kept moving. I was a little concerned about hypothermia, but I was never cold, thanks to that warm wind and polypropylene, Polarfleece, and Gore-Tex that wicked away most of the moisture from my body. The wind dried me from the outside in, but my feet remained wet and uncomfortable and made squishing sounds every time I shifted my weight.

The steady rhythm of the dogs' feet padding along the trail hypnotized me. Or it might have been the chill of being dunked in the icy stream. Or the fatigue factor might have been setting in. At any rate that night I became very, very sleepy. I began to drift off for a moment or two with my eyes wide open, and sometimes with my eyes closed. I would awaken, and my body would be draped over the handlebar.

The moon played peekaboo behind the clouds. Even in the darkness, with just the tunnel of light from the headlamp, I could sense the open country becoming more confining, with willows and brush crowding both sides of the trail. And then I began to hallucinate. I saw people standing beside the trail, never anyone I recognized. They talked and laughed among themselves like they were waiting for my arrival at a nonexistent checkpoint. I turned and as the light of my headlamp swept over them they stopped talking and turned their heads to stare at me as we passed. Sometimes they were back from the trail and I only heard voices, catching snippets of conversations, never any intelligible words, but I assumed they were talking about me, or my team.

Even though my rational mind told me these people did not exist, it was strange and perplexing and incredibly spooky to deal with. I tried to drink some water and managed to choke down a Reese's peanut butter cup and a handful of trail mix. I had difficulty swallowing.

We came to a series of small hills. To set a good example for my dogs I ran every upgrade. On the downhills I rode the runners. Dawn was beginning to color the eastern sky and all I wanted was sleep. Eventually I got my wish and when I awoke, slumped over the back of the sled, I saw my dogs curled up in the snow. I had no concept of how much time had passed. Paul came back to see where I was and we decided, since my dogs were already settled in and not inclined to move, that we would rest. I shared some Gummi Bears with Paul and we both grabbed short naps.

When we pushed on we discovered the settlement of Iditarod was only a couple of miles from where we had camped. The town of Iditarod, all I saw, consisted of two old cabins, a new mushers' cabin, and an outhouse. Inside the mushers' cabin was a diesel stove, cranked up and hot. The warm air hit me like a punch in the stomach. A screen was suspended above the stove where mushers had laid gear to dry. I got out of my clothes, pulled on a pair of dry long underwear, and hung everything that was damp by the stove to dry.

Mushers, volunteers, and race officials were milling around and talking. All the commotion made my head spin. The heat made me drowsy. Everyone was so nice and asked questions about my experiences. I tried to formulate answers, but my mind was numb, as though it were still out somewhere on the trail and had not quite caught up with the rest of me. After feeding my dogs a hot meal and tending to personal matters, I climbed up into the loft in the cabin and slept six straight hours.

When we were ready to leave I dropped Karelan. He had not been contributing to the team. Mostly he just goofed off and ran with a slack tugline, letting the other dogs do the work. He had become a liability.

We had reached the halfway point in the race. I remembered someone telling me if I made it past the first three days on the Iditarod the going would get easier because the dogs and I would become hardened to the trail. Others said that at the halfway point the trail became easier mentally because you knew you had the toughest half under your belt and that in another six days or so it would all be over. I was not so sure.

IDITAROD TO SHAGELUK—65 MILES

We followed the Iditarod River for a few miles and then entered a succession of rolling hills that lay like random furrows. The trail followed a maddening course up and over these hills. Logically it would seem the best route was between ridges, but most often we had to summit the tall hills and drop down the far side. The wind blew constantly in our faces, and the trail was lousy. The crust had been broken apart by snow machines spinning their tracks going uphill, and on the downhills mushers had ridden their brakes and dug deep gullies.

On the uphills I ran or pumped. It was something like trying to run in a bowl of sugar. At the brow of the hills I was able to catch my breath for a minute or two, riding the brake to keep from running over my dogs. I was working hard, taking frequent sips of water, and scrounging in my pockets for some tidbit to snack on. I ate Gummi Bears, candy, and jerky.

Just when it seemed the hills would continue forever, the trail mercifully began a long, slow descent into a valley cut by the Innoko and Yukon Rivers. When we reached the river ice I heard the distant barking of dogs, and in a few more miles caught the whiff of wood smoke. Both were sure signs we were nearing civilization, or at least the village of Shageluk.

We pulled into the checkpoint at Shageluk, and I frantically searched for my bootie bag, which also included the coats for my dogs. It was not tied on the sled in its usual place. I had lost it on the trail somewhere. I tried to remember when I had seen it last and concluded it had to have been where we dropped out of the hills toward the valley floor.

"I'll run back and check the trail," offered one of the volunteers. "Don't worry. I'll find it." He jumped on his snow machine and departed up the trail with a rooster tail of snow blowing up behind him and the loud whine of his powerful engine.

But I was worried. If I did not have that bag, then my dogs would not have booties to protect their feet. They had to have booties. And we needed the jackets, too, because if the temperature dropped—and it was almost certain to drop as we approached the Yukon River—my dogs would be cold and would burn precious calories staying warm. They needed to save every caloric for the race. I was sick with worry and I blamed myself. I was the one who had lost the bag. I was a terrible person. I should have been more alert. Dang it.

After feeding my dogs I made my way to where we were supposed to sleep. It was a round building, and for some peculiar reason the roundness bothered me so I hiked to the headquarters building and lay on the floor. I still could not sleep because I was too stressed out about losing the bootie bag. A Native woman said she was fixing moose stew and cooking salmon and would let me know when it was ready to eat.

I must have dozed because several kids shook me awake, "Rachael, wake up. Wake up. Dinner is ready, Rachael."

I was so tired I just wanted to lie on the floor and sleep, but I knew the woman had worked hard to fix this special meal so I forced myself to get up and eat. The food was delicious. Afterward I was able to make a call to Mom and then I tried to sleep, but instead of sleeping I started crying because my dogs were sick and skinny and I had lost the bootie bag. I was an emotional baby. I could not seem to snap myself out of it and cried myself to sleep.

"Rachael, I've got your bootie bag," said the man who had ridden up the trail on the snow machine and who now appeared before me. "Sandy McKee found it and picked it up. She gave it to me. Here it is."

I was so grateful that I jumped up, thanked him profusely, and gave him a kiss on the cheek. I lay back down and it was as though a thousand-pound weight had been lifted from me. My muscles went slack and I had the most relaxing sleep of my life. It was only a half hour, but it was all I needed.

SHAGELUK TO ANVIK—25 MILES

I went down the line giving each dog a few words of encouragement. Getting on the runners I pulled the hook and we were on our way. The dogs looked gaunt, but they leaned into their harnesses, and we left Shageluk and its population of slightly more than one hundred people. We dropped off a steep bank to the frozen Innoko River and made a hard turn north toward the Yukon River and one-hundred and fifty miles of what was most likely going to be a difficult part of the trail. On this section it is not uncommon to have sustained winds of sixty miles per hour and temperatures that drop to sixty below zero. On the other hand, if the warm weather held, we were likely to encounter overflow—water on top of the river ice,—and the dogs might refuse to go any farther. Either way, the trail down the Yukon River was sure to be a challenge.

For a few miles the dogs responded to their rest in Shageluk and then they eased off and began to shuffle along. My high spirits quickly dissipated and again I began to have doubts about finishing the race.

We turned off the Innoko River toward the Yukon River and traveled along a narrow, windy trail through swamps and thickets of willows and black spruce. Branches hung across the trail. I was repeatedly slapped across the face. Even though I was desperately tired, the trail was way too gnarly to even think about sleep.

Then, once again, it happened. I began hallucinating. This time it was not something as benign as people standing beside the trail. I saw animals—a rock pile became a bison, a stump became a moose.

Each time I grabbed for my ax and as I pulled it free we slipped past the imagined bison, or moose, and none of them ever moved. When we dropped onto the ice of the Yukon River the hallucinations went away.

ANVIK TO GRAYLING—18 MILES

Anvik was a friendly settlement and after signing in at the checkpoint, and caring for my dogs, I gulped a cup of coffee and ate reindeer sausage with the locals, a first for me. I found reindeer sausage to be sweet and spicy at the same time. I was in 67th place. We were still in this race, and after only twenty minutes we bailed out of Anvik.

The trail over the Yukon River ice was solid and stable. I had to change my frame of mind. Gone was the excitement of running the narrow, winding trails through the woods, pulling the hills, and the exhilaration of downhill runs. Traveling on the Yukon was monotonous. There were long stretches when nothing seemed to change. I knew that for a team of sick dogs this might prove to be our undoing. It would be up to me to keep the dogs from getting bored and discouraged. Even though the scenery did not change I tried to liven things up. I sang, handed out hot dogs, and told my dogs how wonderful they were and that they were looking great. I encouraged them to keep up their hard work.

Pia, a rock solid dog that made the other dogs around her work just as hard as she did, was not her typical self. Normally, if the dog running next to her did not pull his weight, Pia yapped and even nipped at the slacker to coax a little more effort. She was my coach on the team. But her shoulders were sore. She had diarrhea. She ran with her head down, aware only of her own misery.

And I was worried about Dugan. He was the skinniest dog on my team. If a sudden cold snap hit, he did not have the reserves to stay warm and keep running. I would have to carry him to the next checkpoint.

I have never—I will never—run a dog that is injured or has lost the heart to run. I was considering dropping both Pia and Dugan.

We came off the river and climbed up the hill to Front Street and the village of Grayling. The gray sky opened and rain began falling. The village dogs howled and carried on as if we were the first outside team they had ever seen. We passed trees and log homes and then we arrived at the checkpoint.

Trying to ignore the rain I laid out fresh straw for the dogs and got as much fat down them as I could, then I went inside. I laid out some of my clothes to dry, ate pancakes, and grabbed an hour of sleep.

Sandy McKee, who was the only racer behind me, came in. She told me she could not continue and was scratching. That meant I was in sole possession of last place. When I went outside, the temperature had dropped several degrees, the rain had switched to wet snow, and the wind had picked up. I dropped Pia and Dugan, which meant I was down to ten dogs.

GRAYLING TO EAGLE ISLAND—60 MILES

Ten solid dogs would be sufficient to finish the race. But I had ten sick dogs. And as we departed Grayling that night and returned to the Yukon River ice, I watched my dogs in the light from my headlamp, searching for the telltale signs that my dogs had had enough and wanted to call it quits. Some dogs will give their feelings away by the way they hang their heads, or their gait, or the way they drop their tails, or even something as subtle as how they hold their ears. If a dog's ears flop down, it means they are unhappy and disheartened. Every dog is different. With a little encouragement some will respond, dig down, and find a hidden reserve; others will not. The ultimate job of every musher is to read the dogs and calculate exactly what they are capable of achieving.

The Yukon drains a huge area, all the interior of Alaska from the Brooks Range to the Alaska Range. Cold air, moving like water, courses along over the ice and the wind mimics the cold. A cold wind greeted us, blowing straight into our faces. I knew this was going to make it more difficult and was glad I had put coats on all the dogs.

Before we departed Grayling, Paul gave me one of his ski poles, and I used it to push off as we traveled. I worked the ski pole and helped the dogs, but several times fatigue overtook me and I caught myself napping. I would awaken but even in my sleep I continued to push with the pole. And then one time I awoke to find that the ski pole was gone. I had dropped it. There was no one behind me who could pick it up. I was the last musher in the race. If I managed to hold on, and finish the race, I would win the red lantern, the award given to the last team to reach Nome.

We ran through the long night. I pumped with one leg for a while and then the other, not only to help the dogs but also to help me stay awake. As morning dawned, my concern for my dogs and my own fatigue, as well as the blasting of the constant wind and the bleak whiteness of the landscape, merged to form a white blur. Occasionally, as we flat-tracked near one side of the river or came upon islands, I was aware of the deep green of spruce and the light-colored birch trees. My dogs never seemed to take notice. They kept to their languid pace. They were tired and sore and disheartened. I could sympathize with them. I had an assortment of aches and pain of my own. My face was windburned and my lips were chapped. My hip and finger still bothered me. The muscles in my forearms were sore from gripping the handlebars. I had scrapes, nicks, and cuts. When I pulled off my gloves my hands looked like working man's hands. And my feet were bruised and wet and cold. I was groggy, scatterbrained, and hushed. But I could deal with my discomforts. What bothered me was the deteriorating health of my dogs. I stopped often, dispensing treats and words of support and confidence.

The dogs finally decided they had had enough. They stopped and lay down on the ice, immediately curling up with their backs to the wind. There was nothing I could do except give them the break they demanded. I plopped myself down on the front of my sled. I figured to be there a minute or two but I fell asleep. Half an hour passed. I had foolishly not been wearing gloves nor did I tuck my hands into a protective pocket. When I awoke my fingers were cold and useless. If it had been really cold and I had made such a critical mistake, I could easily have lost my fingers.

I tucked my hands under my armpits to warm them enough to be functional. My dogs never moved, and I was not sure if we could continue. I was depressed and desperate, wanting something, anything, to go my way for a change.

It was then that Jay Rowan, my friend who had died in a tragic swimming accident, spoke to me. He was not a hallucination. I sensed his presence and he spoke to me, but not the way two people talk. His words simply formed in my mind.

"Rachael, the leaders are only three hundred miles ahead of you. You can do this. I know you're hurting. I know you're discouraged. But you're going to get back on that sled and you're going to pick off the stragglers ahead of you one by one. You're going to finish this race. Get going, girl."

Jay's words inspired me. I got up, pulled on my chore gloves, and got my dogs on their feet. I gave each a quick massage and some love. Paul doubled back and asked how I was doing. I told him we had taken a short break and we were about ready to go. When I called to my dogs they moved forward.

As we traveled I evaluated my dogs with a critical eye. Angel was the only dog in my team that seemed the least bit interested in leading and she was now my thinnest dog. She had the heart but not the physical stamina to continue. Bernard, Ned, and Dutchess were nearly as skinny. If I dropped all four at Eagle Island I would be down to six dogs and have no leaders. A dog team without at least one strong leader is not a dog team. Of my remaining dogs—Eyes, Possum, Jovi, Mandy, Brick, and Seth—none was capable of carrying the team.

I did some soul searching, trying to determine if I was strong enough mentally and physically to hold six dogs together. Cim Smyth had done it, running the last five hundred miles to Nome with only five dogs. And he had set the record for the fastest time from Safety to Nome. But I was not Cim Smyth. I was a rookie and I was fried. I had been holding this team together since Takotna and I was not sure how much longer I could pull off such a miracle.

I continued to pump, pushing off with my right leg ten or twenty times and then switching to my left. I would have a tough decision to make when we reached Eagle Island. I have always been told to never consider scratching going into a checkpoint; that you always take care of your dogs, eat and sleep, and then look at the world from a fresh perspective. I might decide, okay, maybe I could hold them together to Kaltag. And if we made it to Kaltag, then maybe we could limp into Unalakleet, and on to Shaktoolik, Koyuk, and Elim. If we made Elim, we would only be a hundred miles or so from Nome. A hundred miles—now that was definitely doable.

Breaking a race down like that is a distance runner's trick. In the middle of a 3000 you tell yourself, "Only five laps to go," and you count them down: 4, 3, 2, 1, and done. I played the same game in the Iditarod. Go one lap at a time, or as John Patten had drummed into my head, "Small bites are easier to swallow."

We reached Eagle Island checkpoint. It was nothing more than a single tent set up especially for the race in an endless sea of wilderness. I gave the dogs an absolute smorgasbord, and they turned their noses up at the lamb, chicken, and salmon and the hot dogs and beef fat, too. The only thing they were the least bit interested in was the Atta Boy kibbles. But they only nibbled at it. That was a bad sign.

It was obvious from the thinness of the dogs, but the veterinarian was trying to make conversation and asked if the diarrhea medicine had helped. I was honest. There was really no sense in trying to be deceitful. My team was in trouble.

"I haven't been able to keep weight on them, not since Takotna. That's where the diarrhea started getting bad and they began losing weight. Until now they've eaten pretty well, but it doesn't matter how much they eat, or how much fat I pump into them, it all goes straight through their systems. And now they don't have an appetite for anything, not even the treats."

I decided to take some time for myself. I had heard about Eagle Island, and the word from other mushers was that the wind always blew and the checkpoint was nothing more than a dismal tent with a little Coleman heater that never kicked out enough heat to warm the place. But that was in years past. I ducked through the canvas flap and found a palace in the form of a four-wall room made of plywood and a heater that could melt the polar ice cap. I had the heater to myself. I hung up my clothes and dropped a Ziploc bag with Becki's special taco soup into a pan of boiling water. It was one of the finest meals I have ever eaten. When Paul came in I told him he was going to enjoy his food. He soon confirmed my view, saying he had never eaten taco soup but that he was now an enthusiastic convert.

After that, with warm food in my belly and a cocoon of warm air surrounding me, I flopped down on one of the bunks and slept several hours. Jim Gallea, a musher I first met when he ran the Atta Boy 300, woke me. He had run three Iditarod races, but I remembered he was going to medical school at the University of Washington and would not participate this year. I was momentarily confused as to why he was there, but quickly grasped that he was an official.

"We need to talk," Jim told me. He said the veterinarian was of the opinion I should drop four of my dogs.

"But that will put me down to six."

"I know," Jim said, understanding my dilemma.

"Six dogs," I repeated. It did not seem fair. I had given Paul six of my best dogs, and five of them were still on his ten-dog team. If I had had those dogs . . . I stopped myself from thinking of what might have been and faced the fact I was down to six dogs. I had no front end, no leaders. And several of the six were thin and sick. If I continued, I would be putting a tremendous amount of pressure on those six dogs. In good conscience I could not do that to the dogs I loved. I had raised them from puppies, trained and watched them develop into the athletes they had become. It was not right for me to push them past the point where the race was no longer a fun experience.

I spoke with Mark Nordman—the Iditarod race marshal—on the satellite telephone, and he left it up to me, the decision to try to continue or to pull out of the race. It was my decision alone. If I pushed my dogs too far, I would have to live with the consequences of that. And if I pulled out, I would have to live with that, too.

I stepped outside to talk to my dogs and wrestled with my decision. When I saw my spent team and saw the way they were curled up on the straw, how skinny they had become from the diarrhea-causing virus, my decision was made for me. There was only one choice I could make.

I looked upward into the sodden sky. "I held them together as long as I could. My dogs are sick. If there was any way for us to go on, you know I would. I have to scratch. I'm sorry, Jay."

After I had made peace with Jay I went inside the tent, sat on a bunk, and cried. Paul came over and wrapped a beefy arm around me. He knew without my having to say the words. He felt bad for me. I told him, "You better get going. You can pass a few teams on the way in. Or you can stay where you are, in last place, and collect the red lantern." I tried to smile.

"I don't think so," he said. "It wouldn't be the same without you. Besides, I'm the kind of guy who believes in leaving with the same girl he brought to the dance."

I remembered something Dave Sims told me before I left Central Oregon. One day we were sitting on the couch talking about the Iditarod and he said, "If you go up there and you don't finish, then you *have* to do it again. If you finish, you *can* do it again, if you want to."

I said, "I just don't want anybody to make this a sight thing. Saying I pulled out because of my vision. This is a dog thing."

"Don't worry about that," Jim Gallea said. "Nobody doubts you. You proved what you could do. You passed all the tough places with flying colors. Anyone can scratch because their dogs got sick. Look at Rick Swenson and Charlie Boulding, two of the most famous men in our sport. They pulled out when their dogs got sick. It happens. You can come back next year and you'll get to Nome."

All that remained of my 2005 Iditarod run was to make it official. Jim got a piece of paper and a Sharpie. He wrote my name and the words "Scratched at Eagle Island." I signed it.

Then I called Dad on the satellite phone and told him. He said, "I'm sure you made the right decision. I'm proud of you, and, honey, I love you."

Having to scratch from the Iditarod was a setback, but I've dealt with adversity all my life. I'll come back. I always do. I will complete the Iditarod. Next year—the year after—the year after that—the only thing that really matters is to finish what I started. I will accomplish this goal that I have set for myself.

When Mitch Seavey won the Iditarod in 2004, he made the comment that the Iditarod Sled Dog Race was all about overcoming adversity. Each musher who leaves the starting chute is guaranteed to come face-to-face with an array of hardships, misfortunes, and out-and-out disasters. Sleep deprivation. Injuries. Wrecked sleds. Collapsing ice bridges. Extreme cold. Sick dogs. And that's not even to mention the hardships you may start with. Martin Buser ran the Iditarod after cutting off parts of three fingers. The year before, DeeDee Jonrowe ran the race while she was still undergoing chemotherapy for cancer. Guy Blankenship, an insulin-dependent diabetic, ran the race nine times. Gary Paulsen is trying to make a comeback after suffering life-threatening heart problems. We all have personal challenges to overcome if we are to finish the race and reach Nome.

In the long run, if my completing the Iditarod helps others in the world broaden their horizons of acceptance, or if I inspire one person to attain something worthwhile in his or her life, then I am thankful. I race dogs because that is what I love to do. I want to take sled dog racing as far as I can. And every time I overcome my personal fears and prove something to myself, I want to set the bar a little higher. I want to challenge myself. In my life, and in all our lives, there should be no limitations, only possibilities.

MUSHING TERMINOLOGY

basket. Main body of a sled, where gear or a dog may be carried.

booties. Socks for dogs, used for protection of the feet and under adverse trail conditions to prevent ice from forming between a dog's toes. Made from a wide variety of materials, including fleece, denim, trigger cloth, and Gore-Tex.

brake. A sharp metal object affixed to the sled or a simple pad the musher stands on to slow down a team.

brushbow. Curved piece in front of the main body of a sled, designed to protect the sled from brush.

Burled Arch. Iditarod Trail finish line in Nome.

checkpoint. Place designated along the route of a race where mushers are required to check in and each dog is examined by a veterinarian. Any dog deemed incapable of continuing the race will be dropped from the team at this point.

dog bag. Zippered fabric bag carried on a race sled and used to confine a sick or injured dog.

dog box. Wooden structure, divided into small compartments, attached to a truck or trailer, and used for transporting dogs. Each compartment holds one or two dogs.

double lead. Two dogs, hooked side by side, leading the team.

drop chain. A short chain used to secure dogs for watering and feeding.

dropped dog. A dog the musher has dropped from his or her team at a checkpoint. The dog is cared for at the checkpoint and returned to the musher after the race.

Easy! Musher's command for the dogs to slow down.

gangline. Main line that connects the dogs to the sled.

Gee! Musher's command for right turn.

handlebar. The part of a sled that a musher grips. Also called a driving bow.

handler. Person who assists the musher.

harness. Webbed fabric, typically made from nylon, that fits a dog snugly and to which the tugline is attached.

Haw! Musher's command for the dogs to turn left.

Hike! Most universal command for the dogs to move forward.

husky. Any mixed-breed dog from the snow country, usually used to denote those bred for sled dog racing.

lead dog or lead dogs. The dog or dogs in the front of a team, noted for their intelligence, strength, leadership qualities, and ability to follow the musher's commands. May be male or female.

Line out! Musher's command to the leader to pull the team in a straight line, typically used while dogs are being hooked or unhooked in a team.

musher. Person who drives a sled dog team.

neck line. Short line that attaches the collar to the gangline.

no-man's-land. Last mile of a race, where a slower musher is not required to give the right-of-way to a faster musher.

On by! Command to go by another team or other distraction

overflow. Dangerous crossing caused by thick ice and water flowing over the ice and freezing into a thin layer.

pushing off or pedaling. Standing with one foot on a runner and using the other foot to push and help move the sled forward.

rigging. Overall term used to denote the collection of lines by which the dogs are attached to the sled.

runners. Narrow skies on the bottom of the sled that come in contact with the snow and upon which a musher will stand. They are usually made from wood and covered with a coating of plastic or Teflon that can be easily replaced during a race.

safety line. Extra line from the gangline to the sled, in case the main fitting breaks.

single lead. One dog in the lead position.

snow hook. Large metal hook, attached to the sled and the gangline by a line, which can be driven into firm snow to anchor a team for a short period of time.

snub or snub line. Rope attached to the back of a sled that is used to anchor the sled to an immovable object. This line is usually fitted with a quick-release mechanism.

stakeout. Main chain with separate short chains to which the dogs are attached.

stanchions. The upright pieces that attach the runners to a sled.

swing dogs or point dogs. Dogs directly behind the leaders and responsible for helping swing the team around corners.

team dogs. Any dogs in a team between the swing dogs and the wheel dogs.

tether. Chain or shout line, with other lines affixed to it, used to stake out a team.

toboggan. Sled with a flat bottom instead of runners and used when deep, soft snow is expected instead of a good trail.

Trail! Musher's request for right-of-way on the trail from a slower musher. A passing musher has the right-of-way.

tugline. Line that connects a dog's harness to the gangline.

wheel dogs. Dogs closest to the sled and responsible for bringing the sled safely around corners and away from any obstacles. These will normally be the heaviest dogs in the team.

Whoa! Command used to halt a team, usually used in conjunction with a heavy pressure on the brake.

CAPTIONS AND CREDITS FOR ARTWORK AND PHOTOGRAPHS

INDEX